IN

D0765081

EVIDENCE

INITIAL EVIDENCE

HISTORICAL AND BIBLICAL PERSPECTIVES ON THE PENTECOSTAL DOCTRINE OF SPIRIT BAPTISM

GARY B. McGEE, EDITOR

HENDRICKSON PUBLISHERS
PEABODY, MASSACHUSETTS 01961-3473

Copyright © 1991 by Hendrickson Publishers, Inc.
P. O. Box 3473
Peabody, Massachusetts 01961–3473
All rights reserved
Printed in the United States of America

ISBN 0–943575–41–9

Library of Congress Cataloging-in-Publication Data

Initial evidence: historical and biblical perspectives on the Pentecostal doctrine of spirit baptism / Gary B. McGee, editor.
    p.   cm.
    Includes bibliographical references and indexes.
    ISBN 0–943575–41–9 (pbk.)
    1. Baptism in the Holy Spirit. 2. Glossolalia.
3. Pentecostalism.   I. McGee, Gary B., 1945– .
BT123.I55 1991
234′.12—dc20   91-32847
                                            CIP

DEDICATION

In honor of my mother,
Velma L. Davis,
and in memory of my
maternal grandmother,
Lucille Hartzell,
whose sterling values and
Pentecostal witness have
shaped my life

TABLE OF CONTENTS

Part II: Initial Evidence and the Biblical Text:
Four Perspectives

CONTRIBUTORS

Stanley M. Burgess, Ph.D. (University of Missouri–Columbia), serves as Professor of Religious Studies at Southwest Missouri State University, Springfield, Missouri. In addition to authoring *The Spirit and the Church: Antiquity* (1984) and *The Holy Spirit: Eastern Christian Traditions* (1989), Burgess edited *Reaching Beyond: Chapters in the History of Perfectionism* (1986), and co-edited the *Dictionary of Pentecostal and Charismatic Movements* (1988). He also contributed a chapter to *Perspectives on the New Pentecostalism* (1976).

David W. Dorries, Ph.D. (University of Aberdeen), is Assistant Professor of Church History in the School of Theology and Missions at Oral Roberts University, Tulsa, Oklahoma, and is pastor of Leonard Christian Fellowship. His dissertation, "Nineteenth Century British Christological Controversy, Centering Upon Edward Irving's Doctrine of Christ's Human Nature," was completed in 1988 and is an examination of Irving's Christology.

James R. Goff, Jr., Ph.D. (University of Arkansas), is Assistant Professor of History at Appalachian State University, Boone, North Carolina. The publication of Goff's *Fields White Unto Harvest* (1988), a work on the life of Charles F. Parham and the missionary origins of Pentecostalism, represents an important milestone in the historiography of Pentecostalism. His other writings include articles in *Christianity Today, Kansas History, Ozark Historical Review, Dictionary of Pentecostal and Charismatic Movements* (1988), and a chapter in *Pentecostals from the Inside Out* (1990).

J. L. Hall, M.A. (Emporia State University), serves as Editor in Chief of Publications for the United Pentecostal Church International, Hazelwood, Missouri. In addition to writing *The United Pentecostal Church and the Evangelical Movement* (1990), contributing articles to the *Dictionary of Pentecostal and Charismatic Movements* (1988), *Doctrines of the Bible* (1991), and various denominational publications, Hall serves as editor of the *Pentecostal Herald*, the official voice of the United Pentecostal Church International.

Larry W. Hurtado, Ph.D. (Case Western Reserve University), is Professor of Religion and Director of the Institute for the Humanities at the University of Manitoba, Winnipeg, Manitoba. His many publications include *One God, One Lord: Early Christian Devotion and Ancient Jewish Monotheism* (1988), *Mark* (New International Biblical Commentary [1989]), and *Text-Critical Methodology and the Pre-Caesarean Text: Codex W in the Gospel of Mark* (1981). He also edited the recent *Goddesses in Religions and Modern Debate* (1990).

Donald A. Johns, Ph.D. (Saint Louis University), is a full time translator for the American Bible Society. He formerly served as Associate Professor and Chairperson of the Bible and Theology Department at the Assemblies of God Theological Seminary, Springfield, Missouri. Johns wrote numerous articles for the *Dictionary of Pentecostal and Charismatic Movements* (1988) and, as a member of a team of translators, has contributed to *A Contemporary English Version* (1991).

Henry I. Lederle, D.Th. (University of South Africa), is Professor of Systematic Theology in the School of Theology and Missions at Oral Roberts University, Tulsa, Oklahoma. His many books include *The Church of Jesus Christ* (1978), the two-volume *Historical Development of the Doctrine of God* (1979, 1980), *Charismatic Theology* (1986), *Treasures Old and New: Interpretations of "Spirit-Baptism" in the Charismatic Renewal Movement* (1988), and *Modern Ecumenism* (1991). He has also contributed articles to the *International Reformed Bulletin*, *Theologica Evangelica*, *Missionalia*, and the *Ecumenical Review*.

Gary B. McGee, Ph.D. (Saint Louis University), is Professor of Church History at the Assemblies of God Theological Seminary, Springfield, Missouri. He authored the two-volume *This Gospel Shall Be Preached* (1986, 1989), a history and theology of Assemblies of God foreign missions, and co-edited the *Dictionary of Pentecostal and Charismatic Movements* (1988). McGee's other publications include articles in *Assemblies of God Heritage, International Bulletin of Missionary Research, Missiology,* and chapters in *Azusa Street and Beyond* (1986) and *Faces of Renewal* (1988).

J. Ramsey Michaels, Th.D. (Harvard University), is Professor of Religious Studies at Southwest Missouri State University, Springfield, Missouri. One of the foremost evangelical New Testament scholars, his books include *The New Testament Speaks* (with Glenn W. Barker and William L. Lane [1969]), *Inerrancy and Common Sense* (edited with Roger R. Nicole [1980]), *Servant and Son: Jesus in Parable and Gospel* (1981), *1 Peter* (Word Biblical Commentary [1988]), and *John* (New International Biblical Commentary [1989]).

Cecil M. Robeck, Jr., Ph.D. (Fuller Theological Seminary), is Associate Dean for Academic Programs and Associate Professor of Church History at Fuller Theological Seminary, Pasadena, California. In addition to having authored many journal articles, he contributed to the *Dictionary of Pentecostal and Charismatic Movements* (1988); he has edited *Witness to Pentecost: The Life of Frank Bartleman* (1985) and *Charismatic Experiences in History* (1985), and he authored the *Role and Function of Prophetic Gifts for the Church at Carthage* (forthcoming). Robeck has also served as the editor of *Pneuma: The Journal of the Society for Pentecostal Studies* since 1984.

EDITOR'S INTRODUCTION

In 1969 an astute observer of Christianity worldwide remarked: "When speaking of Pentecostals, we are not now dealing with an obscure 'sect,' born almost seventy years ago in a small Midwest town, but with a world-embracing movement. . . ."[1] Indeed, when viewed from an international perspective Pentecostalism can now be credited as the most influential revival of the twentieth century.[2] Interestingly enough, however, few could have foreseen in the first decade of this century that its spiritual energies would one day shake the comfortable assumptions of many Christians about the ministry of the Holy Spirit, spark a significant missionary dispersion, or command the attention of church growth specialists and denominational officials in the historic churches. Yet, this renewal movement of the Spirit has crossed racial, cultural, and social barriers, reawakened church life by focusing on the need for every believer to be Spirit-baptized for Christian witness, and encouraged the ministry of the gifts of the Spirit (1 Cor. 12, 14) within many communities of faith.

On the North American scene, it has come to be identified with labels like Apostolic, Apostolic Faith, Assemblies of God, Church of God (Cleveland, Tenn.), Church of God of Prophecy, Church of God in Christ, Fellowship of Christian Assemblies, Foursquare Gospel, Full Gospel, Open Bible Standard, Pentecostal Assemblies of Canada, Pentecostal Holiness, and United Pentecostal. To these could be added the names of thousands of independent congregations.

The occurrence of revival at the Bethel Bible School in Topeka, Kansas, in January 1901, plunged the radical holiness preacher Charles F. Parham and his followers into a renewal movement that soon spread throughout the Midwest. Subsequent revivals drew their inspiration from the happenings in Topeka, but, most notably, from the influential Azusa Street revival in Los Angeles. But despite the revival's obscure origins, the news spread with amazing speed, especially after 1906. Zealous supporters soon heralded the news that the Pentecostal "latter rain" was being poured out in the last days before the imminent return of Christ, just as the Old Testament prophet Joel had predicted (Joel 2:28–29). Important revivals in Wales (1904), India (1905), and Korea (1907) were considered to be showers compared to the downpour of power from the Holy Spirit that believers soon reported from such far away places as Chile, South Africa, China, Estonia, Germany, Scandinavia, and England. Participants in the fledgling movement testified to receiving Spirit baptism just as the early Christians had in the book of Acts.

To early Pentecostals, the New Testament church in all its apostolic power and purity was being restored. The September 1906 issue of *The Apostolic Faith*, published by leaders at the Azusa Street mission from where the young movement began to acquire international dimensions, excitedly announced that "Pentecost has surely come and with it the Bible evidences are following, many being converted and sanctified and filled with the Holy Ghost, speaking in tongues as they did on the day of Pentecost. . . . and the real revival is only started."[3] Indeed, within just a few decades, Pentecostalism proved to be an astonishingly vigorous new force in Christendom, noted for its remarkable successes in evangelization.

The historical roots of Pentecostalism are traced to John Wesley and John Fletcher, who maintained that each believer should have a post-conversionary experience of grace. Wesleyan holiness advocates defined this as the sanctification of the believer, providing deliverance from the defect in the moral nature which prompts sinful behavior. Christians, therefore, could mirror the "perfect love" of Jesus, having received a perfection of motives and desires (1 Cor. 13). Labeled as the baptism in the Holy Spirit (the "second blessing"), it lifted Christians to a plateau of (gradually upward) spiritual maturity. Followers of the controversial Fire-Baptized brand of holiness envisaged three experiences of grace, with the second for sanctification and the third (baptism of the Holy Spirit and fire) for spiritual empowerment. Some from the Reformed tradition, however, discerning sanctification to be a lifelong process, advised that the subsequent (second) experience (baptism in the Holy Spirit) equipped believers with power for Christian witness.

While many adopted various shades of holiness theology in the nineteenth century and professed to be "sanctified," questions naturally arose about the "evidence" (both inward and outward) of this experience.

When Parham and his Topeka students testified to speaking in tongues (i.e., xenolalia [unlearned foreign languages]), they believed they had found the solution to the evidence question, having been furnished with foreign languages to expedite the evangelization of the world. Along with tongues came a greater love for the lost as well as empowerment for witness. Having discerned a paradigm for the expansion of the church in the book of Acts, Pentecostals concluded that the biblical data confirm the necessity of tongues (later considered by many to be glossolalia [unknown tongues]). Although Mark 16:17–18 and 1 Corinthians 12 and 14 also served as vital sources in the development of Pentecostal theology, the appeal to the "pattern" in the book of Acts has remained paramount, providing the apostolic model for this worldwide movement.

Pentecostalism, therefore, is certainly more than the designations of its followers, the sociological make-up of its constituents, the hodgepodge of polities that characterize its organizational structures, and the enthusiastic worship that has marked its church services. Regardless of other characteristics that could be legitimately cited, one cannot fully understand the dynamic behind the movement without examining its spiritual heartbeat: the core emphases on baptism in the Holy Spirit and "signs and wonders" (exorcisms, healings, prophecy, tongues and interpretations, word of knowledge, etc.). For millions of Pentecostals, Spirit baptism means empowerment for Christian witness; and a large portion of them insist that this work of grace must be accompanied by speaking in tongues as exemplified by the early disciples in Acts 2, 10, and 19. Indeed, leadership opportunities in many Pentecostal denominations and local congregations are frequently offered only to those who have experienced glossolalia, perhaps marking the only time in Christian history when this type of charismatic experience has been institutionalized on such a large scale.

From this vantage, glossolalia represents a "language of experiential spirituality, rather than theology,"[4] catalyzing a deeper awareness of the Spirit's guidance and gifts in the individual's consciousness to glorify Jesus Christ and build his church. How then do Pentecostal theology and evangelical theology differ? Obviously, they share many beliefs: confidence in the trustworthiness and authority of Scripture, the forensic understanding of justification by faith, the Trinity (with the exception of Oneness Pentecostals), the virgin birth, resurrection, and second coming of Christ, as well as other standard doctrines which can be traced to the early church, the Protestant Reformation, and later Protestant revivalism. Pentecostal beliefs about Spirit baptism and contemporary manifestations of the gifts of the Spirit, however, have generally refused to fit comfortably within the rationalistic boundaries of much evangelical theology and spirituality.

Moreover, Pentecostals need to engage in further theological reflection in order to explore the full dimensions of the work of the Holy Spirit in biblical theology, correcting the neglected dimension of the Spirit's ministry in Christian theology.[5] Nonetheless, Pentecostals have been carried along by an eschatological urgency to evangelize and have had little time or interest in academic discussions of theology. With notable exceptions in recent years, they have generally left biblical and theological exposition to evangelical scholars, confident of their integrity when dealing with the issues of the day, but naively assuming that Pentecostal teachings could be easily integrated with some of these formulations without undermining the credibility of Pentecostal beliefs. Even more injuriously, by neglecting reflection and research and by continuing to emphasize personal experience above academic inquiry, Pentecostals allow an underlying anti-intellectualism to continue to pervade the movement.[6]

Just as the quality of human life is enhanced by sound nutrition and exercise, so the continued vitality of key doctrines (e.g., baptism in the Holy Spirit) in communities of believers is sustained through ongoing study of the Scriptures and theological reflection, in addition to the practice of piety. Several important factors, therefore, lie behind the publication of this collection of essays.

First, the role of glossolalia in Spirit baptism has remained a point of controversy through the years. Meanwhile, historians have gained new insights into past charismatic movements. They have examined afresh the theological perspectives of the towering figures of early Pentecostalism, Charles F. Parham and William J. Seymour; and they have studied the development of Pentecostalism's distinctive teachings and the viewpoints of charismatics—the nearest relatives to Pentecostals—concerning the role of glossolalia in the life of the believer. In addition, a new generation of Pentecostal biblical scholars approaches its task with considerably more theological and exegetical expertise than its forebears, without necessarily differing on the hallmarks of doctrine. Accordingly, these studies can enrich the doctrinal self-understanding of the Pentecostal movement.

Second, while the confessional statements of most Pentecostal denominations and agencies cite tongues as the initial evidence of Spirit baptism, the actual practice of speaking in tongues has declined within the ranks. Statistician David B. Barrett suggests that only 35% of all members in Pentecostal denominations have actually spoken in tongues or have continued it as an ongoing experience.[7] If this percentage is only remotely accurate, it still demonstrates a certain ambivalence about the constitutive nature of tongues. Even within the ranks of the clergy, hesitancy has been detected—a recent survey of ministers within the Pentecostal Assemblies of Canada found:

> A group of Pentecostal ministers is emerging which is noticeably different from the traditional norm. They are 35 years or younger and are well educated in areas of theology. They basically affirm all of the important doctrines, but are less dogmatic in their support of them. For example, some of them would not insist that one is not filled with the Spirit unless he or she has spoken in tongues.[8]

And of considerable importance is the fact that church leaders in denominations such as the Assemblies of God (U.S.A.), Church of God (Cleveland, Tenn.), and Open Bible Standard Churches have found it necessary through the years to urge their ministers to remain faithful in preaching and teaching the indispensability of the Pentecostal baptism with speaking in tongues for each believer.

In reviewing the impact of early Pentecostalism on the recent charismatic renewal in the churches, historian H. Vinson Synan notes that "although most of the neo-Pentecostals [charismatics] did not adopt Parham's initial-evidence theology, they nevertheless have tended to pray and sing in tongues even more ardently than their older classical Pentecostal brothers and sisters."[9] One might conclude that traditional Pentecostals, therefore, have become spiritually cold and need reviving. While this possibility should not be discounted, the record of church history demonstrates that doctrinal certitude also diminishes when crucial questions are not adequately answered. Ironically, doctrines may then change from being signposts of spiritual and theological vitality to "shibboleths" of acceptance, serving new and potentially divisive functions within the body of Christ.

The peril of doctrinal ossification is illustrated from an account of the famed Jesuit missionary, Matteo Ricci (1552–1610). According to one historian, when Ricci and his cohorts reached China, they barely found a trace of Christianity left from the work of earlier missionaries. When Ricci heard of people who worshipped the cross, he was told that "not even those who worshipped it knew why they did so, only that over everything which they ate or drank they made a cross with their finger."[10] Even though the details of this story are sketchy, it pointedly warns of the danger of form overtaking meaning. The likelihood of glossolalia disappearing altogether or surviving in form only—the tragic parody of believers reciting glossolalic syllables without the display of the fruit and power of the Spirit in their lives—should give every Pentecostal serious pause. Fortunately, the gifts of scholarship can provide insights into Spirit baptism which may enhance our comprehension of this cornerstone of Pentecostal belief and experience.

Third, the larger church world knows little of this pneumatological distinctive. Most Christians do not believe in a post-conversionary experience of the Holy Spirit and are probably unfamiliar with the teaching. They may also be unaware that millions of believers around the world, comprising an enormous sector of contemporary Christianity, fervently profess that Spirit baptism will inevitably be signalled by glossolalic utterances—denoting a crucial factor in their spiritual bonding and unique ecumenical fellowship. It would be hoped that these historical and biblical essays will help outside observers understand the spiritual dynamics of this fast-growing movement and better comprehend the issues that relate to its most distinctive teaching.

To explore the Pentecostal doctrine of Spirit baptism and initial evidence requires thoughtful reflection and honest appraisals of its historical formulation and exegetical foundations. For this reason, the contributors to this volume present a variety of opinions, particularly in the biblical essays. All of the writers come from a Pentecostal background with the exceptions of David W. Dorries (Southern Baptist), Henry I. Lederle (Reformed), and J. Ramsey Michaels (American Baptist). Each one has been invited to express freely the conclusions of his own research; for that reason, opinions do not necessarily represent those of other contributors, the editor, or the publisher.

The first unit of the book focuses on the historical development of the doctrine. In spite of the restorationist orientation of Pentecostalism, Pentecostal apologists, beginning with Charles Parham, readily turned to the pages of church history to identify themselves with past charismatic movements from the Montanists to the Irvingites.[11] In two chapters, Stanley M. Burgess assesses historical precedents for linkages to modern Pentecostalism. David W. Dorries examines the pneumatology of Edward Irving, a significant nineteenth-century figure who witnessed a revival of the charismata, including tongues, which Irving saw as the "standing sign" of Spirit baptism. James R. Goff, Jr., provides an insightful look into the theological evolvement of Charles F. Parham. With his premillennial moorings and confidence in xenolalic tongues as evidence of baptism in the Holy Spirit, Parham envisioned the speedy evangelization of the world. By drawing this connection between Spirit baptism, tongues, and eschatology, he molded the course of the Pentecostal movement, although the actual influence of his leadership in other respects waned quickly. Notwithstanding, the importance of William J. Seymour, pastor of the Apostolic Faith Mission on Azusa Street in Los Angeles, rivals that of Parham. Cecil M. Robeck, Jr., carefully reviews the steps of Seymour's spiritual pilgrimage and the contours of his thoughts on initial evidence.

My first chapter examines the ways in which early Pentecostals, in keeping with the hermeneutical precedent of other restorationists, looked to the book of Acts for theological truth. Through their analysis of key passages, Acts became a model for faith and practice. Although Pentecostals reached different conclusions about the importance of glossolalia in Spirit baptism, those who have contended that Luke is teaching initial evidence (through implication) in his narrative have challenged the traditional perspectives on biblical interpretation molded by Protestant scholasticism. The next chapter permits earlier Pentecostal apologists to speak for themselves and contains excerpts from a variety of publications. Finally, Henry I. Lederle surveys charismatic perspectives on the issue and calls for dialogue between Pentecostals and charismatics in order to encourage greater unity in the body of Christ—a logical goal given their close kinship.

The second unit includes four exegetical essays on initial evidence from different angles. Donald A. Johns's chapter contains a contemporary classical Pentecostal's exploration of the doctrine and offers some key hermeneutical paths that should be considered for further study. The view of Spirit baptism taught by many (but not all) within the large Oneness family of Pentecostalism is provided by J. L. Hall.[12] Not espousing baptism in the Holy Spirit as subsequent to conversion, Hall links the event to repentance from sin and to water baptism in the salvation of the believer. The chapter by Larry W. Hurtado, while supportive of present-day manifestations of gifts of the Spirit, nevertheless challenges the biblical foundations of a subsequent work of grace and the claim that tongues must accompany it. He suggests that glossolalia can be normal in the lives of Christians, but should not be expected of everyone. Finally, J. Ramsey Michaels, looking at the debate from the stance of a non-Pentecostal, warmly expresses appreciation for the witness of Pentecostalism to the power of the Spirit. He suggests, however, that rather than appealing to a particular phenomenon as proof (e.g., glossolalia), New Testament writers affirmed the possession of the Spirit by Christians to be the empirical evidence for the reality of God and his workings in individuals and communities of believers.

These essays will undoubtedly trigger many responses. The faith and presuppositions of some will be confronted by recent historical findings or opposing biblical expositions of the doctrine. Others, however, may discover new meaning for their charismatic experiences of glossolalia, or they may perhaps be forced to reconsider their assumptions about Spirit baptism. In any case, if this limited examination of the Pentecostal baptism and the doctrine of initial evidence prompts further discussion, dialogue, research, and better understanding within the body of Christ, it will have abundantly served its purpose.

NOTES

1. P. Damboriena, S.J., *Tongues as of Fire: Pentecostalism in Contemporary Christianity* (Washington, D.C.: Corpus Books, 1969), vii.

2. E. E. Cairns, *An Endless Line of Splendor: Revivals and Their Leaders from the Great Awakening to the Present* (Wheaton: Tyndale House Publishers, 1986), 177; G. B. McGee, "The Azusa Street Revival and 20th Century Missions," *International Bulletin of Missionary Research* 12 (April 1988): 58–61.

3. "Pentecost Has Come," *Apostolic Faith* (Los Angeles), September 1906, 1.

4. For a brief description of the Pentecostal and charismatic movements, their similarities and differences, as well as tensions between them, see S. M. Burgess, G. B. McGee, and P. H. Alexander, "The Pentecostal and Charismatic Movements," *Dictionary of Pentecostal and Charismatic Movements* (Grand Rapids: Zondervan, 1988), *DPCM*, 1–6.

5. For an insightful discussion, see P. A. Pomerville, *The Third Force in Missions* (Peabody, Mass.: Hendrickson, 1985), 79–104.

6. For a description of classical Pentecostalism, see H. V. Synan, "Classical Pentecostalism," *DPCM*, 219–21. See also Gary B. McGee, "The Indispensable Calling of the Pentecostal Scholar," *Assemblies of God Educator* 35 (July–Sept 1990): 1, 3–5, 16.

7. D. B. Barrett, "Statistics, Global," *DPCM*, 820.

8. C. Verge, "Pentecostal Clergy and Higher Education," *Eastern Journal of Practical Theology* (Eastern Pentecostal Bible College, Peterborough, Ontario, Canada) 2 (Spring 1988): 44.

9. H. V. Synan, "The Touch Felt Around the World," *Charisma* (January 1991), 85.

10. A. C. Moule, *Christians in China Before the Year 1550* (New York: Macmillan, 1930), 4.

11. C. F. Parham, *A Voice Crying in the Wilderness* (Baxter Springs, Kan.: Apostolic Faith Bible College, reprint of 2d ed., 1910), 29; B. F. Lawrence, *The Apostolic Faith Restored* (St. Louis: Gospel Publishing House, 1916), 32–37; S. H. Frodsham, *With Signs Following* (Springfield, Mo.: Gospel Publishing House, 1926), 230–36.

12. J. L. Hall, *The United Pentecostal Church and the Evangelical Movement* (Hazelwood, Mo.: Word Aflame Press, 1990); for Oneness believers ("Apostolics," "Pentecostals") unrelated to the United Pentecostal Church International, consult *Clarion*, the official publication of the Apostolic World Christian Fellowship with headquarters in South Bend, Indiana.

I

INITIAL EVIDENCE
IN HISTORICAL PERSPECTIVE

1

EVIDENCE OF THE SPIRIT:
THE ANCIENT AND EASTERN CHURCHES

Stanley M. Burgess

In studying modern Pentecostalism, I have become aware that the uniqueness of the movement is not just that it stresses glossolalia (speaking in tongues) or a baptism in/with the Holy Spirit. Admittedly, the emphasis on tongues is somewhat rare, but tongues did exist before in various Christian contexts. The expectation of a baptism in the Spirit actually has been rather common in Christian history, although for most Christians it early became institutionalized into sacramental form. Instead, it seems to me that the real historical distinctive of modern Pentecostalism is its insistence that tongues be viewed as the "initial physical evidence" for Spirit baptism.

My purpose then is neither to study the history of speaking in tongues,[1] nor merely to examine the history of the experience which Pentecostals and many charismatics call "the baptism of the Holy Spirit." Rather, it is to search out historical precedents for the linkage which these modern enthusiasts make between the two and to examine what Christians past have accepted as evidence of Spirit baptism or Spirit indwelling.

RECEPTION OF THE HOLY SPIRIT: THE ANCIENT RECORD

From the second century, Christians were teaching that a person received the Holy Spirit in the waters of baptism.[2] There may have been a rite separable from baptism which involved prayer and the imposition of hands (Acts 8:14–20) by which the Spirit was given, but we have no postscriptural witnesses to this earlier than the third century. In that century, Christian teaching directly identified the time of Spirit reception to a separate rite which was consequent to baptism. It was some time later that the specific terms, "chrismation" in Eastern churches and "confirmation" in the West, were added.

The Early Western Church

In the early Western church, no one insisted on a dramatic physical manifestation of the spiritual change which accompanied the reception of the divine Spirit. This was simply accepted by faith, much as the modern Pentecostal accepts the salvation experience by faith, without requiring additional evidence for validation. An increase of sanctifying grace was anticipated, so that the recipient was enabled to profess fearlessly the faith and to resist temptation. In addition, the confirmed person was expected to receive gifts of the Holy Spirit—which in the Roman church tended to be identified with the Isaiah 11:2 gift list (wisdom, understanding, knowledge, counsel, piety, fortitude, and fear of the Lord).

Tertullian, the late second- and early third-century North African theologian who seems to have been the early church father most aware of the Holy Spirit's activity, and who late in life joined the prophetic Montanist sect, is the first to identify a rite separate from baptism which marked the reception of the divine Spirit. In his writing, *On Baptism*, Tertullian teaches that in the water the believer is cleansed and prepared for the Holy Spirit. After coming from the font, the newly baptized is "thoroughly anointed with a blessed unction . . . and the hand is laid on [that one], invoking and inviting the Holy Spirit through benediction." This he supports by the implied typology of Genesis 48:14, where Jacob lays his hands in blessing on the heads of Ephraim and Manasseh, and by the incident of the Ephesian disciples in Acts 19:2.[3]

And what for this early proto-Pentecostal was identifiable evidence of the reception of the Spirit? Tertullian declares that the dove of the Spirit will bring the peace of God and a divine spiritual modulation. In addition, from this point on, the soul will be illuminated by the Spirit.[4] The latter is consistent with Tertullian's Montanist inclinations, which included the reminder that Jesus had informed his disciples insofar as they were able to bear, but he had promised that when the Spirit of truth would come, the divine Spirit would then lead into all truth (John 16:12–13).[5] Montanists saw this fulfilled with their own New Prophecy.

Our first evidence from the church at Rome comes from the *Apostolic Tradition* of Hippolytus (d. 235). While Hippolytus sometimes associates the reception of the Spirit with baptism, on occasion he links this with the laying on of the bishop's hand with prayer and unction with oil. He especially associates the latter with the anointing of new church leaders, including the bishop, the presbyter, and the deacon.[6] Clearly, the effect of their Spirit reception is empowerment for service.

Cyprian (d. 258), another important North African father, more clearly identifies anointing with oil after baptism as the moment for the Spirit's entry. He asserts, "Now . . . they who are baptized in the Church are brought to the prelates of the Church, and by our prayers and by the imposition of hands obtain the Holy Spirit." Again, he declares the distinction between baptism and chrism: "Two sacraments preside over the perfect birth of a Christian, the one regenerating the man, which is baptism, the other communicating to him the Holy Spirit." The result of Spirit baptism is that recipients are "perfected with the Lord's seal."[7]

Hilary of Poitiers (d. ca. 367) also distinguishes between "the sacraments of baptism and of the Spirit,"[8] but never directly identifies the latter as chrism or unction. He does make one highly unique suggestion, however. He conjectures that the baptism of the Holy Spirit actually awaits us in the future, either in the purification of martyrdom or in cleansing fires beyond the grave.[9]

Ambrose, bishop of Milan (d. 397), declares that where the Spirit of God is, there is life. The Spirit brings the recipient a more abundant life of holiness, purity, creativity, and conformity to the image of God. The Spirit is the stream flowing from the living fount of God, who brings God's blessing to the human race.

For Ambrose, life in the Spirit begins with the sacraments. In baptism the Spirit renews and resurrects; in confirmation the Spirit seals the soul and provides his sevenfold gift (Isaiah 11:2); and in the Eucharist the Spirit actualizes the Incarnation and anticipates the Resurrection.[10]

The Early Eastern Churches

Early Eastern Christians understood chrismation to be an extension of Pentecost. The same Spirit who descended visibly on the apostles now descends invisibly on the newly baptized. Through chrismation every member becomes a prophet and receives a share in the royal priesthood of Christ. With the reception of the Spirit, all are called to act as conscious witnesses to the truth ("Ye know all things" [1 John 2:20, AV]).

Eastern Christian fathers tend to view the Holy Spirit's work primarily as that of perfecting the saints. This can be seen in the writings of Cyril of Jerusalem (d. 386), one of the great Eastern Christian authorities on baptism and chrismation. He reports that after coming up from baptismal waters, the recipient is given an unction which is the Holy Spirit. "The body is anointed with visible ointment, but the soul is sanctified by the Holy and life-giving Spirit." One is anointed on the forehead to be delivered from the shame of sin, on the ears in order to hear the mysteries of God, on the nostrils to smell the sweet savour of Christ, and on the breast so that one will put on the breast-plate of righteousness to stand against wicked forces.[11] Reception of the divine Spirit, then, results in a growth in holiness, in spiritual sensitivity, and in strength to combat nefarious powers.

Included in a sacramentary or missal ascribed to Serapion, bishop of Thmuis in Egypt (ca. 360), is a prayer over the chrism with which those already baptized are anointed. God is requested to make the chrism a divine and heavenly operation, so that every adverse power is conquered, and, by receiving the gift of the Holy Spirit, the recipient may remain firm and unmovable, unharmed, and inviolate.[12]

Basil of Cappadocia (d. 379), the most significant early Eastern writer on the Spirit, makes no distinction between baptism and chrismation. For him, baptism, or the entry of the divine Spirit, marks the beginning of life in the Spirit. All Christians are baptized in one body into one Spirit.[13] But one must be detached from the world before it is possible to receive the Holy Spirit. Once the Spirit is received, the first stage is purgation or purification by the Spirit, followed by divine illumination by the Spirit; and, finally, the soul is lifted by the Spirit to a state of perfect union with God.[14] In addition, all the divine gifts are poured out on those who are possessed by the Spirit—but these are always instruments of virtue, to be used for the benefit and blessing of others.[15] For Basil, then, the reception of the Holy Spirit is the beginning of a process of spiritual growth or perfecting, as well as the inception of a life as a pneumatophor—a carrier of the Spirit—lived in the Spirit for others.

A lifelong friend of Basil, Gregory of Nazianzen (A.D. 330–389) distinguishes between John's baptism with water and the baptism of the Spirit which Jesus gives. The latter is the perfect baptism.[16] The indwelling Spirit creates a spiritual koinonia, revealing the things of God. Hereafter, the recipient of the Spirit opens his mouth to draw in the Spirit, and speaks divine mysteries, words of wisdom, and divine knowledge. In obedience to the Spirit's beckoning, he lives, he moves, he speaks, or is silent.[17] As with Basil, Gregory of Nazianzen understands the baptism of the Spirit as entry into the Spirit life.

The highly mystical Ephrem of Syria (ca. 306–373), called the "Harp of the Spirit" by his countrymen, teaches that the recipient of the Spirit is enabled to transcend the temporal realm, thereby entering sacred or liturgical time (eternity). Baptism, which for Ephrem is the moment of the Spirit's entry, is the gateway to paradise or the kingdom of heaven, in which the "not yet" becomes the "already."[18] Life in the Spirit is allowing the divine Third Person to effect this entry into sacred time at every moment of life. At the same time, the Spirit removes scales from eyes so that the Christian can recognize the world as transfigured and the kingdom of God as existing within. The indwelling Spirit is central in the blending of heaven and earth, of time with the timeless, and of known with the unknown.

Ephrem did not limit the Spirit's work to the sacraments. He recognizes that the Spirit's activities are beyond defining; they spill over all boundaries of human expectation. Those baptized in the Spirit enjoy the "medicine of life" and the several gifts. Ephrem personally is said to have received the gift of tears in such abundance that it was as natural for him to weep as it was for others to breathe.[19]

The writings of Pseudo-Macarius (who may or may not be the famous anchorite, Macarius of Egypt, of the late fourth century) are concerned with the spiritual life, and especially the Holy Spirit's work in the church. Pseudo-Macarius recognizes that an individual begins the Christian life with the laying aside of sin and the putting on of the "soul of the Holy Spirit."[20] At this point, the Christian begins a new life in the habitation or heavenly house of the divine Spirit, and puts on Christ, the Pearl of Heaven, who cannot be worn by one who has not been begotten by the Spirit.[21]

For Pseudo-Macarius, evidence of the new life in the Spirit includes spiritual metacognition or awareness of the divine process in oneself.[22] It also includes spiritual gifts and Spirit-given inebriation. Dissatisfied with mere head knowledge, Pseudo- Macarius insists that the indwelling Spirit of God is to be experienced. After all, the Christian's mind is in heavenly flame because of the indwelling Spirit's light.[23] Spiritual experiences will range from great rejoicing, to that of the bride with her bridegroom, to lightness in body, to spiritual intoxication, to weeping and lamentation for fellow humans, to consuming love for humanity.[24] Finally, the reception of the Spirit is the beginning of the path towards perfection, in which one is translated from glory to glory, from joy to perfect joy.

Isaac, bishop of Ninevah (late seventh century), is one of the leading East Syrian or Assyrian (popularly known as "Nestorian") spirituals. He recognizes that God is beyond human intellect. By the Spirit one gains spiritual knowledge and begins living a virtuous life, successfully struggling with passions. By the Spirit, the soul is raised to God, enters a state of ecstasy or spiritual drunkenness, and receives the gift of tears. God's word comes alive. Finally, when one receives the gift of the Comforter and is secretly taught by the Spirit, there is no need of material things.[25]

It must seem obvious to the reader that ancient Christian writers are not overly concerned with external evidence of Spirit infilling. While they describe the effects of the Spirit's presence in the Christian life, these are not intended as proofs of Spirit baptism—for they needed no such proof. As a matter of faith they understood that the Holy Spirit enters in the initiatory sacraments, whether at baptism or subsequently at confirmation/chrismation. No proof was required beyond that demonstrated in the character and spirituality of the recipient.

AUGUSTINE: A REJECTION OF TONGUES AS INITIAL EVIDENCE

I am not suggesting that the early Fathers totally ignored the issue of tongues accompanying Spirit baptism. In fact, the greatest of the Western fathers, Augustine of Hippo, actually deals directly with this relationship on several occasions. But each reference suggests a negative, rather than a positive, correlation for the church of his day. While the descent of the Spirit at Pentecost was marked by the "tongues of many nations," Augustine specifically denies that the gift of tongues continues as a signal of the reception of the divine Spirit to his own day. "In the laying on of hands, now, that persons may receive the Holy Ghost, do we look, that they should speak with tongues?" " . . . [w]hen we laid the hand on these infants, did each one of you look to see whether they would speak with tongues, and, when he saw that they did not speak with tongues, was any of you so wrongminded as to say, These have not received the Holy Ghost?"[26]

Augustine goes even a step further. He argues that a spiritual work should not need external proof. "It is understood that invisibly and imperceptibly, on account of the bond of peace, divine love is breathed into their hearts, so that they may be able to say, 'Because the love of God is shed abroad in our hearts by the Holy Ghost which is given unto us.' "[27] The very idea that there should be a sign of the Spirit's reception prompts a strong reaction: "God forbid that our heart should be tempted by this faithlessness." Furthermore, tongues are no longer needed because "the Church itself now speaks in the tongues of all nations."[28]

That Augustine on at least five occasions rejects the concept that tongues should be anticipated as a sign of Spirit reception is highly suggestive. Clearly he does not reject gifts of the Spirit generally, for he reports positively a variety of miracles, including divine healings, in his own Hippo congregation. One can only speculate that, in specifically denying the "evidence" of tongues, he might have been reacting against contemporary enthusiasts of whom we have no historic record.

THE RADICAL DUALISTS: SPECIAL SPIRIT BAPTISM WITH ACCOMPANYING EVIDENCE

While the notion that the reception of the Holy Spirit should be evidenced by tongues or other extraordinary gifts was rejected by Augustine and did not seem to occur to other mainstream church fathers, it *was* taken seriously by one category of Christians. These were the radical dualists—individuals who believed that the cosmos was experiencing a great ongoing conflict between the forces of good and evil. So-called mitigated dualists believed that the evil force was a creature inferior to God; but absolute dualists posited two equal and coeternal deities.

According to the radical dualists, humans were in a difficult position; their souls were spiritual and therefore good, but they must seek to liberate their souls from the flesh as effectively as they could. By living the proper life, they could escape the flesh. Therefore, dualists exaggerated and distorted the ascetic, world-renouncing texts of Scripture and postulated an evil material creation. For many dualists, flesh was itself a creation of an evil God or a fallen creation. Matter was inferior to the spiritual—that which was beyond human sensory perception. The ultimate purpose of existence was to escape from the evil material world.

Consequently, radical dualists throughout history have rejected the world around them, including the mainstream church, as wicked. They have viewed the church as apostate and certainly powerless to cope with the great cosmic struggle against evil. This resulted in a belief that it was impossible to live in the world without becoming part of that world. Radical asceticism was practiced— especially a rejection of marriage which would perpetuate the human body. Usually, extreme dualists were divided into two classes, namely, those who fulfilled the ascetic practices of their group, and those who could not or would not do so, and were, therefore, merely adherents.

Radical dualists also tended to deny the Incarnation—God taking human flesh—the propitiatory work of Jesus Christ on the cross, and the resurrection (why would anyone want to resurrect something as vile as human flesh?). They also rejected the sacraments of the church, insofar as they use evil matter—water in baptism, as well as bread and wine in the Eucharist (although I have not found any open rejection of the oil of chrismation). In other words, the church's "means of grace" were flawed and ineffectual against the powerful hordes of evil.

For several groups of radical dualists, what was needed was an extra-sacramental act—a separate baptism, not of water, but of the Spirit. The fire of the divine Spirit alone could counter the hordes of darkness. And, of course, with so much at stake, it was reasonable to them that there be evidence of Spirit baptism.

Gnostics

Christian Gnostics were the first dualists to distinguish between water and Spirit baptism. In the *Gospel of Philip*, for example, we read:

> If one go down into the water and come up without having anything and says, "I am a Christian," he has borrowed the name at interest. But if he receive the Holy Spirit, he has the name as a gift. He who has received a gift does not have to give it back, but of him who has borrowed it at interest, payment is demanded.[29]

Again, chrism or anointing of the Holy Spirit is viewed as superior to water baptism. The author even goes so far as to suggest that Christians gain that appellation from the word "chrism."[30]

But extant Gnostic texts, which include glossalalia-like passages,[31] make no specific connection between Spirit baptism and tongues. They do suggest, however, that the gifts of the divine Spirit are exercised by those who have received special "gnosis," or knowledge.[32]

Montanists

The Montanists, another group with strongly dualistic tendencies, emerged around A.D. 155. Their founder, Montanus, reportedly a pagan priest of Cybele, converted to Christianity and shortly thereafter, claiming to be possessed by the Holy Spirit, he began to prophesy. Eusebius of Caesarea later reports that Montanus "became beside himself, and being suddenly in a sort of frenzy and ecstasy, he raved, and began to babble and utter strange things, prophesying in a manner contrary to the constant custom of the church handed down by tradition from the beginning." Another critic, Epiphanius of Salamis suggests that Montanus pretended to have a fuller revelation of the Spirit than that possessed by the church.[33]

Montanus was joined by two women, Maximilla and Prisca (or Priscilla), who also prophesied, "talking wildly and unreasonably and strangely."[34] Together with Montanus, they taught a severely ascetic lifestyle, based upon their apocalyptic belief that the New Age of the Paraclete had arrived with them and that the parousia was to occur shortly thereafter at Papuza in Asia Minor. They contended that the apostles had received the perfection of the Spirit in limited measure, but that the full and final gift of the Spirit lay reserved for their own group.

The Montanists rejected as fornication second marriages for Christians. They increased the number of fast days on which they abstained from fresh food, juicy fruit and wine, as well as bathing. Idolatry, murder, fornication, and adultery were irremitable sins for which absolution should never be granted.[35]

This perfectionist lifestyle was accompanied by a spirit of intolerant exclusiveness. The Montanists understood that the Holy Spirit had been given to them in even greater measure than to the apostles. They denied that the Spirit's gifts were present in the church because of its moral laxity. Furthermore, only the "church of the Spirit" would forgive sins, not the corrupted institutional church.[36]

The Montanist reception of the Holy Spirit meant to them that a new era, the Age of the Paraclete, had dawned. This would, in turn, usher in the second coming of Christ. Further, the coming of the Spirit was evidenced by their own prophetic utterances, which became for them a new canon, superseding both Old and New Testaments. Although some modern Pentecostals find "tongues" in Eusebius' description of Montanus' "babbling and uttering strange things,"[37] this may simply have been a reference to his prophecies, which must have seemed nonsensical and strange to those who did not identify with him. In any event, there is no sure indication that tongues played any real role in Montanism, let alone served as an evidence of the Spirit's presence among them.

Messalians

Another heretical dualistic sect, the Messalians, originated in eastern Syria (in Edessa and surrounding parts of Mesopotamia) ca. A.D. 360, and survived until the ninth century. They also were known as Euchites, or "praying people." The Messalians believed that every person was possessed from birth by a personal demon. Even the body of Christ had to be purified from devils by the Logos (the Second Person of the Trinity), although through glorification Christ became like the Father.

Water baptism, which the mainstream church saw as an antidote to demonic forces, did not satisfy the Messalians. The sacrament of baptism was not sufficient because it cut away only former sins, leaving the root of wickedness untouched. They believed that it was possible for Satan and the Holy Spirit to dwell together in a human being—presumably after baptism.[38] Eventually, the individual demon must be driven out through asceticism and unceasing fervent prayer.

The Messalians expected direct evidence, both for the expulsion of the evil spirit and for the entry of the Holy Spirit. The former was perceived visually, with the appearance of images as smoke, black serpents, or a sow with her litter.[39] But indwelling of the divine Spirit also was perceived through sensory experiences. These were likened to sexual intercourse: "It is necessary for the soul to feel such communion with the heavenly bridegroom as the wife feels while having relations with her husband."[40] On occasion, the Holy Spirit was seen to enter the soul with the appearance of an innocuous fire.[41]

It was not enough for believers to confess that they possessed the Holy Spirit in faith through baptism. The Messalians refused to admit any divine activity not present to consciousness. Water baptism was inefficacious because it changed nothing in the psychological state of the person baptized. There had to be experiential evidence that the Spirit had been received "with all certainty and in every operation."[42] True Christians were to receive "a share of the sensation of the Spirit" through prayer and the imposition of hands in a fiery baptism.[43] Only after they had a direct and recognizable experience of the Spirit could they be considered "filled with the Holy Spirit" and freed from their demons.

Having participated in this rite of passage, the Messalian claimed to be able to discern evil spirits and to have prophetic gifts so as to read the hearts of others. Devoting themselves completely to prayer and ascetic works, they had no time for work—an activity which they considered inappropriate for true Christians. They had contempt for churches, of which they felt no need. After all, had they not personally experienced the Holy Spirit? In such a state of grace, they claimed to be partakers of the divine nature and capable of reaching such a level of perfection that they were equal to God and unable to commit sins.[44]

Because of their radical teachings, the Messalians suffered intense persecution. Stamped out in the eastern Mediterranean world by the ninth century, the movement reappeared in Armenia and around Byzantium under the name Paulician, and in the Balkans under the name Bogomil.[45]

SYMEON THE NEW THEOLOGIAN'S "BAPTISM IN THE HOLY SPIRIT"

The radical dualists called for a baptism of the Spirit because, in their opinion, the institutional church's water baptism was flawed and inadequate to equip a Christian for participation in the cosmic struggle against evil. In contrast, the great Eastern spiritual, Symeon the New Theologian (949–1022), argues the need for both water and Spirit baptism. Symeon recognizes that water baptism confers grace through the indwelling of the entire Holy Trinity. Yet a fuller possession of the Spirit comes through a life of faith, through trials and tribulations, and through a second baptism, which he calls "the baptism in the Holy Spirit." He based this theology of two baptisms on the account of the apostles at Jerusalem who sent Peter and John to Samaria to pray for those who already had been baptized (in water) so that they might receive the Holy Spirit, "for he had not yet descended on any of them" (Acts 8:14–17).

Symeon agreed with the Messalians that a person was not in grace without directly experiencing God. It is not enough that the Christian believe that Christ or the Trinity lives within. That divine presence must be operative in a way that is consciously experienced. To Symeon, an ongoing, personal experience of God was essential. The greatest heresy of his day was the notion that Christians no longer could intimately experience God as they had in the early church.

Symeon illustrates the baptism in the Holy Spirit with Plato's Allegory of the Cave in *The Republic*.[46] The great Greek philosopher pictures a prisoner locked in a dark dungeon after birth. The prison is illumined by a small lamp, so that it is difficult to see nearby objects. He is totally unaware of the glorious sun shining outside and of the objects outside illumined by the sun. But after many years in this dark cell, the prisoner is freed to go out into the full sunlight, where he experiences ultimate reality. So it is with life in the Spirit. The Christian suddenly becomes aware of the divine light which dwells within and which possesses him.

In his *Discourses*, Symeon reports numerous personal experiences of God. As a man of twenty, he prostrated himself in prayer, pouring out tears in abundance as he sought God to have mercy on him and to grant spiritual vision to his soul. He then experienced his first vision of God as light.

He lost all awareness of his surroundings and forgot that he was in a house or that he was under a roof. He saw nothing but light all around him and did not know whether he was standing on the ground. . . . Instead, he was wholly in the presence of immaterial light and seemed to himself to have turned into light. Oblivious of all the world he was filled with tears and with ineffable joy and gladness.[47]

It appears that Symeon continued to enjoy similar theophanies throughout his life.

Not content to enjoy his new life in the Spirit in solitary, Symeon exhorted his fellow monks to repent and know a conversion of heart. They then could experience a baptism in the Holy Spirit, as evidenced by the gift of tears.[48] "Seek the Spirit!" he pleads; "Leave the world . . . do not be concerned about the present life."[49]

Symeon's efforts to reform his fellows and encourage them towards a life in the Spirit met considerable resistance. His theology, which implied that spiritual leadership could be based solely on a personal experience of the Spirit rather than on ecclesiastical position, threatened the institutional church. He was accused of being a Messalian. In A.D. 1009 he was forced into exile by an anti-charismatic archbishop, acting on the complaints of Symeon's monks. When finally released from exile, he decided to finish out his days in guiding others and in writing, rather than in assuming administrative responsibilities which were offered to him.

What then were the evidences of this baptism in the Holy Spirit? Clearly, tongues were not in Symeon's mind, although he himself spoke in tongues.[50] Baptism in the Spirit results in an intensified experience or sensation of the indwelling Trinity. In addition, the recipient of the indwelling Spirit experiences the gift of tears and a heightened sense of compunction or remorse for sins. Further, the fruits of the Spirit (those in Galatians 5 and other ascetic virtues) will accompany the presence of the Holy Spirit, for these also are his gifts.[51] Under the power of the Spirit, the Christian will be able to keep Christ's commandments and will be able to better comprehend the things of God. Finally, reception of the Spirit opens the door to a new and vital interior life and to all the divine graces. Symeon associates these graces with *theosis* or deification of the Christian (becoming God-like).

Symeon's stress on a baptism in the Holy Spirit and his call for Christians to return to a radical living of the gospel—to the charismatic and prophetic life of the primitive church—bear striking resemblance to modern Pentecostal and charismatic emphases. But the evidence which he offers for the Spirit-filled life is far broader than the Pentecostal "initial evidence" of tongues. It more closely resembles that of many modern charismatics.

EASTERN CHRISTIANITY: A HOUSE DIVIDED BETWEEN EXPERIENTIAL AND SACRAMENTAL EMPHASES

The division in Eastern Christendom between those who maintain that the divine Spirit works in and through the sacraments (or "mysteries") and those who insist on extra-sacramental mystical endowments of the Spirit has continued to modern times. The first group is represented by Nicholas Cabasilas; the second by Seraphim of Sarov.

Nicholas Cabasilas

Of all Eastern Fathers, Nicholas Cabasilas (d. ca. 1371) is most concerned with the work of the Holy Spirit in the sacraments or "mysteries." Like Symeon the New Theologian and his spiritual successor, Gregory Palamas (a fourteenth-century defender of the experiential Hesychasts), Cabasilas taught the concept of God as Uncreated Light. But he did so in moderated form. God is to be experienced as light in the mysteries, rather than in extra-sacramental mystical experiences as taught by Symeon and Palamas.[52] According to Cabasilas, mystical union with Christ or a personal transfiguration experience occurs in the mysteries of baptism, chrismation, and the Eucharist. Those who are spiritually born in baptism must also be energized and animated. This occurs in chrismation, which Nicholas calls "participation in the Holy Spirit." The effect of chrismation is the imparting of the energies of the divine Spirit. As it was on the day of Pentecost, some individuals receive the ability to foretell the future, to cast out demons, and to heal diseases through their prayers. But all Christians receive gifts at chrismation, including godliness, prayer, love, and sobriety. Unfortunately, many individuals do not realize or exercise the divine gifts received at chrismation.

The Spirit also shares his gifts during the Eucharist, after he is invoked in the *epiklesis*. He transforms bread and wine into the Body and Blood of Christ, and transforms the participants as he grants to them remission of sins.

For Cabasilas, evidence of the Spirit's presence is the perfection of the saints, known as *theosis*—becoming one with divine light (literally, "deification," although with Gregory Palamas's distinction between divine "essence" and "energies," it is clear that what is meant here is becoming

God-like, not sharing in divine "essence"). Reception of the divine Spirit brings the character of God. The Christian is holy because of the indwelling Holy Spirit.[53]

Seraphim of Sarov

One of the great saints of the Russian church, Prokhor Moshnin—better known as Seraphim of Sarov (1759–1833)—practiced the experientialism of Symeon the New Theologian. Of weak body, he frequently experienced miraculous healings, as did many who sought his prayers. He was granted a powerful gift of prophecy, as well as the ability to know the needs of his supplicants before they told him. But of greatest importance for our study is his recorded conversation in November 1831 with Nicholas Motovilov concerning the reception of the Holy Spirit.[54]

The pious Motovilov inquires of Seraphim as to the goal of Christian living. The latter responded that prayer, fasting, and works of mercy were only the means, not the end of the Christian life. The true end is the acquisition of the Holy Spirit. The Spirit's presence brings the kingdom of God and all the blessings of the present and future life to the recipient. The Spirit is given only on the condition that the believer knows how to acquire him. This is done primarily by prayer. One must pray until God the Holy Spirit descends.

Motovilov inquires how it was possible to know that the Holy Spirit is present in a person or not. In turn, Seraphim asks why his visitor is not looking at him. Motovilov responds that he cannot, because Seraphim's face and eyes are brighter than the sun and, therefore, he is dazzled. Seraphim reported that his visitor also was shining in the same transfigured manner, and that Motovilov would not have been able to see him as such had he not received the fulness of the Spirit.[55]

Seraphim's "evidence" for a baptism in the Spirit, then, is a transfiguration experience—being transformed while still in the flesh into divine light. This to the Eastern mystic is the process by which *theosis* is achieved. The Holy Spirit, then, is the divine agent who returns humanity to the image of God.

NOTES

1. The standard study is G. H. Williams and E. Waldvogel [Blumhofer], "A History of Speaking in Tongues and Related Gifts," in M. P. Hamilton, ed., *The Charismatic Movement* (Grand Rapids: Eerdmans, 1975), 61–113.

2. K. McDonnell and G. T. Montague, in *Christian Iniation and Baptism in the Holy Spirit from the First Eight Centuries* (Collegeville, Minn.: Liturgical Press, 1991), insist that baptism in the Holy Spirit was integral to Christian initiation in the early church. They therefore reason that it must be viewed as normative, both then and now.

3. Tertullian, *On Baptism* 7–8, in *Ante-Nicene Fathers* (Grand Rapids: Eerdmans, 1976), 3:672, 673 (henceforth ANF).

4. Tertullian, *On the Resurrection of the Flesh* 9, ANF 3:551.

5. Tertullian, *On the Veiling of Virgins* 3.1, ANF 4:27.

6. Hippolytus, *Apostolic Traditions* 2.1, 3.1–7, 7.2–5, in Burton Scott Easton, trans. (Cambridge: Cambridge University Press, 1934), 33–39.

7. Cyprian, *Letters* 72, 73; ANF 5:381, 388.

8. Hilary of Poitiers, *Commentary on Matthew* 3.14; PL 9: col. 926.

9. Hilary of Poitiers, *Homilies on the Psalms* 118; PL 9: col. 519.

10. Ambrose, *On the Mysteries* 7.42, 9.59, in *Nicene and Post-Nicene Fathers*, 2d series (Grand Rapids: Eerdmans, 1975), 10:322, 325 (henceforth NPF); *On the Holy Spirit* 3.10.68, NPF 2d series 10:144; *On the Sacraments* 5.17, in *Corpus scriptorum ecclesiasticorum latinorum* (Vindobonae, apud C. Geroldi filium, 1866–1913), 73:65.

11. Cyril of Jerusalem, *Catechetical Lectures* 21 ("On the Mysteries III: On Chrism"), NPF 2d series, 7:149–50.

12. J. Wordsworth, ed., *Bishop Serapion's Prayer-Book*, in Early Christian Classics (London: SPCK, 1899; New York and Toronto: Macmillan, 1923), 74–78.

13. Basil of Cappadocia, *On the Holy Spirit* 26.61, NPF 2d series, 8:39.

14. Ibid., 9.23; NPF 2d series 8.16.

15. Basil of Cappadocia, *The Small Asceticism* 3, in Jacques Paul Migne, ed., *Patrologia cursus completus. Series Latina* (Pariis, J. P. Migne, 1844–1904), CIII: col. 495.

16. Gregory of Nazianzen, *Oration on the Holy Lights* 8, NPF 2d series 7:381.

17. Gregory of Nazianzen, *Oration* 12: "To his father" 1, NPF 2d series 7:245.

18. See S. M. Burgess, *The Holy Spirit: Eastern Christian Traditions* (Peabody, Mass.: Hendrickson, 1989), 178.

19. Gregory of Nyssa, *Vita atque eucomium*, in Jacques Paul Migne, ed. *Patrologia cursus completus. Series Graeca* (Paris, J. P. Migne, 1859–87), 46:col. 830.

20. Pseudo-Macarius, *Homily* 1.9, in A. J. Mason, *Fifty Spiritual Homilies of St. Macarius the Egyptian* (London: SPCK, 1921), 8.

21. Pseudo-Macarius, *Homily* 32.1, Mason 172.

22. Ibid., 5.5, Mason 42.

23. Ibid., 5.4, 27.12; Mason 40, 206–7.

24. Ibid., 18.7, Mason 154–55.

25. A. J. Wensinck, *Mystical Treatises of Isaac of Nineveh* (Amsterdam: Verhandelingen der K. Akademies, 1923), 36, 117, 330. Cf., Burgess, *Holy Spirit: Eastern Christian Traditions*, 102–9.

26. Augustine, *Homily* 6.10 (on the Epistles of St. John), NPF 1st series 7:497–8; *On Baptism* 3.16.21, NPF 1st series 4:443.

27. Augustine, *On Baptism*, loc.cit.

28. Augustine, *On the Gospel of St. John* 32.7, NPF 1st series 7:195.

29. *Gospel of Philip* 2.3.64.12–30; in James M. Robinson, ed., *The Nag Hammadi Library in English* (New York: Harper & Row, 1981), 139 (henceforth NHL).

30. Ibid., 2.3.74.12–23, NHL 144.

31. See S. M. Burgess, *The Spirit and the Church: Antiquity* (Peabody, Mass.: Hendrickson, 1984), 41.

32. *The Interpretation of Knowledge* 9.1.15–17, 20; NHL 432–4.

33. Eusebius, *Church History* 5.16.7–9, NPF 2d series 1:231; PG 40:col. 875.

34. Ibid., 5.16.8, NPF 2d series 1:231.

35. Tertullian, *On Modesty* 1, 4–5; ANF 4:75, 77–78.

36. Ibid., 21, ANF 4:100.

37. E.g., W. H. Horton, ed., *The Glossolalia Phenomenon* (Cleveland, Tenn.: Pathway Press, 1966), 77.

38. Timothy of Constantinople, *De iis, qui ad Ecclesiam accedunt* ("The Reception of Heretics," 2, 7), in *Patrologia Syriaca* (Paris, ediderunt Firmin-Didot et socii, 1926), 3/1:cols. ccxiii, ccxxiv; John of Damascus, *De Haeresibus Compendio* 80.3, 5, English trans. in F. H. Chase, Jr., *St. John of Damascus: Writings*, vol. 37 of *The Fathers of the Church* (Washington, D.C.: Catholic University of America, 1958, 1970), 132; Augustine, *De haeresibus ad quodvultdeum liber unus* 57, PL 42:col. 41.

39. Augustine, ibid., 57, PL 42:cols. 40–41; Timothy 3, PS 3/1:col. ccxxii; John of Damascus 80, PS c/1:col. ccxxxvi, Chase 133.

40. John of Damascus, ibid., 80, PS 3/1:col. ccxxxii, Chase 132; Timothy 4, PS 3/1:cols. ccxxiii–ccxxiv.

41. Augustine 57, PL 42:cols. 40–41.

42. John of Damascus 80.17, PS 3/1:col. cxxxv, Chase 133.

43. Ibid., 80; PS 3/1:col. cxxxvi; Chase 134.

44. Jerome, *Prologue in Dialogum adversus Pelagianos*, PS 3/1:cols. clxxix–clxxx, NPF 2d series 6:448–449.

45. S. Runciman, *The Medieval Manichee: A Study of the Christian Dualistic Heresy* (Cambridge: Cambridge University Press, 1947), chapters 2, 4, and 5.

46. Symeon the New Theologian, *Traites Ethiques*, 1, 12, 350–378, in Jean Darrouzes, ed., *Sources Chrétiennes* (Paris: Les Editions du Cerf, 1967), 129:298–300.

47. Symeon the New Theologian, *The Discourses* 22.89–105, in Classics of Western Spirituality, ed. C. J. deCatauzara (New York: Paulist Press, 1980), 244–46.

48. *Discourses* 29.5, 313. See G. A. Maloney, *Symeon the New Theologian: The Mystic of Fire and Light* (Denville, N.J.: Dimension Books, 1975), chapter 2 "Baptism in the Holy Spirit," and Burgess, *Holy Spirit: Eastern Christian Traditions*, 58–61, for further discussion.

49. G. A. Maloney, trans., *Hymns of Divine Love by St. Symeon the New Theologian* (Denville, N.J.: Dimension Books, 1976), 98.

50. P. Thompson, "A Prayer to God of St. Symeon the New Theologian," *Sobornost* n.s. 6 (June 1936): 2.

51. *Discourses* 10.50–59, 163.

52. Nicholas Cabasilas, *The Life in Christ* (Crestwood, N.Y.: St. Vladimir's Seminary Press, 1974), 103–7.

53. Ibid., book 6, 173–89.

54. V. Zander, *St. Seraphim of Sarov* (Crestwood, N.Y.: St. Vladimir's Seminary Press, 1975), 83–94; A. F. Dobbie-Bateman, trans., *St. Seraphim of Sarov: Concerning the Aim of the Christian Life* (London: SPCK, 1936), 42–60.

55. Zander, *St. Seraphim*, 95; Dobbie-Bateman, *St. Seraphim*, 58.

2

EVIDENCE OF THE SPIRIT: THE MEDIEVAL
AND MODERN WESTERN CHURCHES

Stanley M. Burgess

The great medieval Roman Catholic theologians had very little to add
to the Augustinian synthesis with regard to a baptism of the Spirit and
to any "evidence" which might accompany an infilling of the divine
Spirit. In part, this may have resulted from their veneration for the
Father from Hippo. It also stemmed from their preoccupation with the
filioque controversy—namely, whether the Holy Spirit proceeded from
the Father through the Son (the Eastern Christian position) or from
both Father *and the Son* (the Western position). Again, the divine Spirit
was seen as an agent of Christ in redemption, and, therefore, was emphasized less than in the Eastern churches, where the Spirit was the agent
for perfecting the saints. Finally, for most theologians—other than the
mystics—there seems to have been more concern for scholastic inquiry
than for experiential spirituality. Of course, in addition to the mystics,
several fringe groups, including the radical dualists, showed considerable interest in a pneumatology of experience.

Spiritual gifts as described by Paul in 1 Corinthians 12 were exercised
widely in the Catholic West during the Middle Ages. But most Catholic
theologians taught that it was not to be expected that they would function in all believers. Instead, these were extraordinary gifts reserved for

the ministries of the most pious, and so they marked the lives of saints. Certain of the saints reportedly spoke in earthly languages not their own, and a few allegedly spoke in the language of angels.[1] In addition, other charismatic gifts were apparent in the lives of the saints— including gifts of knowledge and discernment, of healing, and of prophecy. These often received high profile from the Roman church, which listed them in support of the elevation of these individuals to the status of saints. Although they are frequently cited as indicators of the spiritual life, they never are viewed as "evidence" of Spirit infilling. This can be illustrated in the life of Hildegarde of Bingen.

Medieval Catholic Mystics

Hildegarde of Bingen (1098–1179). The German mystic Hildegarde became the leader of a convent near Bingen. She is said to have exercised many spiritual gifts, including singing in unknown tongues to the extent that her biographer refers to these occasions as "concerts."[2] She also experienced visions, which increased in frequency as she grew older. One of these is pictured in the first miniature of the famous Rupertsberg illuminated manuscript, in which Hildegarde's head is pierced by the flames of the Holy Spirit as she writes down her visions on a wax tablet.[3] This is a remarkable self-portrait of her infilling with the Holy Spirit, with obvious reference to the experience of recipients on the day of Pentecost. She reports that this occurred when she was forty-two years and seven months old. A burning light of tremendous brightness coming from heaven poured into her entire mind. It was like a flame that does not burn but kindles. It set her entire heart on fire. As a result of receiving the Spirit she writes as the Spirit directs.

Hildegarde's principal writing, *Scivias*, recounts twenty-six visions and evidences an apocalyptic emphasis dealing with creation, redemption, and the church. In addition, she wrote saints' lives, two books of medicine and natural history, homilies, and hymns. Several of these books are written in Latin, a language virtually unknown to her. Among her published hymns is *De Spiritu Sancto*, which expresses her deep understanding of the creative and re-creative work of the divine Spirit:

> Holy Spirit, making life alive,
>> moving in all things, root of all created being,
>> cleansing the cosmos of every impurity,
>> effacing guilt, anointing wounds.
> You are lustrous and praiseworthy life,
>> You waken and re-awaken everything that is.[4]

Were Hildegarde to have been asked what evidence exists for the presence of the Holy Spirit, her answer would not have centered on spiritual gifts. Rather, she would have spoken of her writings, which she believed were directed by the divine Spirit. But she also would have recognized that the Spirit's presence is not restricted to any individual but is cosmic in character. Therefore, she would have pointed to all of nature—to the universe which was created jointly by the Trinity and which is sustained by the divine Spirit.

> Holy Spirit.
> Through you clouds billow, breezes blow,
>> stones drip with trickling streams,
>> streams that are the source of earth's lush greening.
> Likewise, you are the source of human understanding,
> You bless with the breath of wisdom.
> Thus all of our praise is yours,
>> you who are the melody itself of praise,
>> the joy of life, the mighty honor,
>> the hope of those to whom you give the gifts of the light.[5]

Bonaventure (ca. 1217–74). Chief among medieval Western mystics was Bonaventure, whose overriding purpose as a writer was to portray the journey of the inner person inward and upward into the mystery of the triune God. For him, this journey was a growth in the Spirit, an expansion of the heart in love and other great virtues through the three stages of purgation, illumination, and perfection.[6] Bonaventure personally wrestled with the Spirit and received a mystical ecstasy that gave rest to his intellect and made natural affections of little concern to him.

Bonaventure greatly revered his mentor, Francis of Assisi, and the workings of the Spirit in and through him. In his biography of Francis,[7] he portrays the saint as a man of the Spirit. Francis' first experience of the Spirit came as he gained assurance that his sins had been completely forgiven. He was rapt in ecstasy and totally absorbed in a wonderful light. In this state he was able to see what would transpire for him and his followers in the future.

Francis learned that the presence of the Spirit for whom he longed was granted more intimately to those who seek him and withdraw from the noise of worldly affairs. He frequently was lifted up by the Spirit into ecstasy (also described as "drunk in the Spirit"), and he thereby gained a greater devotion to the crucified Christ. For Francis, to know Christ and him crucified was a gift of the Spirit. Wherever Francis went, he exercised gifts of wisdom, knowledge, and prophecy, and performed miracles of great power.

Julian of Norwich (1343–1413) and Margery Kempe (ca. 1373–post 1439).
Among the most influential Catholic mystics of the High Middle Ages
were Julian of Norwich and her disciple, Margery Kempe. Julian probably was an anchoress, living outside the walls of St. Julian's church in
Norwich. On May 8, 1373, as she remained in a state of ecstasy for five
hours, she received a series of fifteen revelations. One other vision
followed the next day. Twenty years later, Julian related her meditations
on these visions in a book, *The Sixteen Revelations of Divine Love (The
Showings).*[8] She became famous in her own time and was sought out,
especially by those who also had similar mystical experiences. Among
these was Margery Kempe.

After almost twenty years of marriage and fourteen children, forty-year-
old Margery Kempe began to have visions of Christ. She also felt compelled to live a celibate life, in preparation for a pilgrimage by foot to
Jerusalem. Whenever Margery heard preaching on the crucifixion of
Christ, she broke out in tears. Some clergy complained against her emotional outbursts. As a consequence, Margery visited Julian of Norwich in
her cell to determine whether her tears were from God or merely from
human emotions. In her autobiography, Margery relates this visit. Julian
gave Margery real support, confirming that her gift of tears was not
against the Spirit, but was a token of the Spirit's indwelling: " . . . when
God visits a creature with tears of contrition, devotion, and compassion,
he may and ought to believe that the Holy Ghost is in his soul. . . ."[9] In
addition, Julian insists that those who are chaste are properly called
temples of the Holy Spirit.

Ensley's Sounds of Wonder

Eddie Ensley argues that, from the ninth through the sixteenth centuries, spontaneity of worship, songs of jubilation, clapping of hands, and
even dance movements were apparent in the lives of many ordinary
believers.[10] Ensley uses the term "jubilation" to refer to the language of
spiritual inebriation—going beyond ordinary speech into a transcendent
language of praise—which he views as the equivalent of speaking in
tongues. Ensley also suggests that it was common to hear group singing
in the Spirit, as practiced in the present-day charismatic renewal.

This was accompanied by popular devotion to the Holy Spirit, with the
writing of such hymns as "Veni, Creator" ("Come, Creator Spirit") and
"Veni, Sancte Spiritus" ("Come, O Holy Spirit"). Churches, hospitals,
hospices, and even towns were dedicated to the divine Third Person in
this period. Confraternities of the Holy Spirit to care for the poor and
for deserted children, appeared in the Auvergne.

Whether one accepts Ensley's "jubilation as tongues" thesis, it is abundantly clear that the Western medieval church experienced a not inconsiderable share of Spirit activity. Nowhere, however, is glossolalia linked to Spirit reception.

Joachim of Fiore: The Apocalyptic Age of the Spirit

Perhaps the most important prophetic figure in Western medieval Christianity, Joachim of Fiore (ca. 1130–1202), experienced a series of visions which helped him to understand the meaning of the Scriptures, and from these he developed a dispensational system that he applied to human history.[11] Joachim divides history into three periods: the age of the Father (from creation to Christ), the age of the Son (reaching from the ninth or seventh centuries B.C. to A.D. 1260), and the age of the Spirit (from ca. A.D. 500 to the end of the world). The three ages represent ongoing spiritual progress.

Because the dispensation of the Spirit is a time when the corporate church will be blessed by more intensive Spirit activity, this age does not equate with a baptism of the divine Third Person, which is normally understood in highly individualistic terms. But Joachim sees spiritual graces emerging in the full body of Christ with the advent of the Spirit— graces which are remarkably similar to those anticipated by the church when an individual is filled with the Holy Spirit.

During this age, the Holy Spirit will complete the teachings of Christ and impart to each one knowledge and grace to achieve perfection and to persevere in it. Humankind as well as the church will be perfected, and the world will be evangelized. All peoples will learn to despise this world and worldly things. The spiritual person will know the truth without veil and will receive directly from the Holy Spirit all the charismatic gifts necessary for perfection. The institutional church will be transformed into the true spiritual church, and the kingdoms of this world will yield to the kingdom of God. Heaven will descend upon earth.

In a very real sense, Joachim understands that the age of the Spirit will be "evidenced" in both corporate and individual dimensions. The coming of the divine Spirit will lead to the perfection of the church and its members, with the exercise of all spiritual gifts (for the good of all). Interestingly, this is in keeping with Eastern, rather than Western, Christian spirituality.

THE CATHARS: MEDIEVAL WESTERN RADICAL DUALISTS

Catharism, which seems to have links to earlier dualistic heresies such as Paulicianism (and perhaps also to Bogomilism), appeared in western

Europe in the eleventh century.[12] Because of its proselyting, it became the most powerful heresy in the West by the thirteenth century. At the Fourth Lateran Council (1215), the Roman church initiated a crusade against the Cathars. Under persecution, the movement began to decline, disappearing altogether during the fourteenth century.

Like other radical dualists, the Cathars posited two opposing forces in the world, one good and one evil. The God of the Old Testament created the world (matter) and was, therefore, the evil god. The Old Testament was to be rejected, except for certain prophetic statements which were believed to have predicted the coming of Christ.

The Cathars were docetists, arguing that Christ could not have had a true human body since the divine would not have clothed itself in a garment of evil flesh. His suffering on the cross was therefore an illusion, as was his resurrection. Like the gnostics, the Cathars also considered Jesus as less than very God; thus the doctrine of the Trinity was denied. Jesus' mission was not to redeem through his passion, but rather to convey to human prisoners of the flesh instructions for escaping from the body.

Because Christ's body was an illusion and the Eucharist was matter, that sacrament was a delusion. The cross and all Catholic images were matter, and therefore contemptible. Water baptism also was considered as unprofitable for salvation. Instead, the Cathars believed that to enter the company of their elite, the *perfecti* or *cathar,* it was necessary to take the *consolamentum* or initiatory sacrament. This was a baptism with fire and the Holy Spirit, performed by the imposition of hands.

The *consolamentum* combined baptism, confirmation, and ordination into a priestly caste, with confession, penitence, absolution and even extreme unction for the dying. Through this rite, the Cathars believed that mortal sins were forgiven and the Holy Spirit was received. The expectation of this baptism with the Spirit was that recipients would become members of the *cathar* (or the "perfect").

Preliminaries to attaining this status were arduous. The candidate had to be approved by other *perfecti* and had to have shown fitness to undertake the life by a year's probation. During this time severe food fasts were undertaken. All sexual contact was forbidden; and especially in the last days of the movement, even the most harmless physical contact between man and woman was rigorously excluded. If married, a candidate was obliged to abandon his or her partner; if unmarried, lifelong celibacy was the rule.

During the ceremony the candidate promised never to touch the opposite sex again, never to kill an animal or to eat meat, eggs, or anything made with milk. The candidate further agreed to do nothing without first saying the Lord's Prayer, and never to travel, spend the night anywhere, or even eat without a companion. In addition, the candidate was never to sleep unclothed; and, finally, the initiate pledged never to betray the faith even though faced with the worst of deaths.

Having passed through the *consolamentum,* Cathars were allowed to say the *Pater Noster* ("Our Father") and to participate fully in the life of the *perfecti.* At the same time, they faced a lifetime of rigid observance of the precepts of this life. Cathars met regularly for mutual encouragement, self-examination, and confession of sins, as they battled for perfection in their way of life. No breach in their code was allowed for the "perfect" ones. For the Cathars, asceticism was not, as with the Roman Catholics, merely a means to perfection. It was the sole means of salvation.

The baptism of fire and of the Spirit, then, was entry into a rigid ascetic life, the exercise of which would bring one to perfection and ultimately to salvation. They are particularly important to our study for their linkage of Spirit infilling and a life of holiness.

THE REFORMATION ERA

The Magisterial Reformers

The sixteenth-century Protestant revolt brought a new stress on the Scriptures, and with that an emphasis on the primacy of faith for salvation. In their recovery of the gospel, both Luther and Calvin underscored the indispensable role of the Holy Spirit in the event of justification. The Spirit makes Christ and his atoning sacrifice and imputed righteousness available to every believer. Hence, sanctification necessarily follows justification, and both are works of the Spirit of God. For Luther and Calvin, therefore, the presence of the Spirit is evidenced by both salvation and righteousness.

Martin Luther (1483–1546). For Luther, the outpouring of the Holy Spirit on the day of Pentecost freed the disciples from their fear and sorrow, changing and renewing their hearts, and inflaming them with boldness to preach Christ. This also would occur for later Christians, as they are confronted by the Spirit through preaching. They are called, gathered, enlightened, sanctified, and preserved.[13] They are equipped by the Spirit with the word of proclamation and with courage and power to fight the devil.[14] The Spirit mediates the living and resurrected Christ in such a way that Christ becomes the new subject of the believer's life. Pentecost also brought a new meaning for prayer; from Pentecost on, prayer was offered with a spirit of supplication.[15]

Following Augustine, Martin Luther argued that "new tongues" had been a sign and a witness to the Jews. However, in his own day, Christianity no longer required confirmation by such signs. Tongues had ceased. But Christians might expect to receive one of several other gifts of the Holy Spirit, although only "fanatical spirits and sectarians" would seek to have all these gifts.[16]

One of Luther's contemporaries, Andreas Bodenstein von Carlstadt, argued that Paul's directives to the Corinthians concerning tongues excluded preaching in Latin. Luther, in response, insisted that Paul was not forbidding speaking with tongues (for Luther this meant reading, teaching or preaching in a foreign language) when it was accompanied by an interpretation. In the absence of an interpreter, no language other than the appropriate vernacular should be utilized.[17]

According to Luther, the Holy Spirit is given only to the anxious and distressed heart. Obviously, no one should boast of possessing the divine Spirit—as certain proud fanatics did—because even the most pious still must strive against sin.[18] These self-proclaimed "prophets" (including Carlstadt and the three prophets from Zwickau) do not have the "signs" of Pentecost. Indeed, Luther declares, there is no revelation of the Holy Spirit outside the Scriptures.[19]

John Calvin (1509–1564). For the great Genevan Reformer, John Calvin, the Holy Spirit serves to create faith in Christ through the word of God in the heart of the predestined elect person. The Spirit also gives "inner witness" to authenticate Scripture.

The evidences for the Spirit's work, then, are faith in Christ and in the Scriptures, but not in overt spiritual gifts. Like Luther, John Calvin seems to have been personally unacquainted with the more "visible" spiritual gifts, including glossolalia. In the New Testament church, tongues had facilitated preaching in foreign languages, but in Calvin's view had been corrupted by human ambition at Corinth. God therefore had chosen to remove such utterances from the church rather than have them further abused.[20] Calvin concludes that the divine Spirit is given to us for a better use, namely, that we may believe with the heart unto righteousness.

Calvin does insist that the genuine fruits of the Spirit—love, joy, peace, patience, kindness, goodness, faithfulness, gentleness and self-control (Gal. 5:22–26)—are the operational basis in practice for the genuine exercise of the gifts of the Spirit. And indeed certain (nonvisible) gifts do remain, including the word of knowledge, the word of wisdom, and the discernment of true and false spirits. Perhaps most appealing to Calvin is the gift of prophecy, which he correlates with outstanding inspired preaching. More important to Calvin than all of these is the inner testimony of the Spirit, which convinces Christians that they must listen obediently to the Scriptures.[21]

The Radical Reformers

Unlike the teaching Reformers, the Radical Reformers (Enthusiasts, Anabaptists, and other groups) emphasized the "inner voice" of the Spirit and gave less credence to any "external word," which for some included the Bible.[22] In a manner reminiscent of the Montanists, they taught that the advent of the Spirit evoked prophecy, which conveyed prescriptions for Christian living and new eschatological understandings. For example, the Hutterites (followers of Jacob Hutter) taught common ownership and shared utilization of goods. The Melchiorites (followers of Melchior Hoffmann) prophesied the approaching last judgment. A second generation Melchiorite, Jan Matthys, was a violent fanatic who took over the city of Munster, which he declared to be the New Jerusalem over which he as prophet-king would rule.

Other Radical Reformers included Sebastian Franck who taught that Christians should follow the inner leadings of the Holy Spirit. Franck distinguished between "the true church"—the invisible body of Christ— and all organized churches, which were evil. Kasper von Schwenckfeld also stressed inner experiences, especially that of rebirth (a sixteenth-century "born again" Christian), which was accomplished by the divine Spirit. The pacifist Menno Simons (1496–1561) taught that the Spirit guides into all truth, justifying, cleansing, sanctifying, reconciling, comforting, reproving, cheering, and assuring children of God.[23]

It should be noted that glossolalia broke out among a few groups during the Radical Reformation, including those at Appenzell, St. Gall, Fulda, and Munster.[24] But glossolalia remained incidental and occasional, with prophecy and the "inner light/word" being the expected evidences for the coming of the Spirit.

THE SEVENTEENTH CENTURY

The concluding decades of the Reformation Era found the Western church, both Roman Catholic and Protestant, engaged in producing detailed confessional statements. At the same time, much of their energy was depleted from fighting protracted religious wars. The Holy Spirit, considered of prime importance by the early Reformers, was now obscured in long debates over minute doctrinal details. But several Christian fringe groups that developed during this period did focus heavily on the work of the divine Third Person. These included the Quakers and the Prophets of the Cevennes (Camisards).

The Quakers ("The Religious Society of Friends")

The Society of Friends was founded by George Fox (1624–1690) in mid-seventeenth-century England, which had been torn by civil war and considerable religious ferment. As with many of their precursors among the Radical Reformers, the Quakers' central doctrine was the "inner light" (or "inner word"), in which the Spirit speaks directly to the human mind. Through the "inner word" Christ is revealed, as is the Christian's relationship to God, the nature of Christian doctrine, and the correct interpretation of Scripture ("the outer word").

The Quakers developed a unique form of corporate worship, sitting in silence and waiting for God to speak through one or more of them. Early Quaker literature records visions, healings, and prophecies which they likened to the day of Pentecost. There is even evidence of tongues-speech among them, although Fox eventually discouraged such ecstatic utterances.

In contrast to the contemporary Puritans—who were highly biblicist—the Quakers taught that experiencing the divine Spirit was the only basis for true Christianity. Robert Barclay, their leading first generation theologian, declared that without the Spirit, Christianity was no more than a corpse, once the soul and spirit have departed.[25] Every true Christian minister, whether ordained or not, is endowed by the divine Spirit. For the Quaker, then, the Holy Spirit's presence brings revealed truth concerning all things relating to the Christian life.

The Prophets of the Cevennes (Camisards)

The Camisards were French Protestant resistance fighters provoked to revolt by the brutal repression of all public practices of their faith following the revocation of the Edict of Nantes in 1685. They were persecuted mercilessly by the French government, and their revolt finally was suppressed in 1705. Some found sanctuary in England and formed a small sect known as the "French Prophets."

The Camisards claimed to be directly inspired by the Holy Spirit. Their prophets were inspired by apocalyptic writings and personal revelations to predict the end of time and to wage war against King Louis XIV (1643–1715). Among their leaders was a respectable intellectual, Pierre Jurieu, and a glassblower, M. du Serre; they gathered young children of both sexes from the peasantry, and breathed into their mouths the gift of Pentecost. Eventually, large numbers of children (from the ages of six months up!) were reported to have prophesied. The Spirit also was received after individuals fasted several days and then received a holy kiss.

The Camisards maintained that "God has no where in the Scriptures concluded himself from dispensing again the extraordinary Gifts of His Spirit unto Men." Joel's prophecy was to have an even greater fulfillment in their time than in the early church.[26]

Camisard enthusiasts are reported to have been seized by ecstatic inspiration, during which time they struck themselves, fell on their backs, and shut their eyes. After remaining in trances, they came out with twitches, uttering strange and often amazing things. Sometimes they spoke in human languages of which they had no knowledge, but more frequently in unknown tongues.[27]

THE EIGHTEENTH CENTURY

The Jansenists (17th–18th centuries)

Approximately twenty years after the Camisards were finally dispersed in 1710, a similar enthusiasm broke out within the Jansenist community. The Jansenists, who took their name from Cornelius Jansen, the bishop of Ypres, were a radically Augustinian movement in the Roman Catholic church. Their teachings undercut the sacramental and hierarchical claims of the church and were condemned in 1653 by Pope Innocent X. The early Jansenists, especially those at Port-Royal, were given to dependence on signs and wonders, but this tendency reached its peak among the convulsionaries of eighteenth-century Saint-Medard.

The Roman church viciously persecuted the radical Jansenists in an effort to stamp out the movement. They were kicked, trampled, pressured by heavy weights or squeezed, beaten with clubs, pricked with swords, and crucified. The persecuted were known for their spiritual dancing, for healings, and for prophetic utterances. When seized by convulsions, some reportedly spoke in an unknown tongue and understood languages in which they were addressed.[28]

While it is impossible to judge fully their understanding of the Holy Spirit's work, since most of their primary sources have never been studied critically, it seems likely that their pneumatology was shaped by their persecutions. In this event, the presence of the Holy Spirit was evident not only by spiritual gifts but also by an ability to suffer for their truth. In short, the Jansenists seem to have had much the same understanding as early Christian martyrs.

Isaac Watts

One of the greatest of Christian hymn-writers, the English non-conformist Isaac Watts (1674–1748) did much to make hymn-singing a powerful devotional force at a time when the use of music was regarded with suspicion. While he seems to have tended towards Unitarianism late in his life, the subject of the Holy Spirit was important in his earlier writings. Most interesting is his essay, "The Gift of the Spirit."[29]

Watts declares that the significance of the gift of the Spirit was to make saints of the rebellious and sinful, as well as to confer power on them to reverse the laws of nature and to imitate creation by giving eyes to the blind and by raising the dead. Furthermore, Watts insists that this same Spirit is given to all divine subjects, without regard to time frame. And where the Spirit is, miracles occur—the sinner is transformed into a saint, blind eyes open, human nature is recreated, and the dead receive divine life. He also states that the Spirit "teaches Egypt and Assyria, and the British Isles, to speak the language of Canaan." It is this gift of the Spirit which the Son sends down to us continually from the Father. Reflecting one of the great concerns of many eighteenth-century spirituals, Watts implores, "May all the temptations which we meet from men of reason, never, never baffle so sweet a faith!"

The Moravians

The Moravian Brethren were direct descendents of the Bohemian Hussites, a group which declined after the Thirty Years War (ending in 1648). They were reorganized in 1722 at Herrnhut under the leadership of Nikolaus Ludwig Count von Zinzendorf (1700–1760) and were strongly influenced by both German pietism and the Lutheran church, of which they considered themselves a part. The group at Herrnhut later was called the "Church of God in the Spirit" by Count Zinzendorf.

Following a time of renewal in 1727, the Moravians became known for their emotionally expressive worship, fervent prayer, and much singing.

Their zeal was channeled into numerous missionary projects. In England they were maligned by one John Roche for reviving the Montanist practices of "strange convulsive heavings, and unnatural postures," and speaking in tongues ("they commonly broke into some disconnected Jargon, which they often passed upon the vulgar, 'As the exuberant and resistless Evacuations of the Spirit . . .' ").[30]

It is particularly interesting to note that Zinzendorf believed (like early twentieth-century Pentecostals) that the gift of tongues had originally been given in order to facilitate the missionary enterprise. But the Moravian leadership did not endorse glossolalia, even though it occurred sporadically in their meetings.

One of the most famous Moravian preachers, John Cennick, delivered a discourse on *The Gift and Office of the Holy Ghost* in Little Sommerford in Wiltshire, England, in 1740.[31] He argues that in his own sinful and degenerate generation, no doctrine was less regarded than that of the Holy Spirit. The Spirit's baptism is the one true baptism, "without which all other baptisms are but faint shadows."[32] This baptism of the Holy Spirit comes with water baptism, but only for those who have truly repented of their sins. Spirit baptism is evidenced by Jesus' threefold promise: "He shall convince the world of sin, of righteousness, and of judgment" (John 16:8). In other words, Spirit in-filling results in a greater awareness of God's work within his people. The divine Third Person "allays fears of death, hell and judgment, wipes the tears away, and eases us in all trials, temptations and burdens, and in our last hours bears us up with an holy confidence. . . ."[33] As such, he has merited the name "Comforter." Finally, Cennick encourages his hearers to seek the unspeakable gift of the Spirit. "Only open your hearts and he will come and sup with you, and you with him. . . . Yea may a double portion of this spirit rest upon you henceforth for ever and ever."[34]

Jonathan Edwards

The most important theologian of the first Great Awakening, Jonathan Edwards (1703–1758), recognized a danger in the cleavage which developed between emotional defenders of revivalism and rationalistic critics of revivalist religion. Edwards entered the fray between rationalists and enthusiasts in the uncomfortable position of being a defender of the Awakening as a movement but a critic of both rationalism and enthusiasm. Part of his defense was to separate the true evidences for the Holy Spirit's working from the false.

Edwards recognizes that there are times in Christian history ("Spring seasons") during which the Spirit of God is outpoured and religion is revived. Unfortunately, whenever the Spirit of God is poured out, Satan introduces a bastardized religion or a counterfeit.[35] Mere enthusiasm offers no evidence of the Spirit's working. "Tears, trembling, groans, loud outcries, agonies of body, and the failing of bodily strength," as well as religious "noise," heightened imagination (including states of ecstasy), and irregularity in conduct were not marks of the Spirit's presence and operation.[36] But there *were* reliable indicators. The Spirit of God clearly was at work when Jesus was uplifted, when Satan was attacked, when individuals gained a greater regard for Scripture, and when a spirit of love towards God and other humans was present.[37]

In short, Jonathan Edwards finds little value in what he sees as excessive enthusiasm in the Awakening. He does not expect or desire any restoration of the miraculous gifts (1 Cor. 12).[38] His understanding of the work of the Holy Spirit, then, stands as a precursor of modern Evangelicalism, but not of Pentecostalism.

John Wesley and the Early Methodists

The founder of Methodism, John Wesley (1703–1791) introduced into Protestantism a distinctive pneumatology—an awareness of the person of the Holy Spirit and the Spirit's operation in all of human experience—that was unlike any other in Western Christianity at the time. Actually Wesley's writings on the divine Third Person most closely resemble those of earlier Eastern spirituals, such as Clement of Alexandria, Macarius of Egypt, the Cappadocians, and Ephrem of Syria.[39] This is not surprising, because as a student and a priest at Oxford he had immersed himself in Eastern Christian spirituality.

It would be wrong to suggest that John Wesley was personally given to enthusiastic religion. His own experiences were few and far between. But he *was* extraordinarily tolerant of followers who claimed dreams, visions, healings, and revelations, and of earlier prophetic groups such as the Montanists, whom he described as "real, scriptural Christians."[40] As a consequence, Wesley undeservedly was labelled by certain educated contemporaries as an "enthusiast"—i.e., one who claimed extraordinary revelations or powers from the Holy Spirit, or who demonstrated any kind of religious excitement. Wesley simply countered that he followed Scripture and the early church concerning spiritual gifts, which he thought normative for all ages in the history of Christianity.

On one occasion, his own brother, Samuel, wrote him expressing horror over what he thought were extravagant emotional and physical outbursts in connection with some of John's preaching. John responded by affirming several of the positive outcomes of his followers' enthusiasm—conviction of sins, divine peace and joy, and a sound mind—all of which confirmed the preached word.[41]

It has become fashionable for modern Pentecostals to portray John Wesley as their founding father.[42] Indeed, Wesley did recognize that the gift of tongues was frequently dispensed in his day and that it had existed in other post-apostolic centuries. But he certainly did not see it as the normative evidence for the Holy Spirit's presence. He explained that God imparted his gifts as he chose, and had not chosen to give him this gift which he had granted to some of his contemporaries (including the French Prophets and the Moravians).[43]

As with Eastern Christian spirituals, Wesley taught that the real evidence for the Spirit's working was Christian growth towards perfection (the perfecting of human love in this life; or *theosis* in the East). "We do believe that he will in this world so 'cleanse the thoughts of our hearts, by the inspiration of his Holy Spirit, that we shall perfectly love him, and worthily magnify his holy name.' "[44] It was this emphasis on the Spirit's work of sanctification which gave rise to the modern holiness movement—in which much of Pentecostalism took root.

The Shakers

The Shakers were an early communistic and pacifistic group which took its origin during a Quaker revival in England in 1747. They were known for the physical shaking or trembling which resulted from the spiritual exaltation in their services.

While the Shakers did not teach a separate "baptism" of the Holy Spirit, they clearly believed in a mystical experience of personal union in Christ. In turn, this led to a life in the Spirit, with a number of spiritual gifts. For the earliest Wardley Shakers, all of this was as a foretaste and an immediate precursor to the *parousia*, the second coming of Jesus Christ, for which they longingly waited. Secondly, they believed in the ultimate radical perfectibility of human beings. Life in the Spirit, then, was an equipping for personal perfection and a preparation for the climax of the ages.

When Ann Lee joined with the Wardley Shakers, they began to teach that Christ had indeed returned, and that Ann was the first to experience Christ in glory. Her role thereafter was to inaugurate a consciousness of the *parousia*, as the first one among many to be drawn into the unifying experience of Christ alive and fully present in-through-with us all. With the coming of Ann Lee, life in the Spirit meant experiencing Jesus Christ already returned to earth again.[45]

THE NINETEENTH CENTURY

The Irvingites

Edward Irving (1792–1834), a Scottish-Presbyterian pastor, was founder of the Catholic Apostolic Church, whose numbers were known as the Irvingites. A gifted preacher, Irving early became minister of a fashionable London congregation, which included his lifelong friend, Thomas Carlyle, and numerous prominent government leaders. His interest in prophecy and millenarianism led him to the belief that since the fivefold offices of apostles, prophets, evangelists, pastors, and teachers had been abandoned, the Holy Spirit had, as a result, left the church to its own devices. He was stimulated to seek for and to expect a restoration of spiritual gifts to the church. It was his conviction that he must function as prophet and priest. He toured Scotland, preaching this new message. Prayer groups were established to seek a new outpouring of the Holy Spirit. Early in 1830 parishioners near Glasgow began to experience charismata, especially glossolalia. By 1831 practice of the charismata was part of worship in many of Irving's churches. Irving was later censured by the London Presbytery in 1832 for violating regulations by allowing women and men not properly ordained to speak in the services. Subsequently, he was expelled from his pulpit. Irving then led about eight hundred members to form a new congregation, which would become the Catholic Apostolic Church. In 1833, his status as a clergyman in the Church of Scotland was removed.

Ironically, Irving did not receive the charismata about which he preached. Consequently, he was not able to lead his own new church for long. He was removed from his position of leadership within the movement and in 1834 was sent to Glasgow by "gifted" apostles, where he died shortly thereafter.

It is clear that Irving made a connection between a new outpouring of the Spirit and restored charismata. Further, he called glossolalia the "standing sign" of the presence of the Spirit.[46] But those who insist that he correlated tongues as the initial physical evidence for Spirit baptism may be reading in too much of their own twentieth-century concepts and terminology.[47] It would seem fair, however, to suggest that the Irvingite belief was a milestone in the development of what later became the Pentecostal concept of tongues as the initial physical evidence of Spirit baptism.

The Holiness and Evangelical Movements

Twentieth-century Pentecostalism can be traced in part to an emphasis placed on a "second work of grace," espoused both by Wesleyans and by "higher-life" teachers of the nineteenth century.[48] One of Wesley's contemporaries and a designated successor, John Fletcher (vicar of Madeley and president of Trevecca College in Wales) moved beyond Wesley in teaching that in this age of the Holy Spirit, the believer received perfection ("an entire deliverance from sin, and a recovery of the whole image of God") when "baptized with the Pentecostal power of the Holy Spirit."[49]

John Wesley's emphasis on an experience of sanctification subsequent to conversion as part of the larger quest for perfection led individuals such as Walter and Phoebe Palmer to popularize the holiness message. The National Camp Meeting Association for the Promotion of Holiness, founded in 1867, soon was joined by non-Methodists. Together they stressed a normative Christian experience, which they called variously entire sanctification, second blessing, perfection, perfect love, and the baptism with the Holy Spirit. While few experienced glossolalia, they popularized both the concept of a second work of grace and the terminology which subsequently was adopted by Pentecostalism.

Benjamin H. Irwin (b. 1854), a Wesleyan holiness preacher, received a sanctification experience, followed by what he described as a "baptism of fire" or "a third blessing." Shortly thereafter, he organized the Fire-Baptized Holiness Association. The mainstream of the holiness movement, however, rejected his teachings as the "third blessing heresy."[50]

A second and related doctrinal development came from the "higher-life" teachers (none of whom was associated with the Methodist wing of the holiness revival) who believed that this second experience endued the believer with power for witness and service. These included Dwight L. Moody, Reuben A. Torrey, Andrew Murray, A. B. Simpson, and Adoniram Judson Gordon. But despite their emphasis on a baptism with the Holy Spirit, they taught that tongues had ceased (with the exception of Simpson).[51]

CONCLUSIONS

This survey of the Christian idea of a baptism in/with the Holy Spirit and the evidence(s) for that infilling indicates that, while the concept of Spirit baptism was very common throughout the Christian centuries, the modern Pentecostal identification of glossolalia as the "initial evidence" of such baptism is completely novel until the nineteenth-century Irvingites. Amazingly, in almost two millennia of Christian life and practice, no one from the apostolic period to the early nineteenth century—not even those who placed great emphasis on the study of Scripture— associated tongues with the advent of life in the Spirit. Even tongues-speakers in earlier centuries did not make such a connection. Only Augustine addresses a possible linkage between glossolalia and Spirit entry, and he concludes that the connection ceased in the first-century church.

Historically, the only real concern for "evidence" of the Spirit's presence has been over the validation of prophets. Just as the Scriptures distinguish between "true" and "false" prophets, so the church from its inception has attempted to establish criteria by which to judge (in many cases, to discredit!) its "change agents."

One of the most interesting results of this investigation has been the discovery of a positive correlation between radical dualism and the perceived need for a separate baptism in the Spirit. Certainly, radical dualists throughout Christian history share with modern Pentecostals an awareness of the cosmic dimensions of the struggle between the forces of good and evil. They concur that Christians are unable to face this struggle and to spread the good news of the Kingdom successfully without a special infilling of God's Spirit.

It also should be apparent that few "comfortable" individuals have been concerned with matters of Spirit baptism. Those who have called for a special baptism of the Spirit were persecuted, or voluntarily chose to leave worldly comforts in pursuit of holiness or closeness to God, or were eschatologically motivated. In any event, disequilibrium seems to have been something of a prerequisite for such concerns.

Without question, twentieth-century Pentecostals have shared in this disequilibrium. Eschatologically oriented, they have recognized the need for a special work of the divine Spirit to empower them for service in what they perceive as the last days before the second coming of Christ.

But what *is* unique about modern Pentecostals is that they consider glossolalia to be the litmus test of Pentecostal orthodoxy and *the* valid sign for Spirit baptism. Most of them disclaim all Christian traditions born after the first century. Instead, the Pentecostal experience is seen as a *restoration* of Spirit-outpouring in the apostolic church, evidenced by tongues—an association equally rare since the first century. This study demonstrates that Pentecostals, who rejoice in the novelty of their teachings and experiences, are fully justified in classifying their doctrine of initial evidence as distinctive. Throughout the twentieth century, they have clung tenaciously to this teaching, and it has in turn become their rallying point and source of identity.

NOTES

1. For examples, see S. M. Burgess, "Medieval Examples of Charismatic Piety in the Roman Catholic Church," ed. Russell P. Spittler, *Perspectives on the New Pentecostalism* (Grand Rapids: Baker, 1976), 15–25.

2. *Acta Sanctorum* (AASS), September V, 683.

3. M. Fox, trans., *Illuminations of Hildegard of Bingen* (Santa Fe, N.M.: Bear, 1985), 26–27.

4. Ibid., 9. For Hildegard's *Scivias,* see B. Hozeski's English translation (Santa Fe, N.M.: Bear, 1986), or C. Hart and J. Bishop, trans., *Hildegard of Bingen: Scivias,* in *Classics of Western Spirituality* (New York: Paulist Press, 1990).

5. G. Uhlein, ed., *Meditations with Hildegard of Bingen* (Santa Fe, N.M.: Bear, 1983), 42.

6. E. Cousins, trans., *Bonaventure: The Soul's Journey into God,* in Classics of Western Spirituality (New York: Paulist Press, 1978), 53–116.

7. Ibid., 179–327.

8. E. Colledge and James Walsh, trans., *Julian of Norwich: Showings,* in Classics of Western Spirituality (New York: Paulist Press, 1978).

9. *The Book of Margery Kempe* in E. Clark and H. Richardson, eds., *Women and Religion: A Feminist Sourcebook of Christian Thought* (New York: Harper & Row, 1977), 112–13.

10. E. Ensley, *Sounds of Wonder: A Popular History of Speaking in Tongues in the Catholic Tradition* (New York: Paulist Press, 1977).

11. See discussion of Joachim's apocalypticism in Stanley M. Burgess, "Medieval Models of Perfectionism," in *Reaching Beyond: Chapters in the History of Perfectionism* (Peabody, Mass.: Hendrickson, 1986), 155–63.

12. Among the best introductions to the Cathars are S. Runciman, *The Medieval Manichee: A Study of the Christian Dualistic Heresy* (Cambridge: Cambridge University Press, 1947), chapter 6; and M. Lambert, *Medieval Heresy: Popular Movements from Bogomil to Hus* (New York: Holmes and Meier, 1976), chapter 8. On the *consolamentum,* see J. B. Russell, *Religious Dissent in the Middle Ages* (New York: Wiley, 1971), 59–68.

13. M. E. Stortz, "Let the Spirit Come: Lutheran Interpretation of the Holy Spirit," *GOTR* 31 (3–4, 1986): 311.

14. Martin Luther, *Against the Heavenly Prophets in the Matter of Images and Sacraments,* in Conrad Bergendorff, ed., *Works* (St. Louis: Concordia, 1958), 40:146–149.

15. Luther, *Sermons on the Gospel of St. John*, in Jaroslav Pelikan, ed., *Works* (St. Louis: Concordia, 1961), 24:405.

16. Luther, *Selected Psalms*, in J. Pelikan, ed., *Works* (St. Louis: Concordia, 1955), 12:295.

17. Luther, *Against the Heavenly Prophets*, in Conrad Bergendorff, ed., *Works* (St. Louis: Concordia, 1958), 40:142.

18. Luther, *Sermon on Pentecost* 13–15, in John N. Lenker, ed., *Sermons of Martin Luther* (Grand Rapids: Baker, 1983) 7:334–35.

19. Luther, *Against the Heavenly Prophets*, in Conrad Bergendorff, ed., *Works* (St. Louis: Concordia, 1958), 40:146–49.

20. John Calvin, *Commentaries: The Acts of the Apostles* (1965), 1.51.

21. Calvin, *Commentaries: I Corinthians* 5.24–32; in Ford Lewis Battles, trans., *Institutes of the Christian Religion* 4.8.9 (Philadelphia: Westminster, 1960), 1155–56.

22. The best treatment is in George H. Williams, *The Radical Reformation* (Philadelphia: Westminster, 1962).

23. Menno Simons, *The Complete Works of Menno Simons*, ed. H. S. Bender et al. (Scottsdale, Pa.: Herald Press, 1956), 495–96.

24. Williams, *The Radical Reformation*, 133, 443.

25. D. Freiday, *Barclay's Apology in Modern English* (Philadelphia: Friends Book Store, 1967), 32. An excellent introduction to Quaker teachings is Douglas V. Steere, ed., *Quaker Spirituality: Selected Writings*, Classics of Western Spirituality (New York: Paulist Press, 1984).

26. F. M. Mission, *A Cry from the Desert* (London: printed for B. Bragg at the Black Raven in Pater Noster Row, 1708), v–vi. R. A. Knox, *Enthusiasm: A Chapter in the History of Religion* (Oxford: Clarendon Press, 1950); chapter 15 presents a critical view of Camisard spirituality. B. L. Bresson, *Studies in Ecstasy* (New York: Vantage Press, 1966), is much more favorable.

27. Ibid., 32.

28. D. A. de Brueys, *Histoire du fanatisme de notre temps* (Paris: F. Muguet, 1692, 1737), 137; Knox, *Enthusiasm*, chapter 16.

29. In D. L. Jeffrey, *A Burning and a Shining Light: English Spirituality in the Age of Wesley* (Grand Rapids: Eerdmans, 1987), 61–2.

30. J. Roche, *Moravian Heresy . . . as taught throughout several parts of Europe and America by Count Zinzendorf, Mr. Cennick, and other Moravian teachers . . .* (Dublin: printed by the author, 1751), 44.

31. J. Cennick, *The Gift and Office of the Holy Ghost*, 4th ed. (London: H. Trapp, 1785).

32. Ibid., 8.

33. Ibid., 16.

34. Ibid., 18.

35. Jonathan Edwards, *A treatise concerning religions affections* (1746), ed. John E. Smith (New Haven: Yale University Press, 1959), 185, 287.

36. Jonathan Edwards, *The distinguishing marks of a work of the Spirit of God* (Boston: S. Kneeland and T. Green, 1741), 5–41.

37. Ibid., 41–61. See also Jonathan Edwards, *A divine and supernatural light, imparted to the soul by the Spirit of God, shown to be both a scriptural and rational doctrine* (1734, reprinted Boston, Manning and Loring: n.d.).

38. Edwards, *The distinguishing marks*, 97–98.

39. Burgess, *Holy Spirit: Eastern Christian Traditions,* 149, n. 11.

40. N. Curnock, ed., *John Wesley: Journal* (London: Epworth Press, 1938), 3:496. Note that John's brother, Charles—the great hymnologist—was far less tolerant of enthusiasts.

41. Letter to Samuel Wesley (May 10, 1739), in Jeffrey, *A Burning and a Shining Light,* 241–42.

42. E.g., H. V. Synan, *The Holiness Pentecostal Movement in the United States* (Grand Rapids: Eerdmans, 1971), 13. See Williams' and Waldvogel's [Blumhofer's] discussion, 77–81.

43. John Wesley, *Letters,* 4:379–80.

44. F. Whaling, ed., *John and Charles Wesley: Selected Writings and Hymns,* Classics of Western Spirituality (New York: Paulist Press, 1981), 377.

45. F. W. Evans, *Shaker communism, in tests of divine inspiration. The second Christian or Gentile Pentecostal church . . .* London: James Burns, 1871).

46. Quoted in W. Lewis, *Witnesses to the Holy Spirit* (Valley Forge, Pa.: Judson Press, 1978), 236.

47. E.g., Bresson, *Studies in Ecstasy,* 196, asserts that Irving "seems to be the first person who viewed speaking in tongues as the inital evidence of the Baptism."

48. D. W. Dayton, *Theological Roots of Pentecostalism* (reprint, Peabody, Mass.: Hendrickson, 1991).

49. Letter of John Fletcher to May Bosanquet, dated March 7, 1778, reprinted in Luke Tyerman, *Wesley's Designated Successor* (London: Hodder and Stoughton, 1882), 411.

50. H. V. Synan, "Irwin, Benjamin Hardin," in *DPCM,* 471–72.

51. C. Nienkirchen, "Simpson, Albert Benjamin," *DPCM,* 786–87.

3

EDWARD IRVING AND THE "STANDING SIGN" OF SPIRIT BAPTISM

David W. Dorries

In light of the remarkable Pentecostal occurrences and their rich theological moorings centering around the person of Edward Irving during the 1830s in Great Britain, the "classical" Pentecostal outpouring in twentieth-century America loses some of its uniqueness. Although no direct link theologically and historically has been traced between these two movements, the British expression, which preceded the American movement by more than seventy years, clearly anticipated some of the more significant features of the "classical" experience.

EDWARD IRVING AND NINETEENTH-CENTURY MANIFESTATIONS OF THE SPIRIT

Edward Irving (1792–1834), a Scottish-born and educated pastor and theologian whose theological contributions to the Christian church transcended the narrow confines of his native Scottish Calvinism, came into public prominence during his twelve years of pastoral ministry in London. Controversy seemed to court Irving. In an age when docetic images of Christ dominated the religious world, Irving was committed to the

vivid and vital preaching of Christ's true humanity, rooted in the ancient
incarnational-Trinitarian formulations of the church fathers and recovered by the Protestant Reformers.[1] Irving's efforts to restore christological
balance to the church of his time resulted in a backlash of opposition,
culminating in his deposition from the ordained ministry of the Church
of Scotland in 1833. By then, however, Irving's attention was fixed de-
cisively in a different direction. Erupting first in humble circumstances
in 1830 in the west of Scotland and surfacing next in London in 1831,
occurrences of spiritual gifts, signs, and wonders thoroughly shook the
contemporary religious world and radically altered the future course of
Irving's life and ministry.

West of Scotland Pentecostal Revival

In the spring of 1830, reports began to circulate that certain individuals
had experienced miraculous manifestations of the Spirit. These persons
resided in the Gareloch region in the west of Scotland, where Irving's
influence was well-known. He had preached there for his pastor friends
John Macleod Campbell and Robert Story in the summers of 1828 and
1829. The first in a series of events occurred when Mary Campbell, a
young woman dying of tuberculosis, was healed and exercised the Spirit's
gift of tongues. The story begins in early April of 1830, when the Macdonald family, residing across the Clyde River in Port Glasgow, experienced a miraculous healing as Margaret rose up from her sick bed at the
command of her brother James. His command had been given only
moments after he dramatically announced that the baptism of the Spirit
had come upon him. The Macdonalds were friends of Mary Campbell.
Now that Margaret had been healed, James was prompted to write a letter
to Mary Campbell, not only to report of his sister's healing, but likewise
to command Mary to rise and be healed. In the process of reading James'
letter, Mary Campbell experienced an immediate recovery and spoke in
tongues. James and his brother George also manifested the Spirit's gifts
of tongues, interpretation of tongues, and prophecy.

As news of these events was spread across the land, people began to
converge upon the homes of Mary Campbell and the Macdonalds to
investigate these phenomena. People came from various parts of Scotland, England, and Ireland. Daily prayer meetings were held for months
on end, with gifts of the Spirit manifested regularly from an expanding
number of persons. Several homes were utilized for the meetings, and the
movement continued without supervision from the religious establishment or ordained ministry. As might be expected, intense controversy

erupted within the religious world over these happenings. Widespread interest and attendance at the meetings continued for eighteen months until spiritual manifestations noticeably declined in frequency and power.[2]

The Irving Connection

When Irving first heard reports of the miraculous outpouring, he was not aware that his doctrine had played a role in their occurrence. Only through studying several letters written by Mary Campbell did he come to understand how his preaching had made a difference. His emphasis on the authenticity of Christ's human life and on Christ's holiness as derived from the Holy Spirit's operation rather than his inherent divinity sparked in Mary a discovery that had led to her reception of the gift of tongues and her physical healing. She took Irving's Christology to its logical conclusion, i.e., that the miraculous works of Christ proceeded also from the Spirit and not his divine nature. Therefore, since we are of the same human nature as Christ and indwelt by the same Holy Spirit, we are compelled to do likewise "the works which he did, and greater works than these."

As it dawned upon Irving that a direct linkage existed between his Christology and the appearance of the manifestations, a fresh comprehension of the gospel unfolded for him. He began to understand that the great redemptive work for humankind accomplished by Christ in his incarnation and atonement was preparatory to the chief office he assumed as resurrected Head of the Church, i.e., his role as Baptizer with the Holy Spirit. Stated Irving,

> . . . the peculiar and proper name of Christ, as Head of the Church, is "He which baptizeth with the Holy Ghost," and was not fulfilled till the day of Pentecost, . . . and that the whole body of Scripture speaketh of it as the proper calling of the Church in all ages to put forth the same. . . .[3]

The implications of this profound discovery increasingly captured Irving's attention after 1830. Reports reaching him of continued miraculous manifestations from Scotland took on vital theological significance for him, for they "turned our speculations upon the true doctrine into the examination of a fact."[4] Irving was now not only ready to endorse the surprising events unfolding in his native Scotland, but he earnestly desired a similar visitation in London among his Regent Square congregation. By April of 1831, Irving had decided to open up his church for prayer meetings, to be held Monday through Saturday at six-thirty in the morning. His hopes were shared by many others. Between six hundred and a thousand persons gathered for daily prayer, expecting supernatural manifestations of the Spirit to be visited upon them. In addition to anticipating gifts, signs, and wonders, participants sought for the restoration of the ancient offices of the church. As Irving expressed it,

> We cried unto the Lord for apostles, prophets, evangelists, pastors and teachers, anointed with the Holy Ghost the gift of Jesus, because we saw it written in God's word that these are the appointed ordinances for the edifying of the body of Jesus.[5]

The London Visitation

Approximately three months after the start of these prayer meetings, manifestations of the gifts of tongues, interpretation of tongues, and prophecy occurred. As pastor, Irving assumed the responsibility of "trying the spirits," authorizing only those persons whose gifts had been proven in private to exercise their gifts in public. The manifestations in the early morning services continued for a number of months. During this time, Irving devoted his preaching and teaching ministry to instructing the whole congregation about the proper scriptural principles and practices of spiritual gifts.

Educating his Presbyterian congregation that gifts of the Spirit have a normal place and purpose in Christian worship proved to be a formidable challenge, particularly in light of the lack of precedence for such happenings throughout three hundred years of Protestant church history. Irving should not have been surprised when the most of his trustees were alarmed at the first instance of manifestations disturbing the orderly worship of the Sunday morning and evening services of Regent Square. On October 16, 1831, as words of an unknown tongue filled that great auditorium for the first time during a Sunday morning service, with nearly two thousand people present, bedlam followed. Further chaos erupted that evening as nearly three thousand people packed into the building, many being curiosity seekers and rabble rousers who had come to scoff at the unusual proceedings. After facing two weeks of disorderly disturbances, caused largely by protestors from outside rather than from the members themselves, Irving temporarily halted the expressions of the Spirit during Sunday services. Taking time to reflect further, Irving reversed his policy and allowed the gifts to continue. He concluded that to stifle the gifts would be to quench the voice of the Spirit and to resist Christ's role as Baptizer in the Spirit. However, with the resumption of the gifts, their expressions were restricted to two designated times within the order of worship. Through Irving's wise leadership and continued scriptural instruction, order and harmony were restored to the Sunday services without quenching the voice of the Spirit through the gifted. Yet among the trustees, opposition only intensified towards Irving's policy of authorizing such unprecedented occurrences. These were the same churchmen who had unanimously backed Irving during more than ten years of pastoral ministry. Now they drew the line against him, convinced that he had no warrant for allowing the propriety of Presbyterian worship to be interrupted by what they believed to be the vain babblings of deluded fanatics.

The trustees turned the case over to the London Presbytery on March 17, 1832. The complaint of the trustees can be summarized by the first allegation contained in the libel.

> Firstly, that the said Rev. Edward Irving has suffered and permitted, and still allows, the public services of the said church, in the worship of God on the Sabbath, and other days, to be interrupted by persons not being either ministers or licentiates of the Church of Scotland.[6]

Irving's eloquent personal defense before the Presbytery is exemplified by this initial statement from his testimony: "It is for the name of Christ, as 'baptizer with the Holy Ghost,' that I am this day called in question before this court. . . ."[7] After a week-long trial, the Presbytery reached the following verdict on May 2, 1832.

> [W]hile deeply deploring the painful necessity thus imposed upon them, they did, and hereby do discern that the said Rev. E. Irving has rendered himself unfit to remain the minister of the National Scotch Church aforesaid, and ought to be removed therefrom in pursuance of the conditions of the trust-deed of the said church.[8]

Newman Street Pentecostalism

On the Sunday following the trial, Irving and his congregation found themselves locked out of the sanctuary of Regent Square. The vast majority of the church's membership had thrived under Irving's pastorate, and they were not willing to abandon him now. After more than five months of worship in a temporary facility, the ostracized congregation secured a permanent place of worship on Newman Street in London. Having been forced out of their Presbyterian structure, Irving and his church now were in a position to pursue spiritual gifts and apostolic church government without hindrance. In the new church order that had begun to emerge, Irving retained the office of pastor while others were set apart and ordained as apostles. The first apostolic ordination took place on November 17, 1832. By July 14, 1835, the twelfth and final apostle had been ordained within the church, now named the Catholic Apostolic Church.

Other like-minded churches and pastors throughout Britain began to link themselves with the "Pentecostal" church on Newman Street. It was becoming apparent that a new and expanding movement had been birthed.

With the advent of a new movement that took its impetus from Irving's conviction that Christ's office as Baptizer in the Holy Spirit had been neglected for centuries of church history, London now had become the scene for a Pentecostal outpouring some seventy years before Charles Parham's "classical" Pentecostal formulations and more than seventy-five years before the Azusa Street Pentecostal revival. Armed with the confidence that a new day was dawning for Christendom, Irving continued in his preaching and writing to expand upon the doctrinal and practical implications of baptism in the Spirit.

> Oh, brother! this baptism with the Holy Ghost, which I am about to teach thee of, is the very glory of God in the sight of angels and of men: wilt thou not be the bearer of it? . . . for it is the most glorious and blessed theme of which I have ever yet discoursed, or of which thou hast ever yet heard.[9]

IRVING'S DOCTRINE OF SPIRIT BAPTISM

For Irving, Spirit baptism is the common inheritance of every baptized believer.

> And I say, that every baptized person is privileged to possess this gift, and is responsible for it, and will possess it through faith in God; . . . I say it is knit unto baptism, it is the rubric of baptism.[10]

Both dimensions of Christian baptism, regeneration and Spirit baptism, Irving sharply distinguished from one another, due to their differing functions. Regeneration, which includes remission of sins and union with Christ, can exist in the life of the believer and the church without Spirit baptism.[11] However, where regeneration exists alone without the baptism of the Spirit, a condition of serious deficiency is present regarding baptismal privileges. "They who preach baptism as containing no more than regeneration, are but disciples of John the Baptist; for Christ baptizeth not with water, but with the Holy Ghost."[12]

Spirit baptism is the extension of Christ's life and ministry through the church. It brings "to every believer the presence of the Father and the power of the Holy Ghost, according to that measure, at the least, in which Christ during the days of his flesh possessed the same."[13] It is the triumphant, risen Christ who now baptizes his church in the same Spirit who enabled him while in mortal flesh to minister in the mighty words and works of the Father. Since we are, in Irving's words, wedded to the risen body of Christ: . . . we are the children of the heavenly man, we should exhibit the form and feature and power and acts of the heavenly man, . . . Now, his actings as the risen man are entirely and altogether supernatural. . . .[14]

Spirit Baptism Subsequent to Regeneration and Sanctification

Irving had no intention of minimizing the sanctifying work of the Spirit by seeking to turn the church's attention towards the privileges and responsibilities of Spirit baptism. "Let no one say, then, that we undervalue the sacramental ministration of a cleansed soul and a holy body. . . ."[15] Irving seemed to regard sanctification, being a part of regeneration, as a legal standing of righteousness imputed to the believer by Christ:

> . . . we are baptized into perfect holiness, into the positive and absolute dismissal of all sin, into the burial of the flesh with its corruptions and lusts, the quickening of the Spirit into all holiness.[16]

Yet beyond the justifying faith of believer's baptism, Spirit baptism is a separate and subsequent experience calling for a faith response to activate the manifestations of the Spirit's efficacy.

Enhances Holiness

Before exploring further this dimension of his thought, it should be noted that the believer's legal standing of sanctification must be experientially realized as a lifelong process of the Spirit's enablement. On this point, Irving was convinced that Spirit baptism greatly enhanced the believer's capacity to perfect a life of holiness. The goal of spiritual gifts, after all, was to contribute to the sanctification of the believer and the body of Christ at large.

> Nor is it right to say, that we must wait for perfect sanctification before we ask for the manifestations of the Spirit, which are given to every man to profit withal, to edify oneself, and to edify the church.[17]

In short, the church could no longer afford to ignore her endowment of power.

> So, if the church reviveth, she must act as the Church; which is not in the way of holiness merely, but in the way of power, for the manifestation of the completeness of Christ's work in flesh, and the first-fruits of the same work in glory.[18]

Activation By Faith

As previously noted, Spirit baptism must be activated by the believer's faith response, and it is a separate and subsequent experience from regeneration. Regeneration is inherently contained in believer's baptism, while Spirit baptism is a baptismal privilege that must be "stirred up." States Irving: "Timothy is more than once exhorted not to neglect, but to stir up" the gifts of the Spirit. "For when the power of God—the signs and wonders, and divers miracles, and gifts of the Holy Ghost—were [*sic*] seen to attend upon men," it was because they had adopted the "childhood way of learning, which is by faith."[19] Irving held that the childlike prayer of faith, exercised with importunity, would be rewarded by the baptism of the Spirit.

> . . . it is the Holy Ghost in his largest and fullest operation, in all his power and efficacy, in all his gifts and graces, which is thus liberally offered and undoubtingly assured to every one who with sincerity asketh, with earnestness seeketh, and with importunity knocketh.[20]

Irving encouraged the church to approach Spirit baptism and the accompanying signs and gifts with the simple desire to ask and receive obediently, refraining from the tendency to understand them first. Irving

> call[ed] upon all and every one of the members of Christ to covet earnestly, and fervently to pray for, spiritual gifts, speaking with tongues and prophesying; and this whether they understand these expositions or not. For faith standeth in the receiving and obeying of the word of God; and understanding followeth the possession of what we pray for.[21]

INITIAL EVIDENCE AND SPEAKING IN TONGUES

Can it be said that Edward Irving held to a theory of "initial evidence" for determining that the believer had received the baptism in the Spirit? The answer is *yes*. However, it must be noted that Irving would have been uncomfortable with the term "evidence," due to his disdain for certain "evidence writers" of his day who considered the sole value of the miraculous to be the raw power they represented. These "evidence writers" disconnected miracles from considerations of the nature of the gospel and the character of Christ's redemption.

> These miracles they make to stand merely in their power: and so, say they, they demonstrate God to be with the worker of them: . . . Now, be this granted, and what to do hath it with Christ?[22]

Irving detected this "empirical spirit" as motivating the common Protestant proclivity to dispensationalize the miracles of the New Testament. These empiricists viewed miracles as having only a temporary, utilitarian function. The miraculous works of Christ and the church served merely as supernatural proofs of the authenticity of New Testament events until the completion of the canon of Scripture. Serving no further purpose, miracles were withdrawn permanently from Christendom. Irving revealed the chief failure of these empiricists: ". . . there is no recognition of Christ as the doer of the work; there is no recognition of the work itself being part and parcel of Christ's redemption."[23] Irving realized that the miracles of the New Testament were far from being accidental, seasonal occurrences. He viewed the revelation of God in Christ and the very nature of God's kingdom as altogether and essentially supernatural from start to finish.

Tongues the Standing Sign

Preferring the term "sign" or "gift" rather than "initial evidence," Edward Irving nonetheless clearly taught that the reception by the believer of Spirit baptism was evidenced or confirmed by the manifestation of unknown tongues. Irving identified the manifestation of tongues in Scripture as being both a sign and a gift. Tongues comes as a sign when the receiver is in the presence of unbelievers. Tongues comes as a gift when the receiver is in private or with other believers. In either case, the manifestation of tongues evidences that the receiver is baptized in the Holy Spirit. Note the following direct references from Irving's writings: ". . . the baptism with the Holy Ghost, whose standing sign, if we err not, is the speaking with tongues."[24] "No doubt the baptism with the Holy Ghost, whereof the sign is speaking with another tongue. . . ."[25] Referring to Spirit baptism, he noted "the introductory sign of the unknown tongue."[26] Speaking of those baptized by the Spirit, Irving says "we find it always to have been the gift first bestowed upon the baptized. . . ."[27] Among all the gifts of the Spirit, Irving notes that the gift of tongues "is the root and the stem of them all, out of which they all grow, and by which they are all nourished."[28]

Further confirmation in support of the initiatory role of tongues among the Spirit-baptized can be found in Irving's words of encouragement to Christians who have not received the manifestation of tongues. Although he assumes that they have not received the baptism of the Spirit, he encourages them not to "be disheartened, as if we were rejected of the Holy Ghost, and had not the Holy Ghost dwelling in us. . . ." Every Christian has the Holy Spirit,

the only way through which the weary and heavy-laden sinner can come to rest. . . . If any person, therefore, having laid hold of this truth, is living in the faith and enjoyment of it, he is to be assured of his salvation, and to be at peace: yet he is to desire to speak with tongues. . . .[29]

Therefore, without the manifestation of tongues, the believer is in Christ and a possessor of the Holy Spirit, but lacking the empowerment of Spirit baptism.

Tongues as Sign and Gift

To understand possible reasons why Irving designated tongues to be the initiatory manifestation of the church's Pentecostal endowment, a closer examination of the various functions served by tongues is in order. Irving succinctly differentiates tongues in the roles of sign and gift.

> The tongue is but the sign and manifestation to the unbeliever: to the believer it is a means of grace, for the end of edifying himself, that he may edify the whole body of the saints.[30]

As a sign to the unbeliever, tongues is "for the stumbling, and snaring, and taking of the proud and high-minded."[31] This results when unbelievers encounter through the manifestation of tongues "a power not human, but divine," intended to convince them "that God really dwelleth in the Church." This message from heaven, spoken through human instrumentality, "is a fresh evidence which God would give to men for a ground of believing, and which, alas! they would also reject."[32] The humble perceive the message in tongues as divine communication and are moved to repentance and faith in Christ. The proud hear only unintelligible speech and reject God's message to their own destruction.

For Irving, tongues can serve in a missionary function beyond its essential purpose as a sign that God is present and communicating supernaturally through the speaker. As on the day of Pentecost, tongues can be an intelligible message capable of being understood by those who know the language, although the message is not understood by the speaker.

> So far from being unmeaning gibberish, . . . it is regularly formed, well pronounced, deeply-felt discourse, which evidently wanteth only the ear of him whose native tongue it is to make it a very masterpiece of powerful speech.[33]

Unlike the early American Pentecostals under Parham's leadership, Irving apparently did not encourage the widespread use of tongues in its xenoglossic function.[34] Though he was convinced that tongue speech represented a known language, he downplayed this feature.

Tongues for Personal Edification

For Irving, the real significance of tongues did not rest in its xenoglossic function. "It is not material to the question whether these tongues were tongues of men or of angels, or whether they were in use by any creature at all."[35] The higher purpose for tongues from Irving's perspective was the level of communication established by the Holy Spirit with the human spirit of the recipient. This deep level of personal edification enables the believer to become increasingly familiar with the supernatural realm of the Spirit. This is in preparation for heightened availability to other spiritual gifts whereby the entire church may be edified.

> Therefore it is nothing to be doubted, that tongues are a great instrument for personal edification, however mysterious it may seem to us; and they are on that account greatly to be desired, altogether independently of their being a sign unto others. And to me it seemeth reasonable to believe, that they will be conferred in private exercises of devotion, and earnest longings after edification; and, being given, ought especially to be occupied in secret actings of the soul towards God. . . . But, withal, there is an ultimate end to be aimed at, beyond present enjoyment and personal edification, which is, that they may prophesy and edify the church when they shall themselves have been edified.[36]

Irving has a point to prove. The gift of tongues humbles the pride of intellect, revealing that "a person is something more than" a "community of reason."[37] Tongues are a marvel to Irving, for they "show us the reason void, and the spirit yet filled with edification."[38] "What a deep subject of meditation were a man thus employed in secret converse with and enjoyment of God, although his reason be utterly dead!"[39]

Far from being anti-theological, however, Irving simply is asserting the priority of the deeper communion of the human spirit with God's Spirit in relation to the rational dimension. While the pride of mankind boasts of the supremacy of the intellect, the childlike and unintelligible utterances of tongues makes "void and empty the eloquence and arguments, and other natural ornaments of human speech," in order "to show that God edifies the soul, in a manner wholly independent thereof, by direct communications of the Holy Ghost, which is the milk of our babyhood, the power in the word to nourish any soul."[40] This inner dialogue between Spirit and spirit, transpiring on a level beyond rational comprehension, provides the Spirit-baptized believer with an increasingly maturing grasp of spiritual reality that eventually gives expression to rationally comprehended revelations for the edification of others.

> [T]he gift of tongues is a chief means of God for training up the children of the Spirit into the capacity of prophesying and speaking in the Church for the edification of all, whether "by revelation, or by knowledge, or by prophesying, or by doctrine."[41]

The utterances of tongues, incomprehensible to the speaker, are like the mother's nursing of her baby, as she "draws forth the voice of the child into indistinct sounds, then into syllables and words, and finally into the various forms of the discourse of reason."[42]

Interpretation of Tongues and Prophecy

For Irving, the manifestation of tongues for every believer is a necessity. It represents a dimension of practical growth and development in the things of the supernatural in preparation for public manifestation of the gifts of the Spirit. Since gifts of the Spirit are given primarily to the church and intended for the edification of its members, one who is Spirit baptized will mature in use of those gifts that can be exercised publicly. For the gift of tongues to be exercised in the assembly, it must be accompanied by the gift of interpretation. Publicly exercised, tongues is simply "a new form,"[43] "a method"[44] of prophecy, and must always remain "subsidiary to the work of prophesying."[45] Referring to Paul's teaching to the Corinthians, Irving states that

> the apostle puts speaking with tongues, when coupled with interpretation, upon the same level with prophecy: "For greater is he that prophesieth than he that speaketh with tongues, except he interpret, that the church may receive edifying."[46]

This gift of interpretation might be "brought to the spirit of the speaker himself, and then he was his own interpreter; but it was more frequent to bestow that gift upon another."[47] Irving clarifies that the gift of interpretation is "nothing akin to translation," for it does "not consist in their knowledge of the strange words, or the structure of the foreign languages."[48] It is a spiritually discerned interpretation of the tongues message given. Public edification occurs when both gifts are manifested, tongues followed by the gift of interpretation.

> Tongues were a sign of this indwelling of God, but prophesying is the certainty of it; and both together bring the perfect and complete demonstration of the Spirit.[49]

Tongues and Spirit Baptism

Drawing from the wealth of Irving's doctrinal and practical expositions, much more could be said than is possible here concerning the gifts of the Spirit and their function. Since tongues represented the root and stem of all other spiritual manifestations, Irving's elaborations upon this gift are particularly insightful. This mysterious "standing sign" of Spirit baptism captivated Irving's interest and imagination.

> [T]he gift of tongues is the crowning act of all. None of the old prophets had it; Christ had it not: it belongs to the dispensation of the Holy Ghost

proceeding from the risen Christ: it is the proclamation that man is enthroned in heaven, that man is the dwelling-place of God, that all creation, if they would know God, must give ear to man's tongue, and know the compass of reason. It is not we that speak, but Christ that speaketh.[50]

Tongues represents the standing sign of the church's inheritance of that office Christ won through such costly sacrifice, the office of Baptizer with the Holy Spirit. For Irving, tongues was the introductory sign of the church's baptism of the Spirit, ushering in the measure of supernatural empowerment limited only by the expanse of Christ's supreme lordship over all.

It [Spirit baptism] is a sign of that which we preach Christ to be—Lord of all. It is a sign of that which we preach Him as about to do—to cast out devils, to raise the dead, and to liberate the creature. It is a sign of what we, the Church, are, in real uninterrupted union with Him, holding a real power under Him—the arm of His strength, the temple of His presence—the tongue of His Spirit, the manifoldness of His wisdom, the kings and priests of Christ for God.[51]

One lingering question must be addressed. Did the man who gave himself so unreservedly to the restoration of this remarkable theme of Spirit baptism possess this experience for himself? Apparently no documentation exists from Irving's own writings to indicate a definitive answer either positively or negatively. My conclusion is that Irving was Spirit baptized and spoke in tongues. He gave the last years of his life, thought, and energy to the understanding and implementation within the church of this crowning expression of Christ's redemptive work. Irving's writings make clear that Spirit baptism is a dimension of every believer's baptismal inheritance, and awaits only the persevering faith response to be activated. Would Irving have so untiringly committed himself to leading others into the deeper reaches of this dimension of power had he himself been a castaway? Also, Irving's insight into tongues as the childlike language of the Spirit, given for the personal edification of all believers, is conveyed with an authority that only a partaker could express.

Catholic Apostolic Church

The Catholic Apostolic Church was in its infancy when Irving met an untimely death at age forty-two. The structure and liturgy of this fledgling movement largely were unformed when its followers found themselves suddenly bereaved of their pivotal leader. As the church developed, practices were added that were not present originally under Irving's influence. A "high church" format was adopted, including liturgical worship, uniform vestments, candles, and incense. Nevertheless, place was given during each service for the manifestations of the Spirit. The Catholic Apostolic Church expanded into a worldwide movement under the leadership of its twelve apostles. Yet because of a limited apostleship, when the last of the twelve died in 1901, no provision existed for future ordination of pastors. Thus, the congregations of this movement dispersed, one by one, as existing pastors died. The Catholic Apostolic Church virtually disappeared.

New Apostolic Church

In the 1860s, as the Catholic Apostolic Church was experiencing promising growth on the Continent, a German constituency began functioning independently from the mother church after being denied the right to expand the number of apostles beyond the original twelve. They formed a separate organization named the New Apostolic Church. This new church ordained its own apostles and dropped some of the "high church" features of the mother church. These adjustments enabled it to expand successfully among a broader range of classes and cultures. The New Apostolic Church, with headquarters in Zurich, Switzerland, has experienced remarkable worldwide growth, today numbering nearly six million adherents.[52]

CONCLUDING ASSESSMENT

The twentieth-century Pentecostal movement traces its "classical" origins to Charles Parham. This movement's claim to uniqueness has centered upon its emphasis upon tongue speech as the initial evidence of the baptism in the Spirit. Yet in the first half of the nineteenth century, a Pentecostal movement emerged in Great Britain undergirded by a strikingly "classical" doctrine of Spirit baptism articulated by Edward Irving. The British movement possesses a tradition of its own which spans into the present. This tradition, completely unconnected with the twentieth-century movement, predates the modern expression by more than seventy-five years. Despite modern Pentecostalism's claims to uniqueness, it would seem that two historically separate revivals with Pentecostal manifestations, one in Britain and the other in the United States, served as the spawning ground for two separate Pentecostal traditions that have co-existed side by side to the present day. Both traditions trace their roots to a doctrinal recovery of the theme of Spirit baptism as a subsequent experience to Christian regeneration, and both view tongues as an initiatory sign of this experience. The existence of these separate yet similar traditions within the post-Reformation period of the church leads to the conclusion that no singular group or movement may claim exclusive or "classical" ownership of the Pentecostal message. Perhaps this study will encourage Christians everywhere to recognize that the experience of Spirit baptism is the common heritage of the church and available to all who will stir up the Gift that is within them.

NOTES

1. "Docetism" is the tendency either to deny or minimalize the true human body and incarnate nature of Jesus Christ. For an extensive study of Irving's Christology and a defense of its orthodoxy, see David W. Dorries, "Nineteenth Century British Christological Controversy, Centering Upon Edward Irving's Doctrine of Christ's Human Nature," Ph.D. thesis, University of Aberdeen, 1988.

2. For a detailed account of the west of Scotland revival, see Robert Norton, *Memoirs of James and George Macdonald of Port-Glasgow* (London: John F. Shaw, 1840).

3. "Facts Connected with Recent Manifestations of Spiritual Gifts," *Fraser's Magazine*, March, 1832, 204.

4. *Fraser's Magazine*, January, 1832, 757.

5. *The Trial of the Rev. Edward Irving, M.A. Before the London Presbytery* (London: W. Harding, 1832), 24.

6. Ibid., 3.

7. Ibid., 19.

8. Ibid., 88.

9. *The Day of Pentecost or the Baptism with the Holy Ghost* (Edinburgh: John Lindsay, 1831), 29.

10. *Speeches, &c.*, in *Pamphlets Connected with Edward Irving*, vol. 2 (n.p., 1831), 4.

11. *Day of Pentecost*, 25.

12. *Fraser's Magazine*, April, 1832, 319.

13. *Day of Pentecost*, 39.

14. "On the Gifts of the Holy Ghost, Commonly Called Supernatural," in *The Collected Writings of Edward Irving in Five Volumes*, vol. 5, ed. Rev. G. Carlyle (London: Alexander Strahan, 1864), 523.

15. "The Church, with Her Endowment of Holiness and Power," in *The Collected Writings of Edward Irving in Five Volumes*, vol. 5, ed. Rev. G. Carlyle (London: Alexander Strahan, 1864), 505.

16. Ibid., 457.

17. *Day of Pentecost*, 116.

18. "The Church," 502.

19. "On the Gifts," 543.

20. *Day of Pentecost*, 112.

21. "On the Gifts," 557.

22. "The Church," 466.
23. Ibid., 466.
24. *Day of Pentecost*, 28.
25. *Fraser's Magazine*, January, 1832, 759.
26. Ibid., 761.
27. "On the Gifts," 539.
28. *Fraser's Magazine*, April, 1832, 316.
29. "On the Gifts," 559.
30. Ibid., 559.
31. *Speeches*, 31.
32. "The Church," 497.
33. *Fraser's Magazine*, March, 1832, 198.
34. "[X]enoglossa is speaking a known foreign language without having gained a prior knowledge of that tongue. . . . Parham, and virtually all early Pentecostals, assumed tongue-speaking to be specifically xenoglossa. Taking a utilitarian approach, they theorized that this new gift from God signaled the dawn of a missionary explosion." James R. Goff, Jr., *Fields White Unto Harvest* (Fayetteville: University of Arkansas Press, 1988), 15.
35. "On the Gifts," 550–51.
36. Ibid., 548.
37. "The Church," 493–94.
38. Ibid., 494.
39. Ibid., 495.
40. "On the Gifts," 557.
41. Ibid., 541.
42. Ibid., 540.
43. *Day of Pentecost*, 66.
44. Ibid., 65.
45. "On the Gifts," 546.
46. "The Church," 490.
47. Ibid., 495.
48. Ibid., 495.
49. "On the Gifts," 553.
50. "The Church," 498.
51. Ibid., 465.
52. "The New Apostolic Church" (Zurich: The New Apostolic Church International, 1990), 3.

4

INITIAL TONGUES IN THE THEOLOGY
OF CHARLES FOX PARHAM

James R. Goff, Jr.

Debate over who was the most important Pentecostal pioneer has been a consistent theme since historians became interested in the movement some three decades ago. A number of individuals have received attention, yet none is more controversial—or was more colorful during his career—than the itinerant Methodist-turned-holiness faith healer, Charles Fox Parham. Parham's importance to the movement is clearly recognized, particularly his central role in establishing the doctrine that tongues is the initial evidence of Spirit baptism. Nevertheless, whether he ranks as the most significant early pioneer is questioned, especially since he held theological positions that did not become a part of later orthodox Pentecostalism—most notably his emphasis on triune immersion, his espousal of the racist British-Israel theory, his belief in the utter destruction of the wicked, and his insistence that all tongues were actual foreign languages.

Yet arguments that Parham was not the founding father of Pentecostalism, in the end, are not very convincing. What his detractors fail to recognize is that the Pentecostal movement for the volatile first generation period, and indeed throughout much of its subsequent history, never held to a consistent theological platform. Rather, the movement has been free-wheeling; indeed, much of its dynamic growth can be attributed to this interpretive freedom. Thus matters like baptismal modes—or no water baptism at all—have always been a nonissue, despite the fact that individuals felt strongly about their own persuasion. The same holds true for pseudo-scientific theories such as the British-Israel theory. Most Pentecostals knew little about the arguments for or against such a position; it mattered little even for those who did. What did matter was the crux of the Pentecostal message—the baptism of the Holy Ghost. Spirit baptism was understood by all Pentecostals as their identifying badge, and the consensus formed quickly that this experience came to a believer with an accompanying biblical sign, speaking in tongues. Parham, and all Pentecostals before 1908, believed that these tongues were actual languages. That belief fit a peculiar understanding of their own place in God's divine plan. Though the experience would later be broadened to include glossolalia (unintelligible syllables or "heavenly languages") as well as xenoglossa (known or actual foreign languages), the movement never lost the unique interpretation that tongues is intrinsic to Holy Spirit baptism. As a result, Parham's position as the initial Pentecostal theologian and the most prominent spokesman of the pioneering generation cannot be obscured. If we are to know what those first Pentecostals believed and why they believed it, we will find the most vital clues in the life and theology of their most controversial leader.[1]

Charles Fox Parham was born June 4, 1873, in Muscatine, Iowa. A child of the American frontier, he grew up during the boom years of the Midwestern wheat harvest as real estate hawkers proclaimed the region a veritable paradise for the American farmer. His father, William M. Parham, secured at least a respectable existence within the community as a house painter and horse-collar maker and then gambled it all on the fortunes of the wheat harvest in southern Kansas. In 1878 he moved the family to the Sedgwick County community of Anness, where he joined only a handful of settlers in a decade of unprecedented prosperity. By 1883, the gamble had paid off; he was a member of the local school board, served as postmaster, and, while not rich, enjoyed a comfortable lifestyle from income in the cattle industry. A description of William Parham's holdings is preserved in Alfred T. Andreas's *History of the State of Kansas.* Andreas reported that Parham's 160–acre farm "contains sixty acres in cultivation. His outbuildings are very large and commodious. He has every facility for the care of stock, in which he largely deals."[2] Beset by perilous weather patterns, William Parham also endured the setbacks of the late 1880s when drought and economic depression created havoc in the newly found Garden of Eden. Still, he had arrived early enough to survive the struggle and hoped for a more enduring success for his five sons.[3]

The third of William Parham's sons, however, faced even more threatening hardships. Almost from birth he suffered a succession of medical setbacks ranging from infant encephalitis to tapeworms. The most serious condition struck him at age nine and plagued him intermittently for the rest of his life. Rheumatic fever weakened his heart even as it caused painful periods of inactivity and, on occasion, left him near death.[4] Significantly, the disease placed him in the constant care of his mother. Though Parham later claimed that his parents were "not religious," his mother seems to have nonetheless instilled in him the importance of religious devotion. Upon her death in 1885, the as yet unconverted Parham promised that he would meet her in heaven.[5]

Parham's conversion came the following year through the evangelistic efforts of the local Congregational church. Parham formally stood and accepted Christ, though he later recalled that "real conversion" came after the revival meeting when, feeling conviction over personal sin, he underwent a genuine "Damascus road" experience.[6] Shortly thereafter Parham began teaching Sunday School in the local Methodist church and, by the age of fifteen, even held revival meetings. In 1890, at seventeen, he entered Southwest Kansas College in Winfield, Kansas, to study for the ministry.[7]

Parham's college career lasted three academic terms. Less than a year into the program he "backslid," reevaluated his occupational priorities, and decided to study medicine. However, a recurrence of rheumatic fever during the spring semester of 1891 convinced him of the error of his ways, and following a dramatic series of personal healings, he reentered the ministry with a vigor. As a student, Parham began holding successful revivals in the agricultural communities of southeast Kansas, and in March 1893 he received a local minister's license from the Winfield District, Southwest Kansas Conference of the Methodist Episcopal Church, North. By the beginning of the 1893–94 academic term, the student-preacher felt ready to launch into full-time ministry. Alienated from college life because of his new-found evangelistic commitment, and hard-pressed for funds due to the Panic of 1893, he accepted a supply appointment at the Eudora Methodist Church outside Lawrence, Kansas.[8]

Parham's career as a Methodist minister was short-lived. He took over the pulpit in June 1893 upon the death of the distinguished Methodist clergyman Werter Renick Davis, who twenty-five years earlier had served as the first president of the influential Baker University. Parham's appointment at the age of twenty was quite a shift for the congregation and quite an opportunity for Parham. That he was reappointed to a full year term the following March—albeit still as supply pastor—was a compliment to the young man's drive. While pastor at Eudora, he organized a second charge in the rural community of Linwood, Kansas, holding services on Sunday afternoons.[9]

Yet, under the surface, Parham's position within Methodism was far from secure. Already he had been infected with the radical theology of the holiness movement. Certain that a second work of grace was available to free the believer from the Adamic nature, Parham came to identify the experience with his own dramatic deliverance from rheumatic fever back in 1891. Parham's acceptance of sanctification placed him at odds with the growing trend of the denomination to deemphasize the doctrine, and it branded him among the host of Methodist evangelists seen as troublesome for church leaders.[10]

More problematical for church authorities were Parham's unique theological expressions. Drawing from ideas discussed with David Baker, an elderly Quaker from Tonganoxie, Kansas, Parham began teaching that water baptism was, at best, a meaningless ritual. True baptism was a baptism in God's Spirit which recreated the zeal and commitment of the early church as described in the book of Acts.[11] Parham's emphasis on this spiritual baptism paralleled his lack of emphasis on church membership. He preached a message which downplayed denominational affiliation and encouraged his listeners to join other churches or none at all. He also adopted an unorthodox position on future rewards and punishments. Since eternal life was a gift given only through salvation, he reasoned that the unconverted must receive a punishment of total annihilation.[12]

Such unorthodox views did not completely alienate Parham from Methodism, but they did place a tremendous strain on his relationship with his superiors. Conspicuously, Parham does not seem to have moved toward full ordination within the denomination, despite his laudable work at Eudora and Linwood. While the exact course of events is unclear, it is apparent that both Parham and his supervisors held mutual misgivings about the divine direction of the other party. For Parham's part, he made the initial move. While attending the annual conference on behalf of his parishioners in March 1895, he watched the presiding bishop ordain new conference members. He later reported being "horror-struck at the thought that the candidates were not left free to preach by direct inspiration." He immediately surrendered his local preacher's license and "left denominationalism forever." A new pastor was then appointed to the Eudora-Linwood charge.[13]

Beneath Parham's break with the Methodists lay a genuine rebel attitude complemented by considerable speaking ability and an abundance of youthful energy. His anger was reflected a few years later when, at the tender age of twenty-nine, he noted that "most sectarian schools" were "dominated by back-slidden, superannuated preachers . . . outclassed by younger men of more progressive, and in many cases, deeper spiritual truths."[14] Parham took the break with Methodism as an opportunity to prove his thesis. Without the constraints of outdated church officials, he could be true to the Master's call. Years later he marked the event as a milestone in his career, noting: "I had the confines of a pastorate, with a lot of theater-going, card-playing, wine-drinking, fashionable, unconverted Methodists; now I have a world-wide parish, with multitudes to preach the gospel message to. . . ."[15]

Parham's "world-wide parish" would, of course, take time to cultivate. After leaving Eudora in 1894, he spent the next few years in training, and he learned firsthand the hardships of building an independent ministry. Mixed between the outward results of "hundreds . . . converted, scores sanctified, and a few healed" were innumerable oratorical experiences. Late in 1896, Parham married Sarah Eleanor Thistlethwaite, David Baker's granddaughter. The first of six children followed in September of 1897. The arrival of an infant offered a unique opportunity for a shift in Parham's ministry. Having grown weak from an exhausting schedule and suffering from what a local doctor diagnosed as "heart disease" (probably a complication of the recurring rheumatic fever), he became desperate when his young son also became sick and physicians were unable to prescribe any cure. While praying for someone else to be healed, Parham recognized the irony of his actions and immediately focused on his own need for healing. He reported a surge of God's power and declared that his body had been made "every whit whole." To demonstrate his faith, he discarded all medicines, doctor's addresses, and even life insurance policies. This dramatic act, he felt, resulted in his son's recovery. The incident marked a crucial watershed; though Parham had preached divine healing before, it now became the major emphasis in his ministry.[16]

After a successful campaign in Ottawa, Kansas, Parham spread his ministry into more populated centers and, late in 1898, moved his family and ministerial activities to Topeka. There, on the corner of Fourth and Jackson Streets, he established the Beth-el Healing Home. The home offered a healing retreat for those seeking a faith cure. In addition to daily prayer, Parham offered a variety of services and training sessions to instruct the ailing on how best to secure their own healing. Building on this healing ministry, Parham expanded into an array of religious enterprises including a Bible institute, a temporary orphanage service, a Christian employment bureau, and rescue missions for prostitutes and the homeless. To publicize these efforts, he organized a holiness periodical, the *Apostolic Faith*, and began issuing weekly editions in March 1899.[17]

By the time Parham's star was on the rise in Topeka, he had already collected a strange assortment of religious convictions. In addition to his acceptance of entire sanctification and his unorthodox views on baptism and future rewards and punishments, he had also begun to focus on another experience, the baptism of the Holy Ghost. While most holiness advocates in the 1890s used terms like baptism of the Holy Ghost as a synonym for sanctification, Parham came to see the experience as a distinct event. Apparently influenced by Benjamin Hardin Irwin, an Iowan whose holiness revivals coordinated a series of Fire-Baptized Holiness Associations throughout the South and Midwest, he came, by 1899, to call this experience the baptism of fire. Parham seems to have never personally experienced this fire baptism; at least he never emphasized it from the pulpit. Nevertheless, he felt assured enough of its validity to publish accounts of those who did.[18]

One fire convert who was allowed to publish his experience in Parham's journal was Charles H. Croft. Explaining his own encounter in glowing terms, Croft admonished his readers that "some people are afraid of getting too much salvation and getting too much fire." His answer for those timid souls was to "let the fire of God consume all the dross of self-righteousness, and foolish talking and jesting." He also noted that "the most radical Fire opposers" were "backslidden preachers and elders and bishops and dead, cold professors."[19] Despite their attacks, Croft remained optimistic and boldly predicted the ultimate outcome.

> And they cannot stop the fire; it burns on; and they might as well try to drink the river dry with a spoon as to stop the fire that is spreading so rapidly, and will go on and on unchecked until Jesus comes and catches away his Bride that is rapidly preparing for his coming.[20]

Croft argued that the baptism of fire was the same mysterious experience which descended on the New Testament followers of Jesus in the Upper Room on the day of Pentecost recorded in Acts 2. He was also convinced that its modern outpouring portended the soon return of Jesus Christ. Yet Croft was content to avoid any reference to the miraculous tongue speaking which followed the Jerusalem outpouring. "Cloven tongues like as of fire" were the key to his experience; any need for a glossolalic or xenoglossic event simply escaped his attention. The oversight, however, is not so amazing on second glance. Croft, and probably Parham, could rationalize early on that the new experiences were as valid as those recorded in the New Testament, though now recipients experienced different—and, in the context, more productive—signs. In October 1899, Parham featured an article on divine healing by H. F. Carpenter. Carpenter drew a corollary between the prominence of healing and the absence of tongues in this latter day outpouring of God's Spirit. Predictably, his rationale was utilitarian in nature.

> The Holy Spirit has as many gifts now as it ever had, but it only bestows such as are needful. It does not bestow the "gift of tongues" now because the Bible is now printed and preached in every dialect under heaven, and the gift to speak in the language that is foreign and unknown to the speaker is not necessary. But for the "gift of healing" there will always be a need; as M.D.'s cannot cure all, and often make people worse."[21]

Parham would soon question this interpretation of the absence of tongues speaking in God's latter-day outpouring; however, for the moment his association with the fire movement was sufficient enough for him to include a separate Spirit baptism as a part of his theological creed published weekly in the *Apostolic Faith.* Readers noted that the young evangelist preached and proclaimed

> salvation by faith; healing by faith, laying on of hands, and prayer; sanctification by faith; coming (pre-millennium) of Christ; [and] the baptism of Holy Ghost and Fire, which seals the Bride and bestows the gifts.[22]

Though Parham later dropped the specific reference to fire, probably in the wake of Irwin's resignation from the Fire-Baptized Holiness Church in 1900 amidst public scandal, he nevertheless had accepted the concept of a special Holy Spirit anointing, and he continued to search for confirmation of such an experience to invigorate his own ministry.[23]

Parham's interest in a new Holy Ghost experience paralleled his concern for his own flagging ministerial pursuits in Topeka. Despite the glowing reports of the *Apostolic Faith,* all was not well within the Parham camp. The vision of his ministry in Topeka had far exceeded the results. The paper endured constant financial pressure, and many of the social programs simply failed to attract enough local support for lasting success. By 1900, Parham was severely disillusioned with the state of his ministry. Always interested in the ideas and tactics of other evangelical ministries, Parham now became rejuvenated by the vision of Frank W. Sandford. After hearing Sandford preach in June 1900, he embarked on a twelve-week journey to the evangelist's holiness commune in Shiloh, Maine. Having already accepted the premillennial doctrine of the second coming and the concept of a rapture popularized by the teaching of John Nelson Darby and the Plymouth Brethren, Parham now borrowed from Sandford the conviction that a special Holy Spirit experience would prepare believers, and through their missionary efforts the world, for this momentous event. Sandford's theory provided the utilitarian justification for Irwin's baptism and, in Parham's mind, offered a unique response to H. F. Carpenter's rationale for the absence of tongues. Unlike both Irwin and Sandford, Parham drew great significance from reports of missionaries having been divinely granted xenoglossic tongues to facilitate the transmission of the gospel. That observation ultimately formed within him the germ that would soon develop into American Pentecostalism.[24]

Parham's interest in xenoglossa actually predated his visit with Sandford. Early in 1899, he had read a remarkable report in a holiness journal about Jennie Glassey, a missionary who reported having received foreign language as a gift to aid her missionary work. He enthusiastically informed his readers about this discovery and left no doubt as to the significance of the phenomenon she displayed.

> Glassy [*sic*] now in Jerusalem, received the African dialect in one night. . . . She received the gift while in the Spirit in 1895, but could read and write, translate and sing the language while out of the trance or in a normal condition, and can until now. Hundreds of people can testify to the fact, both saint and sinner, who heard her use the language. She was also tested in Liverpool and Jerusalem. Her Christian experience is that of a holy, consecrated woman, filled with the Holy Ghost. Glory to our God for the return of the apostolic faith.[25]

By the following year, Parham seems to have personally come to the conclusion that language gifts like that given to Glassey would form the nucleus of the worldwide revival. His belief was strengthened by the addition of others interested in the phenomenon. In April 1900, he reported to his readers that a "Brother and Sister Hamaker" were tarrying at Beth-el Healing Home for Jesus to "give them an heathen tongue, and then they will proceed to the missionary field."[26]

Parham's fascination with the xenoglossa idea may have prompted his initial interest in Sandford. If so, he was not disappointed with what he discovered. During the summer spent at Shiloh, he personally witnessed tongue-speaking for the first time. He heard students uttering glossolalic phrases on their way down from the school's twenty-four hour "Prayer Tower." Sandford attached no special meaning to the phenomenon, interpreting it as an occasional manifestation of the endtime revival. Parham, however, attached crucial significance to the glossolalia. Convinced that the second coming would occur on the heels of a worldwide revival, Parham determined that this sign of xenoglossa must be the incontrovertible proof of the new Spirit baptism. With the gift, all recipients became instant missionaries. Though incredulous to most, the concept was logical. It provided both a utilitarian function and a definable sign.[27]

Parham returned to Topeka in September 1900 a new man. His vision restored, he barely paused long enough to note that his healing home had fallen into the hands of competing ministers unwilling to give it up. Optimistically, he secured a large, elaborate structure on the edge of town and opened the Bethel Bible School. There with his family and thirty-four students, he spent the next few months laying the foundation for world evangelism by preparing for the outpouring of God's gift. He taught his students the holiness doctrines of conversion, sanctification, divine healing, and premillennialism, and he advised them that they were the generation raised up specifically for world evangelism. He then convinced them that the true Spirit baptism which would foreshadow this revival had not yet arrived; Parham counseled that the true model for the outpouring was the upper room experience of Acts 2. Gradually, the student body came to accept his new vision. On January 1, 1901, Agnes Ozman spoke in tongues and continued to speak and write in what participants believed was the Chinese language for the next three days. During a more general outpouring on January 3, Parham and about half the students experienced the phenomenon.[28]

Parham's transformation from Topeka reformer to Pentecostal prophet paralleled the ongoing struggle of the Populist movement. Steeped in the politics of agrarian revolt as a child, he drew heavily from Americans disillusioned with the state of American life in the late nineteenth century—especially the changes which threatened their security. The alternative he offered was youthful change and energy; the message of America was valid, only the leadership had lost its inspiration. In that sense Parham mirrored the young Democratic candidate William Jennings Bryan. Like Bryan, he sought to bring change through the force of his own righteous indignation. By the early years of the new century, however, the Populist dream lay in ruins. The thirty-six-year-old Bryan lost in 1896; he lost again in 1900. Youthful vigor and righteousness were not enough in a world controlled by evil. Like many Populists, Parham's dreams shifted inward. The revolutionary goals of social work in the streets of Topeka gave way to a more mysterious, and more powerful, mission. Only God's efforts through the Holy Spirit could change the world and the avenue would be as strange and wonderful as the dramatic success ratio itself. It was thus a new world in which reality and the supernatural were carefully merged. To those clued in only to the sensory world, it seemed strange, even mad. But to the faithful—the ones called to serve in the endtime mission—it was the essence of true reality and justice. Life on the spiritual edge offered a wonderful sense of drama.

Still not everyone at Bethel believed. Reporters learned of the revival when two students, Samuel J. Riggins and Ralph Herrill, defected. Riggins's analysis of the eruption at Bethel was less than complimentary. In an interview with the *Topeka Daily Capital,* he spoke his mind:

> I believe the whole of them are crazy. . . . I never saw anything like it. They were racing about the room talking and gesticulating and using this strange and senseless language which they claim is the word from the Most High.[29]

Local and regional reporters visited Bethel and spread the news of the strange new doctrine. The message created some attention but most observers remained skeptical.

For the remaining students, however, Parham's theory about missionary xenoglossa seemed confirmed, their optimism bolstered by the arrival of the language. While Riggins and some reporters heard only "senseless sounds," others believed they heard actual foreign words. The emergence of such language would have been remarkable to say the least; given the climate at Bethel, documenting it would have been equally remarkable. Most observers were simply not qualified to make a linguistic assessment and, if such observers were present, no record of their findings survives. Yet the mistaking of glossolalia for xenoglossa was due to more than just unfamiliarity with language forms. What seems to have occurred in addition to a false assumption about the character of the utterances was that certain language-like patterns—and possibly even some words—did resemble known foreign language. Through a phenomenon called cryptomnesia, words and sounds previously heard are stored in the subconscious mind without any apparent effort at retention. Then, in a moment of intense stress, the language-like forms emerge though they are seemingly unknown to the speaker.[30]

Due to a high and varied rate of immigration, Kansans frequently made contact with foreign language. Norwegians, Danes, Swedes, and Germans were only a few of those bringing diversity to the state. In 1870, a full fifteen percent of the state's population was foreign-born. On the frontier, native languages flourished in small hamlets of subculture; as late as 1910, over twenty-one percent of the state's foreign-born adults could not speak English.[31] Parham and his students had ample contact with foreign tongues; their expectation of language as an eschatological gift meant that they also would feel the stress capable of creating cryptomnesia.

Unfortunately, the extent of the phenomenon among early Pentecostals cannot be gauged. Nevertheless, it was crucial that the students and

Parham believed that the sounds they uttered were real languages. Ozman's encounter with tongues on the night of January 1 took on increased significance when, on the following day, she spoke in tongues at a Topeka mission and her words were understood by a local Bohemian. Ozman reported that the encounter "encouraged all very much knowing it was a real language."[32] Real language implied authority to the tiny band of Bible students; it meant that they were indeed part of a momentous endtime event.

Parham also stressed that the languages demonstrated an important distinction within the Christian community. Those baptized in the Spirit with the accompanying sign were "sealed" as members of Christ's bride (Eph. 1:13). These triumphant missionaries to humanity's last generation would be spared the awful destruction of endtime tribulation. They would be the Christians snatched away during the Rapture, and at the second coming they would return victorious to help Christ rule his millennial kingdom. As the sign of the baptism, tongues served a crucial role as evidence and also as a utilitarian missions tool.[33]

In late January 1901, Parham and a small band of students headed to Kansas City to spread the word and convert the world. Results, however, were meager, and by the end of February, the crew returned to Topeka. A subsequent effort in Lawrence, Kansas, also proved disappointing. To shore up sagging spirits, Parham planned a huge summer camp meeting in Topeka and publicized the event to holiness people throughout the country. By late spring, however, the vision of most of the students had dimmed. Parham's year-old son died in March, setting an ominous sign for the future of the work at Bethel. During the summer, the Stone Mansion, the elaborate residence that had housed the operation, was sold out from under the renting Parhams, and the Bible school sought new quarters. By the fall, that effort was abandoned and Parham moved his family to Kansas City to start a new ministry there. To define his mission and clear his head, he published *Kol Kare Bomidbar: A Voice Crying in the Wilderness*—the first Pentecostal theology statement.[34]

Over the next few years, Parham regrouped and expanded the Pentecostal revival under the title the Apostolic Faith movement. Retaining the same message, he scored successes at El Dorado Springs, Missouri, in 1903 and Galena, Kansas, in the winter of 1903–1904. Reemphasizing his healing ministry, he drew crowds at the Galena revival as large as 2500.[35] More importantly he attracted a small core of followers who rekindled the dream of an endtime revival through the divine gift of xenoglossa.

Expanding into Texas in 1905, Parham built a substantial following around Houston. Late in 1905, Parham opened the Houston Bible School, again an institution designed to train workers and produce missionaries for the coming revival.[36] From the Bible school, workers fanned out into rural Texas and the Midwest, spreading the Pentecostal message as they went. Significantly, Parham's message reached the black community of Houston, and the *Apostolic Faith* claimed several black ministers in the growing alliance. One of these ministers, William J. Seymour, traveled to Los Angeles and spread Parham's message there. By late in 1906, a Pentecostal revival was blossoming on the West Coast.[37] Paralleling the growth in Houston and Los Angeles was the Pentecostal revival in Zion City, Illinois, where the personal failure of John Alexander Dowie seemed to offer an entire city for the taking. Parham traveled there in September 1906 and quickly amassed close to a thousand followers.[38] From the strategic strongholds at Galena, Houston, Los Angeles, and Zion City, a host of early Pentecostal pioneers would emerge.

Late in 1906, prospects were extremely bright for Parham. Five years of groundwork seemed finally to be paying off, and the anticipated endtime revival seemed ready to erupt worldwide. To coordinate the event, Parham had reissued the *Apostolic Faith* in 1905. In early 1906, he had created a loose organizational model to encourage expansion and had begun issuing ministerial credentials. His total following by the fall of 1906 was 5,000 to 10,000 persons, most of whom were centered in the Midwest. As more and more of these faithful received the Pentecostal experience, Parham expected the revival to spread with hypergeometric proportions.[39]

Pentecostalism did experience steady growth, but the rate was not nearly as fast and did not occur in the fashion Parham had anticipated. Most importantly, as he would discover to his dismay, the movement would grow without him. A heated battle with Wilbur Glenn Voliva for spiritual control of Zion City and a bitter dispute with Seymour in Los Angeles over the character and social implications of the revival there neutralized Parham's position in those centers.[40] More damaging were the rumors of sexual impropriety which emerged late in 1906 and exploded in the summer of 1907 with Parham being arrested on a charge of sodomy in San Antonio, Texas. Though the case never came to trial, and a variety of evidence remains conflicting, the result was the same everywhere. Parham's influence throughout the young movement was destroyed.[41]

Despite the embarrassment and discouragement that followed the scandal, Parham retained his vision of Pentecostal world evangelism. He circulated for the next two decades until his death in 1929 among a small band of several thousand followers located primarily in the south-central states. To the end he maintained a belief in the validity of missionary xenoglossa.[42] Yet most Pentecostals abandoned the specifics of the early vision; tongues-speech came to be understood as glossolalia (termed "divine language"), and xenoglossa, when referred to at all, was considered an extraordinary miracle. Also, many Pentecostals toned down the disturbing connotations implicit in the "sealing of the bride" theology, though the inherent problem of defending themselves against charges of a spiritual superiority complex remained.[43]

Nevertheless, Pentecostalism owes a great debt to the controversial evangelist. Parham had infused the movement with a unique doctrine—Holy Spirit baptism evidenced by speaking in tongues. Equally important had been his emphasis on endtime missions. Though by 1910 most Pentecostals had abandoned his notion of xenoglossa as a missions tool, they never doubted that the revival itself was a manifestation of endtime chronology. Pentecostals poured themselves, and a sizable percentage of their denominational income, into the task of evangelizing the world. Slowly the message spread. Ironically the success of the numbers game was responsible for the rebirth of the man most Pentecostals had denounced in 1907. The growth of Pentecostalism worldwide sparked scholars to reconstruct the historical roots of the scores of denominations and sects that emerged during the two decades after Parham's fall. The result was a focus back on the forgotten visionary from the central Kansas plains. In the end, Parham taught his students well—very well indeed.

NOTES

1. For a more in-depth discussion of the historiographical significance of this doctrine and Parham's contribution to it, see my *Fields White Unto Harvest* (Fayetteville: University of Arkansas Press, 1988). On the rationalization behind the doctrine, see the contemporary explanation by one of the most erudite Pentecostal leaders, J. H. King, *From Passover to Pentecost*, 4th ed. (Franklin Springs, Ga.: Advocate Press, 1976), 152–85.

2. A. T. Andreas, *History of the State of Kansas* (Chicago: A. T. Andreas, 1883), 1415. For examples advertising the celebrated Kansas boom, see L. D. Burch, *Kansas As It Is* (Chicago: C. S. Burch and Co., 1878); and L. T. Bodine, *Kansas Illustrated* (Kansas City, Mo.: Ramsey, Millet, and Hudson, 1879).

3. On the economic ups and downs of the period, see W. F. Zornow, *Kansas: A History of the Jayhawk State* (Norman: University of Oklahoma Press, 1957), 159–73.

4. S. E. Parham, *The Life of Charles F. Parham* (Joplin, Mo.: Tri-State Printing, 1930), 6–9. Though Parham claimed healing from the disease as a young man of eighteen, a medical analysis seems to indicate that flare-ups of rheumatic fever returned in between long periods of remission. Cf. Goff, *Fields White Unto Harvest*, 23–24, 159.

5. Ibid., 1–2.

6. C. F. Parham, *Kol Kare Bomidbar: A Voice Crying in the Wilderness* (Kansas City, Mo.: By the Author, 1902; reprint ed., Joplin, Mo.: Joplin Printing Co., 1944), 15.

7. There is some question as to Parham's intentions upon enrolling at Southwest Kansas College. Technically, he was a part of the Normal School—a fact consistent with an earlier experience teaching in the local village school. Nevertheless, Parham's intentions were also related to his previous "call" to the ministry and his local evangelistic efforts. College records show that he matriculated for three consecutive years (1890–91, 1891–92, and 1892–93) though he never graduated. Letter from Ralph W. Decker, Jr., Registrar, Southwestern College, Winfield, Kan., 25 November 1985.

8. Parham, *Voice*, 15–19; and letter from Joanne Black, Commission on Archives and History, Kansas West Conference, United Methodist Church, Winfield, Kan., 26 November 1985.

9. F. Quinlan, "History of the United Methodist Church in Linwood, Kansas" (Manuscript, Baker University United Methodist Collection, Baldwin City, Kan., 13 August 1970), 1; and Parham, *Life*, 20–21.

10. On sanctification and the resulting turmoil within the Methodist church, see H. V. Synan, *The Holiness-Pentecostal Movement in the United States* (Grand Rapids: Eerdmans, 1971), 45–54; and R. Anderson, *Vision of the Disinherited* (New York: Oxford University Press, 1979), 36–37.

11. Parham, *Voice*, 21–24.

12. Parham, *Life*, 14 and C. F. Parham, *The Everlasting Gospel* (n.p. [1919–20]), 92–95, 111–17.

13. Charles William Shumway, "A Study of 'The Gift of Tongues'" (A.B. thesis, University of Southern California, 1914), 164; and Parham, *Voice*, 19.

14. Parham, *Voice*, 15.

15. Parham, *Everlasting Gospel*, 7.

16. Parham, *Life*, 32; and Parham, *Voice*, 19.

17. Parham, *Life*, 33–48.

18. On Irwin and the Fire-Baptized Holiness Church, see H. Vinson Synan, *The Old-Time Power* (Franklin Springs, Ga.: Advocate Press, 1973), 81–101; and J. E. Campbell, *The Pentecostal Holiness Church, 1898–1948* (Raleigh, N.C.: World Outlook Publications, 1981), 192–215.

19. *Apostolic Faith* (Topeka, Kan.) 1, 7 June 1899, 5.

20. Ibid.

21. Ibid., 18 October 1899, 2.

22. Ibid., 22 March 1899, 8.

23. On Irwin's scandal and resignation, see Synan, *Holiness-Pentecostal*, 61–67; and J. H. King, "History of the Fire-Baptized Holiness Church" (Manuscript, Pentecostal Holiness Church Archives, Oklahoma City, Okla.). King's manuscript was originally published as a serial in the *Pentecostal Holiness Advocate*, 24 March–21 April, 1921.

24. On Darby's prominence in the developing scheme of premillennialism, see T. P. Weber, *Living in the Shadow of the Second Coming* (New York: Oxford University Press, 1979), 17–24.

25. *Apostolic Faith* (Topeka, Kan.) 1, 3 May 1899, 5. See also W. C. Hiss, "Shiloh: Frank W. Sandford and the Kingdom, 1893–1948" (Ph.D. dissertation, Tufts University, 1978), 163.

26. Ibid., 2, 1 April 1900, 7.

27. Shumway, "A Study," 165.

28. *Topeka State Journal*, 20 October 1900, 14; and Parham, *Life*, 53–65.

29. *Topeka Daily Capital*, 6 January 1901, 2.

30. On cryptomnesia, see W. J. Samarin, *Tongues of Men and Angels* (New York: Macmillan, 1972), 115–18 and Shumway, 19–29; cf. R. P. Spittler, "Glossolalia," *DPCM*, 335–41.

31. Zornow, *Kansas*, 174–83; *The Tribune Almanac for 1893*, 5 vols. (New York: Tribune Association, 1893), 5:123; and *The World Almanac and Encyclopedia: 1915* (New York: Press Publishing Co., 1914), 711–12.

32. A. N. O. LaBerge, "History of the Pentecostal Movement from January 1, 1901" (Manuscript, Editorial Files of the *Pentecostal Evangel*, Springfield, Mo.), 3.

33. Parham, *Voice*, 32; and *Everlasting Gospel*, 74–76.

34. Parham, *Life*, 71–81. Also *Kansas City Times*, 27 January 1901, 15; *Kansas City Journal*, 22 January 1901, 1, and *Kansas City World*, 15 January 1901, 7.

35. L. P. Murphy, "Beginning at Topeka," *Calvary Review* 13 (Spring 1974): 9; and Parham, *Life*, 98.

36. Parham, *Life*, 136–41.

37. D. J. Nelson, "For Such a Time as This. The Story of Bishop William J. Seymour and the Azusa Street Revival" (Ph.D. diss., University of Birmingham, England, 1981), 55–59, 182–201; and Anderson, *Vision*, 62–69.

38. *Waukegan Daily Sun*, 28 September 1906, 1.

39. For an in-depth explanation on arriving at an estimate for Parham's following, see Goff, *Fields White Unto Harvest*, 115, 169–70.

40. Shumway, "A Study," 178–79; and Parham, *Life*, 155–56.

41. *San Antonio Light*, 19 July 1907, 1; and Goff, *Fields White Unto Harvest*, 135–42.

42. Parham, *Everlasting Gospel*, 68. Also *Apostolic Faith* (Baxter Springs, Kan.), 2, November 1913, 14; and 2, August 1926, 15–16.

43. For accounts of xenoglossa over the course of Pentecostal history, see R. W. Harris, *Spoken By the Spirit* (Springfield, Mo.: Gospel Publishing House, 1973) and W. Warner, ed. *Touched by the Fire* (Plainfield, N.J.: Logos International, 1978), 51–58, 89–91, 151–57.

5

WILLIAM J. SEYMOUR AND "THE BIBLE EVIDENCE"

Cecil M. Robeck, Jr.

Cars banging, boiler gasping, the great locomotive ground slowly to a halt as the engineer deposited his payload precisely on schedule. The station dock, until then hushed in anticipation, burst to life as men shouted and "cappers" quickly steered their baggage carts toward the train. Children jumped and squealed with excitement. Those waiting for friends and loved ones cast a furtive eye from car to car as doors sprang open and passengers scampered out. It was Thursday, February 22, 1906, and a quiet unassuming, African-American pastor, Elder William Joseph Seymour, bag in hand, descended the steps and made his way from the train.[1]

Los Angeles, a bustling city of 230,000 in 1906, had more than doubled its population in the past six years, increasing monthly by 3,000 residents. Each arriving train now conveyed a batch of hopeful immigrants, many of them southern poor, to the nation's seventeenth largest city.[2] The area provided a cornucopia of possibilities, as local and intracontinental transportation lines were completed, property development boomed, and economic indicators pushed ever upward. It was a city of dreams and ambitions; it was raw, rugged, bawdy, eclectic, a crucible for new ideas.

The city was home to some 5,000 black Americans in 1906,[3] the majority of whom made their homes within walking distance of the railroad tracks.[4] The three largest churches serving the black community, First African Methodist Episcopal (AME) at Eighth and Towne (900 members), Wesley Chapel at Sixth and Maple (500 members), and Second Baptist on Maple between Seventh and Eighth (500 members), were all located in this area. First AME, originally known as Stevens AME, had moved from its old quarters at 312 Azusa Street in 1904, leaving behind an empty wood-framed building destined to become a center of the city's attention in the summer of 1906.[5]

Seymour later wrote that it was "the colored people" in this area who summoned him to Los Angeles to "give them some Bible teaching."[6] Seymour was not called to one of these prestigious pastorates, but to a small, recently established store-front holiness church then being led by Mrs. Julia W. Hutchins. The meetings were scheduled to begin Saturday, February 24, and Elder Seymour was ready to serve.

For the two or three years before his arrival in Los Angeles,[7] Seymour lived in Houston, where he attended a small holiness church led by Mrs. Lucy F. Farrow, a fifty-four-year-old black widow[8] who, in tent-making fashion, earned her livelihood as a cook. Farrow befriended Seymour, and when she accepted temporary work out of town as family governess for evangelist Charles Fox Parham in late August 1905, she placed the mission in Seymour's charge.[9] Seymour proved to be an able pastor.

The name of Charles Parham, for whom Farrow went to work, was widely known in the greater Houston area from July 1905 onward. Newspapers regularly covered his meetings, where his unique blend of Zionism,[10] divine healing,[11] and tongues speaking[12] were guaranteed to lure a crowd. With his emphasis on healing and his talk of "Zion," many associated him with John Alexander Dowie. But unlike Dowie, whose utopian scheme was Zion City, Illinois, Parham's "Zion" was Palestine. Driven by an evangelistic urgency, a commitment to a British-Israel theory, and an infatuation with the international Zionist movement, Parham preached the "Restoration of Religion's Birthplace to Its Rightful Heirs" and attempted to raise money to purchase a national homeland for the Jews.[13]

To be sure, Parham had his eye on Dowie's Zion, and as Dowie's health deteriorated and as he slowly loosened his grasp on his utopian dream, Parham was prepared to capture as much of it as he could.[14] But Parham's chief claim to fame separated him from Dowie. In January 1901, when some of Parham's followers began to speak in tongues, Parham championed this activity as "the Bible evidence" of "baptism with the Holy Ghost."[15] By 1905, Parham had fashioned this phrase, "the Bible evidence," into a *terminus technicus* to describe the relationship of speaking in tongues to the prominent concern which Parham shared with the Wesleyan-holiness movement, the experience of baptism with the Spirit (Acts 2:4). Between 1901 and 1905 Parham held church services and camp meetings, and conducted several short-term Bible schools in Kansas and Texas, where he propagated his views on this controversial subject. This activity brought him in the summer of 1905 to the Houston area, where he hired Farrow. After an absence of two months, during which he conducted a school in Kansas, Parham, Farrow, and an entourage of helpers once again returned to Houston. It was December 1905.

Lucy Farrow, flush with the excitement of having experienced "the Bible evidence" herself, contacted Seymour. Through her vibrant testimony William Seymour was encouraged to enroll in Parham's newest Bible school scheduled to begin in Houston that month. Farrow's intervention with Parham made Seymour's participation possible, and Seymour quickly embraced Parham's theory of "the Bible evidence," though it would be several months before he entered fully into the experience.

While Seymour continued to preach and study his way into the new year, events were shaping up half a continent away that would contribute to his February 1906 move to Los Angeles. Julia W. Hutchins, a forty-five-year-old black had emigrated from Galveston, Texas,[16] to Los Angeles, as early as 1903. Public records indicate that she was well established in Los Angeles by July 1905, when she was denied a permit to conduct meetings at First and San Pedro Streets due to crowded conditions on that corner.[17] But Hutchins's ties to the greater Houston area were multifaceted, since a number of the people who attended her Los Angeles mission, now established at Ninth and Santa Fe, were also from the Houston area. Among them were Richard and Ruth Asberry, who owned a small home on North Bonnie Brae Street, and Ruth Asberry's cousin, Mrs. Neely Terry. While visiting Houston in late 1905, Terry attended Lucy Farrow's holiness church where Seymour preached. Upon her return to Los Angeles she recommended to Hutchins, who by now was searching for a regular pastor for her flock, that William J. Seymour be called to fill that position.[18] Hutchins agreed.

On the surface, Julia Hutchins's decision may appear to be premature, but she trusted Terry's recommendation. Upon a second look, however, it is probable that Hutchins had had some previous contact with William Seymour or with Lucy Farrow. In September 1905, Charles Parham published the words of a song titled "Battle Hymn" in his periodical *The Apostolic Faith* (Melrose, Kan.). It was authored by a Mrs. J. W. Hutchins.[19] How long he had the song before he published it, how he obtained it, and whether the Mrs. J. W. Hutchins who wrote the song is the same person as Mrs. Julia W. Hutchins of Los Angeles are questions all waiting to be answered. The hymn was popular among Parham's students, and it is probable that Julia Hutchins was its author.[20]

Since Hutchins's "Battle Hymn" was apparently first published in September 1905, three possibilities arise by which Parham could have gained access to it. First, Hutchins could have given it to him at some previous time or she could have mailed it to Parham. This would suggest that she had had some personal contact with Parham before moving to Los Angeles, but there is no evidence to support this theory. Second, she could have known Lucy Farrow from her time in the Galveston and Houston areas and might have given or sent her a copy. Since Farrow was with Parham's family at the time the song was published, it would have been a simple thing for her to pass it on to Parham. Third, Neely Terry could have brought it with her from Los Angeles to Houston and shared it with Elder Seymour who, in turn, sent a copy to Lucy Farrow in Kansas. The latter would have passed it on to Charles Parham. In any event, the circle of friends and acquaintances in the black holiness movement appears to have been a small and tightly connected one, and by February 1906, they were all well acquainted with Parham and Seymour.

Seymour had barely settled in when he held his first meeting in Los Angeles on February 24. But during that first week, he touched a theological nerve of some members of his new congregation. Seymour expounded Parham's view of baptism with the Holy Ghost, including the claim that speaking in tongues was "the Bible evidence." This quickly drove a wedge between Seymour and the Holiness Church Association with whom Hutchins and her congregation had some affiliation. Dr. J. M. Roberts, president of the Holiness Church in Southern California and Arizona, was summoned and attended at least one of Seymour's services. He was troubled by this new doctrine, i.e., that sanctification and baptism with the Holy Spirit, evidenced by tongues, are two separate experiences. Roberts and several others, however, found their efforts to convince Seymour that the position of the Holiness Church was correct to be futile, since in Seymour's words, none of them had "the evidence of the second chapter of Acts."[21] As a result, Roberts asked Seymour not to preach this doctrine any longer.

Not everyone in Seymour's little flock was as troubled by the incident as Julia Hutchins was, and as it turned out, even she would ultimately change her mind.[22] But the following Sunday, March 4, Hutchins pad-locked the mission and stood her ground. She refused to allow Seymour to preach. Fortunately, for Seymour, however, the Asberry's invited him to continue leading a prayer and Bible study meeting in their home at 214 North Bonnie Brae Street. In the safety of that setting, Seymour persisted in teaching speaking in tongues as "the Bible evidence" of baptism with the Holy Ghost.

On April 9, six weeks after Seymour arrived in Los Angeles and five weeks after being locked out by Hutchins, he had his first convert, complete with speaking in tongues. Edward S. Lee, a black employed as a janitor at Los Angeles' First National Bank, spoke in tongues.[23] That evening, others in Seymour's Bible study spoke in tongues as well. Word raced through the neighborhood. The following Sunday, Easter, April 15, some of these same people attended First New Testament Church, a thriving congregation led by Joseph Smale. At the end of service, they proceeded to speak in tongues.[24] By Tuesday evening, April 17, a new congregation had been formed. The Bonnie Brae Bible study group had rented the old building vacated by Stevens (now First) AME Church at 312 Azusa Street, and Seymour conducted a service for the "colored people and sprinkling of whites" who made up the congregation. A reporter from the *Los Angeles Daily Times* was present, pen in hand, to break the news to the world of Los Angeles' "newest religious sect."[25] Seymour summoned Lucy Farrow to help him provide leadership to this burgeoning work.

SEYMOUR: THE EARLY YEARS (1906–1908)

In its early years, the Azusa Street Mission was firmly committed to the view that speaking in tongues was "the Bible evidence" of baptism with the Spirit. Any nuance between tongues as the evidence of baptism with the Spirit and the "gift of tongues" eluded the secular press just as it did most early Apostolic Faith people.[26] But from the beginning the mission's paper, the *Apostolic Faith* (Los Angeles), made the connection between "tongues" and baptism with the Spirit. In the first issue of the *Apostolic Faith*, Seymour published what functioned as the mission's Statement of Faith until 1915. It was also distributed in flyer form to inquirers, under-signed by W. J. Seymour. The subjects of sin and salvation, justification, sanctification, baptism in the Spirit, and divine healing were all ad-dressed. "Baptism in the Spirit" was addressed twice, once positively and once negatively as follows:

The Baptism with the Holy Ghost is a gift of power upon the sanctified life; so when we get it we have the same evidence as the Disciples received on the Day of Pentecost (Acts 2:3, 4), in speaking in new tongues. See also Acts 10:45, 46; Acts 19:6; 1 Cor. 14:21. "For I will work a work in your days which ye will not believe though it be told you." Hab. 1:5.

The statement continued:

Too many have confused the grace of Sanctification with the enduement of Power, or the Baptism with the Holy Ghost; others have taken "the anointing that abideth" for the Baptism, and failed to reach the glory and power of a true Pentecost.[27]

Here, Seymour drew the proverbial "line in the sand," clearly distinguishing the Apostolic Faith movement from the historic Wesleyan-holiness movement. By doing so, he identified his own mission with the position articulated by Charles Parham in 1901. This "apostolic" teaching was distinctive, even confrontational to the Wesleyan-holiness status quo. But it was Seymour's opinion that Parham's position provided an important distinction that held profound implications for world evangelization.

The baptism with the Spirit, Seymour asserted, came "upon the sanctified life." This experience brought the power of the triune God to bear upon the people of God, enabling them "to speak all the languages of the world." "We that are the messengers of th[e] precious atonement ought to preach all of it," exhorted Seymour, "justification, sanctification, healing, the baptism with the Holy Ghost, and signs following."[28]

The primary themes of "apostolic" teaching could be found in Seymour's brief exhortation. These included the ability to speak multiple languages for the evangelization of the world. The baptism with the Spirit was a baptism of *power* which came with a commission. In a short, unsigned article in the same issue of the *Apostolic Faith*, the statement was made that "the gift of languages is given with the commission 'Go ye into all the world and preach the Gospel to every creature.' "[29]

While Seymour generally distinguished his position from that typically held by the Wesleyan-holiness people, he was still ambivalent. This was reflected in his occasional use of the phrase "signs following." In "Tongues as a Sign," an unsigned article possibly written by Seymour himself, the author referred to a passage in the so-called longer ending of Mark (16:16–17) with the observation that:

Here a belief and baptism are spoken of, and the sign or evidence given to prove that you posses [*sic*] that belief and baptism. This scripture plainly declares that these signs SHALL follow them that believe.

The author criticized those who "ran off" with blessings and anointings "instead of tarrying until [the] Bible evidence of Pentecost came."[30] Thus, the writer equated the concepts of *signs which follow* with *the Bible evidence* of baptism with the Spirit.

Within blocks of the Azusa Street Mission, Joseph Smale, former pastor of First Baptist Church, was holding services in Burbank Hall. His congregation of about 225 people, the First New Testament Church, advertised itself as a "fellowship for evangelical preaching and teaching and pentecostal life and service."[31] Smale, who had been greatly influenced by Evan Roberts and the Welsh Revival, asserted that the miraculous had departed from the church through the centuries because the church had departed from the faith. He urged his congregation to "grasp the very glory of God, and bring it to the earth," thereby becoming "a church in union and communion with God and reflecting all the splendors of the first Pentecost."[32]

Smale expected a reemergence of the spectacular gifts of 1 Corinthians 12:8–10 among his people. For several months during 1905 and 1906, the congregation had prayed toward that end.[33] When in April 1906 people began to speak in tongues, first on Bonnie Brae Street, then on April 15 in First New Testament Church, Smale was receptive. He called it "a deep work of the spirit[*sic*] of God," and he appealed to the local Christian community for toleration.[34] He also granted considerable freedom to his own parishioners, encouraging them to exercise the gifts of tongues and prophecy, to pray for the sick, and even to exorcise demons.

All went well until mid-September when Lillian Keyes, the daughter of a close and long-time friend of Smale, prominent surgeon Dr. Henry S. Keyes, allegedly prophesied that Smale had "grieved the Spirit." Keyes's charge and Smale's response were exactly what local news reporters wanted. Throughout the latter half of September, the press whipped up public interest as it reported this classic charismatic confrontation.[35] Finally, Dr. Keyes turned against Smale, too, and rallied a group together who wanted more freedom in their worship (the apparent source of the Spirit's "grief"). Elmer K. Fisher, who was serving as an associate to Smale since leaving his Baptist pastorate in Glendale, became the pastor of this small flock. It met first in a hall at 107½ North Main, then quickly moved to 327½ South Spring Street where it became known as the Upper Room Mission.[36] In its initial service, attendance ran "about fifty." About fifteen came from the First New Testament Church with the rest probably coming from Azusa Street.[37]

Like many who had been influenced by Wesleyan-holiness teachers such as W. B. Godbey, Smale continued to believe in a "God-given gift of tongues," but he charged those who had split his congregation with abuses that paralleled the problems in first-century Corinth.[38] He argued that much of the blame for their excesses could be traced to the position taken at Azusa Street. "Those people contend that the gift of tongues is the inevitable evidence of the baptism of the Holy Ghost. I fail to see that idea, . . ." he complained. "The Bible is the rule of faith and practice and what is contrary to its teachings I cannot accept."[39]

That summer the Los Angeles papers had a heyday. In July, the president of the Los Angeles Church Federation warned that certain of the Azusa Street enthusiasts might "lose their reason . . . and become dangerous."[40] Early in September the *Los Angeles Daily Times* carried a scathing article on Azusa Street. Playing the emotional topics of religion, sexuality, and racism to the hilt, the articles' titles alone were worthy of exploitation in the "dime novel." "Women with Men Embrace," they cooed. Then more overtly they gossiped, "Whites and Blacks Mix in a Religious Frenzy." "Wives Say They Left Husbands to Follow Preacher." Finally, they returned the verdict, "Disgusting Scenes at Azusa Street Church."[41] Dr. R. J. Burdette, pastor of Temple Baptist Church, now declared the events of Azusa Street to be "a disgusting amalgamation of African voodoo [*sic*] superstition and Caucasian insanity."[42]

Charles Parham expected to be in Los Angeles by September 15 to visit the mission on Azusa Street. It is clear that he intended to affix his imprimatur to the work there.[43] Lucy Farrow, who from April until August had aided Seymour at Azusa Street, gave glowing reports of the work in Los Angeles when she visited Parham's Brunner, Texas, camp meeting in August.[44] Despite Parham's interest in getting to Los Angeles, he postponed his trip so that he could make a critical visit to Zion City, Illinois, where he hoped to capture much of Dowie's utopia. Delayed for nearly two months, Parham did not arrive in Los Angeles until late October. He was dismayed to find the Apostolic Faith movement, represented by Azusa Street, to be the subject of widespread negative publicity and the laughingstock of the community.

Parham proceeded to Seymour's mission for a firsthand look. He found it difficult to accept the noisy worship style there, but he was especially distressed by the mingling of black and white worshippers.[45] Parham attempted to censure the leadership at the mission for allowing the state of affairs which he now witnessed. The leaders, however, rejected what they perceived to be an audacious intrusion from the outside, and they asked Parham to leave. They would continue without him.[46]

Following his rejection by Azusa Street leaders, Parham quickly began his own meetings elsewhere. He announced daily meetings at 10 a.m.,

2:30, and 7 p.m. at the Women's Christian Temperance Union (WCTU) building on the corner of Temple and Broadway.[47] Parham attempted to portray his version of the Apostolic Faith movement as "non-sectarian" during his daily noontime meetings in Metropolitan Hall, the space occupied by Fisher's Upper Room Mission at South Spring Street.[48]

Parham now attempted to distance himself from Seymour and Azusa Street by appealing to his involvement with Dowie's Zion. He announced to the press that he had "virtually captured the spiritual forces" of Dowie's utopia. He promised to tell of his exploits at the meetings he held at the WCTU building.[49] But he also conducted meetings in nearby Whittier, where an assistant of Parham, Mr. W. R. Quinton announced,

> We conduct dignified religious services, and have no connec ion [*sic*] with the sort which is characterized by trances, fits and spasms, jerks, shakes and contortions. We are wholly foreign to the religious anarchy, which marks the Los Angeles Azusa street meetings, and expect to do good in Whittier along proper and profound Christian lines.[50]

Parham's later accounts of the situation at Azusa Street became successively more strident.[51]

It is fair to say, though, that the boundaries of appropriate glossolalic behavior were under scrutiny by both Parham and Seymour at that time. One practice is a good case in point. Both leaders had followers who had experimented with such eccentricities as "writing in tongues."[52] The argument must have been raised that since "the Bible evidence" or "gift of tongues" was "language" it should be possible to reduce it to a variety of linguistic forms, including written ones. But by the summer of 1907 a note appeared in the *Apostolic Faith* (Los Angeles) that at Azusa Street they were "measuring everything by the Word, every experience must measure up with the Bible."[53] By the following issue, the celebration of "writing in tongues" had turned to skepticism. "We do not read anything in the Word about writing in unknown languages," it announced, "so we do not encourage that in our meetings."[54] The concern was fanaticism, and the observation was that it was questionable whether writing in tongues produced any genuine benefit. Parham was probably more affected by the dominance of a black African-American worship style than with genuine excesses which he found at the mission.

By the middle of 1907, Seymour's thoughts on the appropriate evidence for baptism with the Spirit also began to shift. Through May 1907, the *Apostolic Faith* presented a solid position that the ability to speak in tongues was *the* evidence, "the Bible evidence," of the baptism with the Holy Spirit. Perhaps the pain that Seymour experienced at Parham's public criticism of Azusa Street led him to print an article in September 1907 aimed at the "baptized saints." "*Tongues are one of the signs* that go with every [Spirit-]baptized person," it began, "*but it is not the real evidence* of the baptism in the every day life."[55] Seymour began to argue that perhaps the ability to speak in tongues had lost its uniqueness as *the* evidence. His Wesleyan-holiness background, with its emphasis upon the fruit of the Spirit (Gal. 5:22–23), had an equally important point to make.

> Your life must measure with the fruits of the Spirit. If you get angry, or speak evil, or backbite, I care not how many tongues you may have, you have not the baptism with the Holy Spirit. You have lost your salvation. You need the Blood in your soul.[56]

Was this a criticism of Parham's behavior after he was asked to leave Azusa Street? One can only speculate, but Seymour's language had begun to shift, and Parham's actions would have left him open to a charge by Seymour that he did not have the baptism even if he did speak in tongues.

Charles Parham left Los Angeles in December 1906, returning to Zion City, Illinois. He then traveled to the East before heading back to Kansas and Texas. In July 1907, while in San Antonio, Texas, Parham was arrested and charged with committing an "unnatural offense."[57] It is not possible to confirm whether Parham's arrest spurred Seymour to address the subject of evidence, but within six months the issue was addressed again in the *Apostolic Faith*, this time in a question and answer format. And the answer was well suited for application to Parham's alleged fall.

"What is the real evidence that a man or woman has received the baptism with the Holy Ghost?" it asked.

> Divine love, which is charity. Charity is the Spirit of Jesus. They will have the fruits of the Spirit. Gal. 5:22 "The fruit of the Spirit is love, joy, peace, longsuffering, gentleness, goodness, meekness, faith, temperance; against such there is no law. And they that are Christ's have crucified the flesh with the affections and lusts." This is the real Bible evidence in their daily walk and conversation; and the outward manifestations; speaking tongues and the signs following; casting out devils, laying hands on the sick and the sick being healed, and the love of God for souls increasing in their hearts.[58]

Once again, Seymour appealed to the role of the fruit of the Spirit, but he made room for a variety of charisms, too. It was clear, however, that fleshly "affections" and "lusts" were singled out as unacceptable. While Parham had taught Seymour to expect "the Bible evidence" of speaking in tongues, Seymour had clearly broadened his understanding of Spirit baptism to include an ethical dimension. The words of Elmer Fisher, pastor of Azusa Street's chief competition, the Upper Room Mission (the place where Parham had been allowed to hold noon meetings when barred from Azusa Street), suggest that Seymour's response was, indeed, motivated by Parham's fall. "Don't allow any of the counterfeits of the devil *or the failures of men* to cause you to lower the standard of the Word of God," Fisher warned, ". . . those who receive the full baptism of the Holy Ghost *will speak in tongues* as the Spirit gives utterance *always.*"[59] Fisher implied that Seymour had stepped back from the truth by concentrating more upon human weakness (Parham's alleged fall) than upon the word of God. At the very least, Fisher's response was aimed to silence the kind of revisionism which Seymour raised. Racial patterns alone did not separate Seymour and Fisher; their approach to tongues as evidence of baptism with the Spirit also separated them.

By late 1907 the *Apostolic Faith* incorporated more articles using alternative language, and the phrase "the Bible evidence" began to disappear.[60] In its place came the increasingly popular description of tongues as a "sign" that would follow. On two occasions the subject of baptism with the Holy Spirit was addressed at length. "Tongues are not an evidence of salvation," the first one announced, "but one of the signs that follow every Spirit-filled man and woman."[61]

Seymour addressed the subject one final time in the May 1908 issue of the *Apostolic Faith*. In this particular article, most likely a portion of a sermon he had preached, Seymour represented the mission's official position. He clearly avoided the language of *evidence* when he recalled,

> The Azusa standard of the baptism with the Holy Ghost is according to the Bible in Acts 1:5, 8; Acts 2:4 and Luke 24:49. Bless His Holy name. Hallelujah to the Lamb for the baptism of the Holy Ghost and fire and speaking in tongues as the Spirit gives utterance.

Seymour went on to promise, "So beloved, when you get your personal Pentecost, the signs will follow in speaking with tongues as the Spirit gives utterance. This is true."[62] What is clear from this is that while Seymour did not teach a doctrine of "the Bible evidence," he still believed that when people were baptized with the Spirit, they would speak in tongues. Now, however, he described the ability as a sign which should follow the experience, as the Spirit made it possible. He was convinced that the sovereignty of God's Spirit had to be retained.

SEYMOUR: THE LATER YEARS (1915–1922)

Seymour was not one to encourage the quest of spiritual manifestations. The ability to speak in tongues was fine, but for Seymour it was not the *sine qua non* of Christian spirituality. "Keep your eyes on Jesus," Seymour warned his readers, "not on the manifestations, not seeking to get some great thing more than somebody else. . . . If you get your eyes on manifestations and signs," he warned, "you are liable to get a counterfeit, but what you want to seek is more holiness, more of God."[63]

Manifestations were important, but they could also be problematic. "If you find people that get a harsh spirit, and even talk in tongues in a harsh spirit, it is not the Holy Ghost talking," observed one contributor to the *Apostolic Faith* in May 1908. "His [the Spirit's] utterances are in power and glory and with blessing and sweetness. . . . He is a meek and humble Spirit—not a harsh Spirit."[64]

Harshness was a problem, especially in the relationship with Charles Parham. Parham continued to attack the work of Seymour in Los Angeles in what can only be labeled as vitriolic. Repeatedly throughout 1912, Parham printed charges and accusations designed to undercut Seymour's credibility. He seemed obsessed to set the record straight, a record which favored his own brand of Pentecostal theology.

Parham described the Los Angeles experience as "counterfeit," "a cross between the Negro and Holy Roller form of worship."[65] In his paper, complete with racial slurs, he described Azusa Street as a "hotbed of wildfire," engaging in "religious orgies outrivaling scenes in devil or fetish worship." Their activities included "barking like dogs, crowing like roosters . . . trances, shakes, fits and all kinds of fleshly contortions with wind-sucking and jabbering. . . ."[66] In each subsequent issue, Parham continued his scathing assessment of Azusa Street, finally describing it all as "sewerage."[67]

Seymour had other problems during these years as well. Most of the whites had left the mission, in part, because of racial prejudice, although other factors, such as incorporation of the mission, had played a role.[68] But, like Parham, Seymour had been deeply wounded by the rupture between these men which occurred in 1906. His response came in the form of a ninety-five-page book published in 1915, *The Doctrines and Discipline of the Azusa Street Apostolic Faith Mission of Los Angeles, Cal.*

A cursory reading of this document demonstrates clearly which portions were authored by Seymour and which portions he "borrowed" from other sources. In continuity with his black heritage and the Wesleyan-holiness tradition, Seymour incorporated twenty-four "Articles of Religion." Abridged originally by John Wesley from the "Thirty-Nine Articles" adopted in 1563 by a Convocation and again in 1571 by the English Parliament to govern the doctrinal concerns of the Church of England, the articles came almost verbatim from *Doctrines and Discipline* of the African Methodist Episcopal Church. Seymour's *Doctrines and Discipline* volume would demonstrate Azusa Street's continuity with the historic churches.[69]

Other points were borrowed as well, but with these, Seymour integrated an amended copy of the mission's "Constitution," an "Apostolic Address," extended passages on the sacred nature of the marriage tie, an exposition on the errors of Parham's "Annihilation Theory," as well as an extended statement on what was meant by the phrase the *"Apostolic Faith."* The *Doctrines and Discipline* also demonstrated that as Seymour continued to lead the now much depleted Azusa Street congregation, his position on Parham's evidential theory had hardened into a clear rejection.

Even within the household of faith, deception could take place along doctrinal lines, Seymour argued, and this fact provided the essential data needed to distinguish the ability to speak in tongues from genuine marks of spirituality. In Seymour's mind, that was sufficient reason to prohibit tongues from being accepted as the evidence of the baptism in the Spirit. "We don't believe in the doctrine of Annihilation of the wicked," he announced, and "that is the reason why we could not stand for tongues being the evidence of the Baptism in the Holy Ghost and fire."[70]

At first glance, this kind of argument does not make sense. After all, what does the "Annihilation of the wicked theory" have in common with tongues as the evidence of the baptism in the Spirit? The answer, of course, lies in Charles F. Parham, who propagated both of these theories.[71] Clearly, Seymour had been selective in accepting what Parham had taught when, in 1905, he studied with him in Houston. But the same 1912 papers in which Parham continued his assault upon Seymour and Azusa Street also advocated the Annihilation theory.[72] Seymour believed that at this point he had biblical grounds on which to disagree with his teacher. If tongues was the evidence of the gift of the Holy Spirit, reasoned Seymour,

> then men and women that have received the gift of tongues could not [have] believed contrary to the teachings of the Holy Spirit. Since tongues is not the evidence of the Baptism in the Holy Spirit, men and women can receive it [the ability to speak in tongues] and yet be destitute of the truth.[73]

Throughout his argument, Seymour had Parham in mind. Seymour did not believe that Scripture supported any theory of annihilationism. He therefore concluded that Parham was guilty of believing what was clearly "contrary to the teachings of the Holy Spirit" found in Scripture. But Parham also believed and taught the theory that tongues was the evidence of baptism in the Holy Spirit. How could this be? Seymour wondered. It could be the case only if Parham were mistaken on the second theory also.

A genuine baptism in the Spirit had a sanctifying effect, reasoned Seymour. It could aid in the protective process of the church, enabling it to distinguish or to discern between truth and falsehood. Annihilationism was falsehood. Parham had not been protected; furthermore, concluded Seymour, Parham had himself been deceived into believing that his ability to speak in tongues was evidence that he had been baptized in the Spirit. Seymour would not be deceived similarly: one could be completely destitute of truth, and yet speak in tongues. On the one hand, genuine baptism in the Spirit came upon the sanctified life, and once sanctified there was no room for error. The ability to speak in tongues, on the other hand, was independent of sanctification.

The ability to speak in tongues was not even uniquely Christian. It could be a legitimate expression of the Holy Spirit, but it might be something else. This made it difficult for any congregation to be safe from imitations, but especially those congregations who viewed speaking in tongues as the required evidence of Spirit baptism. Tongues should not be evidential that someone has been baptized in the Spirit, reasoned Seymour. After all, he went on,

> grevious wolves will enter in among the flock and tear asunder the sheep. How will he [sic] get in? They will come in through the sign gift of speaking in tongues, and if God's children did not know anything more than that to be the evidence, the[y] [the wolves] would not have no [sic] hard time to enter in among them and scatter them.[74]

Undoubtedly the counterfeit of any genuine object deserved special scrutiny, evaluation, testing or discernment, and, if necessary, corrective teaching. Seymour, now a (self-proclaimed?) bishop, saw himself as providing aid to his own parishioners by separating the notion of speaking in tongues from any doctrine of sanctification. It was, after all, possible for people to be deceived by those who spoke in tongues.

Part of the difficulty Seymour had with those who understood the ability to speak in tongues as the evidence that they had received the baptism with the Holy Spirit was his pastoral concern with the materialism of this expectation. Jesus had spoken against those who sought for signs (Matt. 12:38–39), and the people of Seymour's day were no different from the people of Jesus' day. "Some people to-day cannot believe that they have the Holy Ghost without some outward signs," he grumbled, "that is Heathenism."[75]

Words of judgment like these were frequent among holiness people, but many Pentecostals must have rejected Seymour on these grounds alone. He embraced speaking in tongues and was even tolerant of signs, but these were not where one should go to find God. "The witness of the Holy Spirit inward," he wrote,

> is the greatest knowledge of knowing God, for he is invisible. St. John 14:17. It is all right to have the signs following, but not to pin our faith on outward manifestations. We are to go by the word of God. Our thought must be in harmony with the Bible or else we will have a strange religion. We must not teach any more than the Apostles.[76]

Signs did have a legitimate place within the Christian faith, he conceded, but a preoccupation with them was unbiblical, even un-Christian.

Imprecision in early Pentecostal language produced another problem, which was compounded if tongues was declared to be the evidence of baptism with the Spirit. Some apparently interpreted Paul's exchange with the Ephesian disciples in Acts 19:2–6 as indicating that one did not even have the Spirit prior to the time when he or she spoke in tongues. In Seymour's view this was wrong. It was contrary to the very teachings of Christ, he argued. But the error was more significant than that alone.

> If we would base our faith on tongues being the evidence of the gift of the Holy Ghost, it would knock out our faith in the blood of Christ, and the inward witness of the Holy Spirit bearing witness with our Spirit. Rom. 8:14–16.[77]

Seymour viewed the atonement as intrinsic to the Christian faith. He had preached the importance of salvation based upon the atonement for years, but the emphasis that some people placed upon the importance of speaking in tongues and the way that they linked it to the initial reception of the Holy Spirit left him in doubt as to whether they believed that the shedding of the blood of Christ had been satisfactory in achieving their salvation. Their denial of the coming of the Spirit at conversion did not fit with Seymour's understanding of Scripture. Furthermore, the linkage between receiving the Spirit and speaking in tongues seemed to bypass totally any need for the atonement. Tongues speaking, in Seymour's mind, while dependent upon the Spirit in its genuine form, was nonetheless to be understood as standing independent of the atonement. By teaching that tongues was the evidence of the Spirit's presence, some might erroneously seek tongues in an attempt to receive the Spirit and miss salvation completely, for it seemed in Seymour's mind to undermine a biblical doctrine of the atonement.[78]

Seymour's arguments against tongues as evidence were inevitably pastoral in nature: the expectation of the evidential nature of tongues sidetracked spirituality, opening those who sought such signs to all forms of potential problems.

> Wherever the doctrine of the Baptism in the Holy Spirit will only being [*sic*] known as the evidence of speaking in tongues, that work will be an open door for witches and spiritualists and freeloveism. That work will suffer, because all kinds of spirits can come in.

Seymour saw only one antidote, that of Scripture. "The word of God is given to Holy men and women, not to devils," he contended. "God's word will stand forever."[79]

William J. Seymour was committed to the final and ultimate authority of Scripture in the lives of all humanity. "God wants us to have faith to take him at this word," he argued. "If we will take the divine word of God, it will lead us right."[80] Like Joseph Smale who had rejected the evidential theory in 1906, Seymour concluded that tongues *might* demonstrate that a person had received the baptism, but to say that tongues is *the inevitable evidence* of the Spirit's baptism was to go beyond the text.

Tongues could not be made the evidence, he concluded, because the doctrine which determined the evidential necessity of tongues was a human construct, a theological formulation which bound God. It limited the way(s) in which the Holy Spirit might choose to work. Ultimately it would undermine the Christian faith.

> Many people have made shipwreck of their faith by setting up a standard for God to respect or come to. When we set up tongues to be, the Bible evidence of Baptism in the Holy Ghost and fire only [*sic*]. We have left the divine word of God and have instituted our own teaching.[81]

Seymour saw a parallel to the theory of tongues as the evidence in Ezekiel 14:9. "When a man set[s] up any idols in his heart and seek[s] the Lord and if the prophet be deceived," he wrote, "he is the one that deceives the prophet."[82] By adopting the initial evidence theory as doctrine, Seymour argued, those who did so were deceived and at the same time became deceivers. They were guilty of idolatry by which they were more concerned to guarantee their own theological conceptions than they were concerned to allow for God to be free to be made self-evident by means other than tongues. In short, Seymour argued, God should be allowed to be God, and as God, he is free to choose whatever manifestation God might wish, including tongues. But insofar as Seymour was concerned, God would not be limited to speaking in tongues for evidence of the Spirit's baptism.

CONCLUSIONS

In the early days of the Apostolic Faith movement, Charles F. Parham set the tone. His phrase "the Bible evidence" became a technical term for that speaking in tongues which accompanied the baptism with the Holy Spirit. Parham's students, on the whole, followed his lead in the use of this phrase, believing that this "Bible evidence" was the "gift of tongues." William J. Seymour, one of Parham's students and founding pastor of the Azusa Street Mission, initially believed that the ability to speak in tongues was evidence of Spirit baptism, just as Parham had taught.

As the movement gained experience and moved toward maturity, however, questions arose that made it more difficult for Seymour to maintain Parham's position. In particular, Seymour questioned the legitimacy of tongues as evidence when the fruits of the Spirit were absent and the lusts of the flesh were present in the person who claimed to be baptized in the Spirit. Seymour came to believe that baptism with the Spirit was not obtained independently of sanctification, but rather, as a gift of power on the sanctified life. That meant that while the ability to speak in tongues might signify or act as a sign that followed baptism with the Spirit, other factors had to be weighed which, in Seymour's analysis, proved to be far more important as genuine evidences of the Spirit's baptism.

Within the context of interaction among William J. Seymour, Charles F. Parham, Joseph Smale, and Elmer K. Fisher, the doctrine of "the Bible evidence" was tested. Parham was joined by Fisher and continued to maintain what would become the normative position of most North American Pentecostals: tongues as *the evidence,* "the Bible evidence," of baptism with the Spirit. Smale quickly rejected the notion that tongues was the evidence, but he continued to believe in a genuine "gift of tongues" which he anticipated would be restored to the church in the last days. Seymour, however, adopted a position which rejected speaking in tongues as "the Bible evidence" of baptism with the Spirit. To be sure, it could serve as a sign, but baptism in the Spirit would have to come first. In short, Seymour would not be acceptable as a Pentecostal today, if the normative standards of the Pentecostal Fellowship of North America were imposed upon him. In light of this, it may be better to understand Seymour as the forerunner par excellence to the modern charismatic renewal on the one hand, and/or the founder of a more broadly defined Pentecostalism on the other. His definition of what constitutes a Pentecostal would surely be a broader one than would Parham's or Fisher's. It would remain more faithful to the Wesleyan-holiness tradition out of which the Pentecostal movement emerged, including a more profound commitment to the ethical dimension of the Christian faith.

The interaction of Seymour, Parham, Smale, and Fisher provided a crucible for testing the experience of speaking in tongues and its relation to baptism with the Spirit. The doctrine of "the Bible evidence" was not developed in isolation, then left alone to provide a normative theological response to the experience, but rather, it was tested in the interface of these four pastors' experience. William J. Seymour came to reject the theory because he could not find consistency in the ethical dimension of those who claimed to have experienced it: the inability of whites to maintain a supportive role in relationship to a black pastor and the ugly spectacle of underlying or incipient racism played a role in the formation of his thought.

Of significance for the present volume is the observation that nowhere in the writings of Seymour in the *Apostolic Faith* (Los Angeles), or in Fisher's paper, the *Upper Room*, does the phrase "the initial evidence," occur. Likewise, Parham continued to employ "the Bible evidence" as his preferred description. The governing adjective was transformed with time, sometimes being totally absent (the evidence), sometimes being modified further (the *full* Bible evidence), and at times being transformed into a predecessor of some later doctrine through such adjectives as "the *inevitable* evidence" or "the *outward* evidence." This latter adjective may well have led to the idea that speaking in tongues was "the physical evidence," and it is not surprising that it was an adjective first used by Mrs. Lydia Piper at the Stone Church in Chicago.[83] In any case, for a decade or more, Pentecostals would follow the lead of Charles Parham and teach that the evidence of baptism with the Holy Spirit must be "the Bible evidence," the ability to speak in other tongues. Seymour was among them for a time, but his experience led him beyond the narrow limits which his teacher prescribed, to a position which today is followed by many black-American and non-North American Pentecostals.

NOTES

1. W. J. Seymour, *The Doctrines and Discipline of the Azusa Street Apostolic Faith Mission of Los Angeles, Cal.* (Los Angeles: W. J. Seymour, 1915), 12.

2. "Population Is Past 230,000," *Los Angeles Herald,* 15 April 1906, 5. The description of Los Angeles as a "metropolis of two million people" in James R. Goff, Jr., *Fields White Unto Harvest: Charles F. Parham and the Missionary Origins of Pentecostalism* (Fayetteville, Ark.: The University of Arkansas Press, 1988), 131, is clearly wide of the mark, though Goff's point regarding its

cosmopolitan character is well taken. Most towns within 30 miles of Los Angeles boasted fewer than 5,000 inhabitants in 1906.

3. In 1900, the black population accounted for 2.1 % of the total, or 2,131, and in 1910 it accounted for 2.4% or 7,599. Based upon an estimate of 2.3% of 230,000 the total number of blacks would be 5,390. Early 1906 figures would be slightly less, hence the estimate of 5,000. Actual figures for 1900 and 1910 may be found in J. McFarline Ervin, "The Participation of the Negro in the Community Life of Los Angeles" (M.A. thesis, University of Southern California, 1931, rpt. San Francisco: R. and E. Research Associates, 1973), 10.

4. J. Max Bond, "The Negro in Los Angeles," (Ph.D. diss., reprint: San Francisco: R. and E. Research Associates, 1972), 26.

5. G. R. Bryant, "Religious Life of Los Angeles Negroes," *Los Angeles Daily Times*, 12 February 1909, 3:7. The move and name change are documented also in the *Los Angeles City Directory* (1904 and 1905).

6. Seymour, *Doctrines and Discipline*, 12.

7. D. J. Nelson, in "For Such a Time as This: The Story of Bishop William J. Seymour and the Azusa Street Revival" (Ph.D. diss., University of Birmingham, 1981), 35, suggests that Seymour settled there about 1903. This assumption is based upon the vague outline of Seymour's life sketched by C. W. Shumway, "A Study of the 'Gift of Tongues' " (A.B. thesis, University of Southern California, 1914), 173, note a. To date, Seymour's actual date of settlement in Houston remains unsatisfactorily documented.

8. In February 1906, Farrow was 54 based upon information given in the Twelfth Census of the United States (1900), Houston, Texas, volume 45, enumeration District 133, sheet 3, line 62.

9. Nelson, "For Such a Time as This," 35.

10. "Rev. C. F. Parham," *Houston Daily Post*, 9 July 1905, 8; "The Zion Movement," *Houston Daily Post*, 17 July 1905, 5; "Jews to Found Own Home," *Houston Chronicle*, 17 July 1905, 6; "Zionist Students," *Houston Daily Post*, 3 August 1905, 5.

11. "Divine Healer," *Houston Daily Post*, 6 July 1905, 4; "At Bryan Hall," *Houston Daily Post*, 29 July 1905, 4; "In Vision Was Told of Cure," *Houston Chronicle*, 8 August 1905, 3; "Houstonians Witness the Performance of Miracles," *Houston Chronicle*, 13 August 1905, 6.

12. The notice, "At Bryan Hall," 4, announced Parham's afternoon sermon titled "Baptism of the Holy Ghost, with the Evidence of Speaking with Tongues." Cf., "Church Notices," *Houston Chronicle*, 29 July 1905, 6; "Zionist Students," *Houston Daily Post*, 31 July 1905, 5; "Houstonians Witness the Performance of Miracles," *Houston Chronicle*, 13 August 1905, 6.

13. "Not Dowieism," *Houston Daily Post*, 3 August 1905, 5; "Rev. C. F. Parham," *Houston Daily Post*, 9 July 1905, 8; "The Zion Movement," *Houston Daily Post*, 17 July 1905, 5; "Jews to Found Own Home," *Houston Chronicle*, 17 July 1905, 6.

14. "Dowie Can't Leave Zion," *Houston Chronicle*, 3 October 1906, 2:14; "Parham Against Voliva," *Houston Daily Post*, 4 October 1906, 11; "In Zion City," *Houston Daily Post*, 5 November 1906, 6.

15. C. F. Parham, *Kol Kare Bomidbar: A Voice Crying in the Wilderness* (Kansas City, Mo.: privately published, 1902, rpt. Joplin, Mo.: Joplin Printing Co., 1944), 25–38, contains a sermon preached by Parham in January 1901

in which he clearly employs this language. It is reprinted in W. F. Carothers, *The Baptism with the Holy Ghost and the Speaking in Tongues* (Houston: privately published, 1906), 5–18. Parham claimed that this was "The first [sermon] upon the baptism of the Holy Ghost in all modern Pentecostal Apostolic Full Gospel movements." Charles F. Parham, "The Latter Rain" in Robert L. Parham, comp., *Selected Sermons of the Late Charles F. Parham, Sarah E. Parham* (Baxter Springs, Kan.: Robert L. Parham, 1941), 79.

16. Twelfth Census of the United States (1900), Galveston, Texas, volume enumeration District 133, sheet 3, line 62.

17. "Want to Preach on the Streets," *Los Angeles Express,* 1 August 1905, 11. Mrs. Hutchins made a joint application to the city with J. W. Slaughter. This application suggests that she was already well established in Los Angeles. Nelson, "For Such a Time as This," 186, claims that Hutchins had attended Second Baptist Church where in the spring of 1905 she was expelled for advocating Christian holiness as a second work of grace. Unfortunately he does not note his source, and I have been unable to corroborate this statement, although I am inclined to believe it.

18. Nelson, "For Such a Time as This," 65.

19. Mrs. J. W. Hutchins, "Battle Hymn," *Apostolic Faith* (Melrose, Kan.), (September 1905), 1:[?] 1. While there is no clear identification of the author of the song with the Los Angeles church founder, several facts point clearly in that direction: (1) They shared the same name, identifying themselves by the same initials; (2) By February 1906 the Los Angeles Julia Hutchins clearly had contact with Parham's group through William J. Seymour; (3) Both were committed to the missionary task. Should these two women be positively identified as the same person, it may shed light on why Hutchins was so willing to summon Seymour to Los Angeles, sight unseen.

20. S. E. Parham, *The Life of Charles F. Parham: Founder of the Apostolic Faith Movement* (Joplin, Mo.: Hunter Printing Co., ca. 1930, rpt. New York: Garland Publishing, Inc., 1985), 129–30, reprints the hymn and notes its popularity among Parham's followers.

21. "Bro. Seymour's Call," *Apostolic Faith* (Los Angeles), September 1906, 1.1. For another eyewitness account of the meeting between Seymour and Roberts, see Mrs. W. H. McGowan, "Another 'Echo from Azusa' " (Covina, Calif.: Mrs. W. H. McGowan, ca. 1956). This tract has since been edited and incorporated in Mrs. R. L. (Clara) Davis, *The Wonderful Move of God: The Outpouring of the Holy Spirit from Azusa Street to Now* (Tulsa: Albury Press, 1983), 54; reprinted as *Azusa Street Till Now* (Tulsa: Harrison House, 1983, 1989), 17. Cf., Nelson, "For Such A Time As This," 187–88. A portion of the position held by the Holiness church is found in J. M. Washburn, *History and Reminiscences of the Holiness Church Work in Southern California and Arizona* (South Pasadena: Record Press, 1912; rpt. New York: Garland Publishing, Inc., 1985), 377–78.

22. J. W. Hutchins was an enigmatic woman who left few long term clues. A strong leader in her own right, she may have invoked the theological issue to cover a deeper seated issue over control of the church. While Seymour was invited to serve as pastor, Hutchins retained the keys. Yet once Azusa Street became a viable mission, she joined it, and by September 15 was commissioned to go as one of Azusa Street's missionaries to Liberia. By November she

reported that numbers were receiving "the Bible evidence" under her ministry. See untitled report, *Apostolic Faith* (Los Angeles), 1:4, December 1906, 1.5.

23. *Los Angeles City Directory* (1905), 862.

24. Nelson, "For Such a Time as This," 58.

25. "Weird Babel of Tongues," *Los Angeles Daily Times*, 18 April 1906, 2:1.

26. Apostolic Faith people are Pentecostals originally associated with Parham, Seymour, et al. The reporter who wrote "Weird Babel of Tongues," 2:1, says simply that "They claim to have 'the gift of tongues.' . . ." W. F. Carothers, *The Baptism with the Holy Ghost*, 20, seems prepared to distinguish an evidential tongue from the gift of tongues as early as 1906 when he writes, "There is a difference between merely speaking in tongues, which accompanies Pentecost, and the gift of tongues, one of the nine gifts of the Spirit. . . ." At Azusa Street, a similar position is stated in "The Enduement of Power," *Apostolic Faith* 1:4, December 1906, 2.2, but this appears to be a minority view. Cf., Mrs. James Hebden, "This Is the Power of the Holy Ghost," *Apostolic Faith* 1:6, February–March 1907, 4.4, wrote, "At first I find that I had tongues as a sign, now as one of the gifts." By far, most reports follow T. B. Barratt's testimony, "Baptized in New York" *Apostolic Faith* (Los Angeles), 1:4, December 1906, 3.2, who claimed to receive "the full Bible evidence,—the gift of tongues."

27. "The Apostolic Faith Movement," *Apostolic Faith* (Los Angeles), 1:1, September 1906, 2.1.

28. W. J. Seymour, "The Precious Atonement," *Apostolic Faith* (Los Angeles), 1:1, September 1906, 2.2.

29. Untitled report, *Apostolic Faith* (Los Angeles), 1:1, September 1906, 1.4.

30. "Tongues As A Sign," *Apostolic Faith* (Los Angeles), 1:1, September 1906, 2.3–4.

31. "Church Services," *Los Angeles Daily Times*, 5 May 1906, 2.6.

32. "Twentieth Century Church Not Needed," *Los Angeles Herald*, 19 March 1906, 7.

33. "Queer 'Gift' Given Many," *Los Angeles Daily Times*, 23 July 1906, 1:5.

34. "New Testament Leader Writes An Open Letter," *Los Angeles Express*, 23 July 1906, 6.

35. "Girl's Message from God Devil's Work, Says Pastor," *Los Angeles Express*, 20 September 1906, 7; "Trouble in Congregation," *Los Angeles Herald*, 21 September 1906, 8; "Spirits Disrupt A Church," *Los Angeles Express*, 22 September 1906, 1; "Sift [*sic*] of Tongues Splits Flock?" *Los Angeles Herald*, 23 September 1906, 4; "Dr. Keyes Faction Meets," *Los Angeles Herald*, 24 September 1906, 9; "Babblers of Tongues Contented," *Los Angeles Express*, 24 September 1906, 1; "Girl Is a Christian, Not Devil," *Los Angeles Express*, 27 September 1906, 1–2.

36. "Sift [*sic*] of Tongues Splits Flock?" 4; "Dr. Keyes Faction Meets," 9; "Babblers of Tongues Contented," 1.

37. F. Bartleman, *How Pentecost Came to Los Angeles* (Los Angeles: F. Bartleman, 1925), 83–84, reprinted in *Witness to Pentecost: The Life of Frank Bartleman* (New York: Garland Publishing, Inc., 1985) notes simply "The New Testament Church had a split about this time. . . . Brother Elmer Fisher then started another mission at 327½ South Spring Street, known as the

'Upper Room' mission. Most of the white saints from 'Azusa' went with him, with the 'baptized' ones from the New Testament Church."

38. "Babblers of Tongues Contented," 1. W. B. Godbey who authored a small work titled *Spiritual Gifts and Graces* (Cincinnati: God's Revivalist Office, 1895, rpt. New York: Garland Publishing, Inc., 1985) 43, predicted that the gift of tongues was "destined to play a conspicuous part in the evangelization of the heathen world, amid the glorious prophetical fulfillment of the latter days. All missionaries in heathen lands," he exhorted, "should seek and expect this Gift to enable them to preach fluently in the vernacular tongue, at the same time not depreciating their own efforts." His position was shared by many in the Wesleyan-holiness tradition of the day.

39. "Sift [*sic*] of Tongues Splits Flock?" 4. Unfortunately, Pastor Smale does not say *how* this doctrine contributed to the problems.

40. "Young Girl Given Gift of Tongues," *Los Angeles Express*, 20 July 1906, 1.

41. "Women with Men Embrace," *Los Angeles Daily Times*, 3 September 1906, 11.

42. "New Religions Come, Then Go," *Los Angeles Herald*, 24 September 1906, 7.

43. "Letter from Bro. Parham," *Apostolic Faith* 1:1, September 1906, 1.1–2.

44. B. F. Lawrence, *The Apostolic Faith Restored* (St. Louis: Gospel Publishing House, 1916; rpt. New York: Garland Publishing, Inc., 1985), 66; Ethel E. Goss, *The Winds of God*, (rev. ed., Hazelwood, Mo.: Word Aflame Press, 1977), 96.

45. Goff, *Fields White Unto Harvest*, 131.

46. Nelson, "For Such a Time as This," 208–10.

47. "Apostolic Faith Meetings," *Los Angeles Record*, 6 November 1906, 1.

48. "Hold Meetings Daily," *Los Angeles Herald*, 7 November 1906, 7. The relationship to Fisher is still unclear, but it appears that Fisher briefly cooperated with Parham in direct competition with Azusa Street. The fact that the Upper Room Mission might benefit from Parham's presence cannot be overlooked. Bartleman's note that Fisher attracted many of the Azusa Street Caucasians suggests racial bias as well. (See above, note 37.)

49. "Zionist," *Los Angeles Herald*, 9 December 1906, 5.

50. "Apostolic Faith People Here Again," *Whittier Daily News*, 13 December 1906, 1.

51. Cf., "Leadership," *Apostolic Faith* (Baxter Springs, Kan.), 1:4, June 1912, 7–8; Chas. F. Parham, "Free-Love," *Apostolic Faith* (Baxter Springs, Kan.), 1:10, December 1912, 4–5.

52. As early as 1901 it was reported that Agnes Ozman engaged in this activity. See the "specimen" of her writing in *Topeka Daily Capitol*, 6 January 1901, 2. In Los Angeles, Dr. Henry S. Keyes allegedly produced a "specimen" including its interpretation by L. C. LeNan in "Baba Bharati Says Not a Language," *Los Angeles Daily Times*, 19 September 1906, 2:1. Azusa Street celebrated the "gift of writing in unknown languages" in an untitled note in *Apostolic Faith* (Los Angeles), 1:1, September 1906, 1.3.

53. Untitled report, *Apostolic Faith* (Los Angeles), 1:9, June–September 1907, 1.4.

54. Untitled report, *Apostolic Faith* (Los Angeles), 1:10, September 1907, 2.4.

55. "To the Baptized Saints," *Apostolic Faith* (Los Angeles), 1:9, June–September 1907, 2.1. Italics mine.

56. "To the Baptized Saints," 2.1.

57. "Evangelist Is Arrested," *San Antonio Light*, 19 July 1907, 1; "Voliva Split Hits Preacher," *San Antonio Light*, 21 July 1907, 2.

58. "Questions Answered," *Apostolic Faith* (Los Angeles), 1:11, October–January 1908, 2.1.

59. E. K. Fisher, "Stand for the Bible Evidence," *The Upper Room* 1:1, June 1909, 3.3. Italics mine.

60. The phrase "the Bible evidence" occurs at least 38 times in *Apostolic Faith* (Los Angeles), but only twice in the last four issues. Cf., "In Washington, D.C.," *Apostolic Faith* (Los Angeles), 1:10, September 1907, 1.1; W. H. Stanley, "Worth Tarrying For," *Apostolic Faith* (Los Angeles), 2:13 [*sic*], May 1908, 3:3. Other phrases which occur, include "the evidence," "the same evidence," "the outward evidence," and "His own evidence."

61. "The Baptism with the Holy Ghost," *Apostolic Faith* (Los Angeles), 1:11, October–January 1908, 4.1. Cf., also untitled report, *Apostolic Faith* (Los Angeles), 1:12, January 1908, 3.2.

62. W. J. Seymour, "The Baptism of the Holy Ghost," *Apostolic Faith* (Los Angeles), 2:13 [*sic*], May 1908, 3.1.

63. "The Baptism with the Holy Ghost," *Apostolic Faith* (Los Angeles), 1:11 (October–January 1908), 4.1.

64. "Character and Work of the Holy Ghost," *Apostolic Faith* (Los Angeles), 2:13 [*sic*] (May 1908), 2.2.

65. Untitled comments, *New Year's Greetings* (Baxter Springs, Kan.), January 1912, 6. This quotation is a remarkable parallel to the description which Dr. Burdette preached in September 1906. (See above, note 42.)

66. "Leadership," *Apostolic Faith* (Baxter Springs, Kan.), 1:4, June 1912, 7.

67. Cf., "Lest We Forget," *Apostolic Faith* (Baxter Springs, Kan.), 1:6, August 1912, 6; untitled note, *Apostolic Faith* (Baxter Springs, Kan.), 1:7, September 1912, 10; "Baptism of the Holy Ghost," *Apostolic Faith* (Baxter Springs, Kan.), 1:8, October 1912, 8–10; and "Free Love," *Apostolic Faith* (Baxter Springs, Kan.), 1:10, December 1912, 4–5.

68. Seymour, *Doctrines and Discipline*, 12.

69. Ibid., 21–24. I would not make too much of the fact that Seymour used the *Doctrines and Discipline* of the AME as the basis for his own. It may be that he used it by design, but the fact that the Azusa Street Mission building had been owned originally by Stevens (now First) AME Church may simply mean that Seymour used what he had found in the building.

70. Seymour, *Doctrines and Discipline*, 52.

71. Goff in *Fields White Unto Harvest*, 35, has shown that Parham embraced the annihilation doctrine as early as 1892.

72. Cf., J. C. Seibert, "Christian Experience," *Apostolic Faith* (Baxter Springs, Kan.), 1:3, May 1912, 10; "Heaven and Hell," *Apostolic Faith* (Baxter Springs, Kan.), 1:8, October 1912, 8.

73. Seymour, *Doctrines and Discipline*, 52.

74. Ibid., 91.

75. Ibid., 8.

76. Ibid.

77. Ibid., 51–52.

78. Dr. Finis E. Yoakum remembered this point and invoked Seymour's support claiming, "the dear old leader of Azusa said the reason the Pentecostal people are so divided today, is because he agreed with me that the Holy Ghost comes in to abide forever, and then speaks '*as He wills*,' giving us tongues or any other gift, but gifts will not save us. 'We are saved by grace, through faith, and that not of ourselves, it is the gift of God' " (F. E. Yoakum, "The Bible Evidence of the Holy Ghost," *Pisgah* 1:25, March 1920, 3, italics mine).

79. Seymour, *Doctrines and Discipline*, preface.

80. Ibid., 91.

81. Ibid.

82. Ibid.

83. Mrs. W. H. Piper, "He Shall Baptize You: Matt. 3:11," *Apostolic Faith* (Los Angeles), 1:10, September 1907, 4.1–2. If the idea of the "outward" evidence was in vogue at the Stone Church, it may lie behind the position eventually adopted by the Assemblies of God of the "initial *physical* evidence," the term "physical" being an "outward" evidence. The Assemblies of God held its second General Council at the Stone Church in 1915.

6

EARLY PENTECOSTAL HERMENEUTICS: TONGUES AS EVIDENCE IN THE BOOK OF ACTS

Gary B. McGee

Beginning with Charles F. Parham and the Topeka, Kansas, revival of January 1901, Pentecostals have assumed that Luke the Evangelist was far more than a historian, functioning also as a theologian through his preparation of the Gospel of Luke and the book of Acts. According to Pentecostals, his recording of the "pattern" of Spirit baptism, with the accompaniment of speaking in tongues (Acts 2:4; 10:45–46; 19:6), not only depicted the experience of the early church, but established a doctrinal and spiritual norm for all believers. After all, Peter had declared on the day of Pentecost: "The promise [of Spirit baptism] is for you and your children and for all who are far off—for all whom the Lord our God will call" (Acts 2:39, NIV). Although citations of biblical passages to support this doctrine have not been limited to Acts, the use of Acts for establishing Pentecostal doctrine has been indispensable.

Notwithstanding, Pentecostal writers seldom questioned whether their approach to the narrative of Acts represented traditional Protestant hermeneutical procedures. It is also important to recognize that they have employed it *especially* with regard to their teaching on glossolalia as evidence for Spirit baptism.

The elevation of implied statements (the "pattern"), however, to the same level of authority as explicit scriptural propositions constitutes a departure from the manner of interpretation advocated by Lutheran and Reformed theologians since the sixteenth century, many of whom have been strongly influenced by scholastic methodology and who sometimes argued for the cessation of the gifts of the Spirit. In his recent *Christian Theology*, Millard J. Erickson includes a list entitled "Degrees of Authority of Theological Statements" in which he states: "Direct statements of Scripture are to be accorded the greatest weight. To the degree that they accurately represent what the Bible teaches, they have the status of a direct word from God." After this, he provides a diminishing scale of levels of authority: direct implications, probable implications, inductive conclusions, conclusions from general revelation, and speculations.[1] Accordingly, for Erickson, the starting point for theological study must be propositional statements. Like other mainstream evangelicals, he dismisses the Pentecostal claim that Luke portrays Spirit baptism as a subsequent experience of grace authenticated by speaking in tongues.[2]

Since most Pentecostals from Charles F. Parham to contemporaries such as Stanley M. Horton, French L. Arrington, and J. L. Hall (chapter 10) have unhesitatingly appealed to the pattern of glossolalic phenomena to prove the validity of the argument that tongues is the initial evidence of Spirit baptism, it is essential that we find the origin of this hermeneutical frame of reference.[3] Have Pentecostals been alone in discovering an important precedent in the book of Acts? What did they discover? And most importantly, did early Pentecostals agree on a Lucan pattern?

The ways in which Pentecostals have hermeneutically developed their pneumatology offers a rich area for further study. The following investigation, however, only begins to explore the subject.

RESTORING PATTERNS FROM ACTS

Heightened interest in returning to the norms of early Christianity can be traced back to ancient and medieval times whenever an individual or group of believers decided that it was time to "restore" the faith and practice of their New Testament forebears (e.g., the Montanist and Franciscan movements).[4] With the emergence of the Protestant revolt in the sixteenth century and the growing proliferation of sects, "restorationism" soon surfaced within this new branch of Christendom. Martin Luther, of course, claimed to recover the true meaning of the gospel through his espousal of the forensic nature of justification by faith.[5] In the Genevan churches, Calvin established four orders of office (pastors, doctors [teachers], elders, deacons) which he maintained Christ had instituted to govern his church.[6]

Anabaptists (e.g., Amish, Brethren, Hutterites, Mennonites) called for radical changes in the form of the church to adhere more closely to the apostolic model mirrored in the Acts of the Apostles. The followers of Jacob Hutter (d. 1536) even followed communal living after the example of the Jerusalem church (Acts 2:44–45).[7] To link themselves with true believers who preceded them and to bolster their courage in the face of adversity, later Mennonites traced their spiritual heritage all the way back to the sufferings and martyrdoms of John the Baptist and early Christians mentioned in Acts through the aid of the seventeenth-century martyrology, *The Bloody Theater or Martyrs Mirror* (1660). Although Luther, Calvin, and other reformers had aggressively addressed issues such as the authority of Scripture, original sin, justification by faith, the sacraments, and the security of the believer, the vitality of Christian discipleship in the churches waned early in the next century, accelerated by the ravages of the Thirty Years' War (1618–1648). Decades later, evangelical revivalism, known as "pietism," began to spread among Lutheran and Reformed congregations in Germany.[8] Reacting to the esoteric controversies and scholastic methodologies (viewed as spiritually barren) which appeared to consume the energies of the theological establishment, some church leaders (e.g., Philipp Jakob Spener [1635–1705] and August Hermann Francke [1663–1727]) earnestly sought to improve piety in church life. Building on the work of the reformers, they focused on the meaning of regeneration in the life of the believer and the church.

Pietists strongly encouraged Bible study. Not surprisingly, with pietism's emphasis on the "heartfelt" or "born-again" experience of conversion, Christians were instructed to study the Scriptures for personal spiritual edification. This new orientation starkly contrasted with the arid (Aristotelian) methodology of Protestant scholasticism that was frequently guilty of "proof-texting" in the pursuit of logical doctrinal conclusions.[9] Brethren scholar Dale Brown suggests that among the pietists, "the Bible became a devotional resource rather than a source of doctrine, a guide to life rather than just the source of belief and faith."[10] Spener himself said, "true faith . . . is awakened through the Word of God, by the illumination, witness, and sealing of the Holy Spirit."[11] By promoting the recovery of New Testament dynamics, pietism naturally cultivated restorationist tendencies: Instructions from the Gospels and Epistles were logically complemented with varying appeals to paradigms of primitive Christianity in Acts.

The Moravian "Pentecost" of August 13, 1727, offers an important example. On that occasion, participants were "baptized by the Holy Spirit Himself to one love" and forged into an effective fellowship of faith and mission.[12] Thereafter, Nikolaus Ludwig Count von Zinzendorf (1700–1760) and the Renewed Unitas Fratrum (Moravian Church) successfully implemented a revolutionary model of the church that diminished barriers between clergy and laity, allowing opportunities for everyone to minister. Before long, and partially through Moravian influence, revivalism swept England under the ministries of John Wesley (1703–1791) and George Whitefield (1714–1770). Although Wesley never left the Church of England, he effectively evangelized the masses and organized small groups of Christians into "class meetings" to enhance discipleship training. In so doing, he altered the spiritual landscape of the nation and the American colonies.[13] Church growth specialist George G. Hunter, III, refers to Wesley as "the apostolic reformer" who "sought no less than the recovery of the truth, life, and power of earliest Christianity, and the expansion of that kind of Christianity."[14]

Unlike Wesley, many who were influenced by pietism were not reluctant to leave the established churches. Indeed, the reawakening of New Testament Christianity necessitated separation from dead and lifeless ecclesiastical forms. Such proponents directly identified their own movements with the theology and practices of first-century Christians, unfortunately separated in time by centuries of spiritual decline. Their sufferings and triumphs were but an extension of those of early believers in their witness of the true faith. Theologian Claude Welch describes the intense personal identification of this mind-set: "the true birth of Christ is his birth in our hearts, his true death is in that dying within us, his true resurrection is in the triumph in our faith."[15]

Restorationism quickly became a powerful force on the American scene, with each advocate claiming some distinctive insight either in doctrine and/or church practice based in part on a model in the book of Acts. Biblical scholars Gordon D. Fee and Douglas Stuart contend that when restorationists interpret the New Testament, they "look back to the church and Christian experience in the first century either as the norm to be restored or the ideal to be approximated."[16] Ironically, however, what each movement has declared to be the definitive pattern of early Christianity or the "plain teaching" of Acts has not been equally apparent to all as the following examples illustrate.

The ministries of Barton W. Stone (1772–1844) and Thomas (1763–1854) and Alexander (1788–1866) Campbell gave rise to what actually became known as "the Restoration movement." Members preferred to be called simply "Christians" (after the earliest designation of believers in the first century, Acts 11:26). Stone and the Campbells birthed several present-day groupings of churches: Churches of Christ, Disciples of Christ, and independent Christians. In regard to their concept about the order of salvation, they heavily depended on the analysis of conversions recounted in Acts; this led to the following essential pattern of conversion: faith, repentance, confession, water baptism by immersion, forgiveness of sins, and the gift of the Holy Spirit.[17] Other features of New Testament practice were also reintroduced.

With roots dating back to the sixteenth century, the Baptists represent another prominent movement bent on regaining the purity of the early church.[18] In his history of the Baptists, written in the nineteenth century, Thomas Armitage, asserted that

> the true historian must fix his eye steadfastly at the beginning of his work, upon the New Testament pattern, and never remove it; because it is the only guide to truth in every age, and the only authority of ultimate appeal. An exact likeness, therefore, of the Apostolic Churches should be sought at the outset. . . . We never can be wrong in following the pattern found in the Constitution of the Apostolic Churches.[19]

One can readily see that Baptist church polity has depended on what has been considered the New Testament precedent for independent congregations, articulated in the Epistles and exemplified in Acts.[20]

The American holiness movement also attempted to restore the vitality of the early church. Influenced by the writings of John Wesley and John Fletcher (1729–1785), holiness advocates stated that after conversion, each believer should pray to receive sanctification, which assured deliverance from the defect in his or her moral nature that prompted sinful behavior. Labeled as the baptism in the Holy Spirit (the "second definite work of grace"), this second work allowed every Christian to reach a plateau of (gradually upward) spiritual maturity, variously called the "deeper" or "higher" life in Christ. Holiness preachers, therefore, taught that the book of Acts depicts the separability of salvation from Spirit baptism, detailing instances where believers received the latter (sanctification) following salvation.[21] Wesleyan theologian Wilber T. Dayton remarks that

> in common with the Old Testament saints, then, the followers of Jesus before Pentecost could be born of the Spirit, helped by the Spirit, and enabled by the Spirit as by One who was with them (John 14:17) but was not yet the fountain of living water gushing from the inner being of a believer who had "received" the "gift of the Holy Spirit" (John 7:38).[22]

Little wonder that among Wesleyans, the examination of Luke's theology has played a vital (but not exclusive) role in doctrinal formulation.[23]

Naturally, holiness believers also exhibited considerable interest in the gifts of the Spirit. This helps to explain why the holiness movement was closely associated with the evangelical healing movement, another controversial nineteenth-century voice of restorationism.[24]

The idea of a "subsequent" work of grace was also adopted by some within the Reformed tradition. While concerned with sanctification, influential voices emphasized the baptism in the Spirit as a means of empowerment for Christian witness. R. A. Torrey, superintendent of the Moody Bible Institute in Chicago, strategically found ample evidence from Acts that "the Baptism with the Holy Spirit is an operation of the Holy Spirit distinct from and subsequent and additional to His regenerating work. . . . primarily for the purpose of service."[25] In regard to the Ephesian "Pentecost" (Acts 19:6), Baptist pastor A. J. Gordon said,

> this passage seems decisive as showing that one may be a disciple without having entered into possession of the Spirit as God's gift to believers. . . . All that need be said upon this point is simply that these Ephesian disciples, by the reception of the Spirit, came into the same condition with the upperroom disciples who received some twenty years before. . . . In other words, these Ephesian disciples on receiving the Holy Ghost exhibited the traits of the Spirit common to the other disciples of the apostolic age.
>
> Whether those traits—the speaking of tongues and the working of miracles—were intended to be perpetual or not we do not here discuss. But that the presence of the personal Holy Spirit in the church was intended to be perpetual there can be no question. And whatsoever relations believers held to that Spirit in the beginning they have a right to claim to-day.[26]

In a similar vein, both A. B. Simpson, founder and president of the Christian and Missionary Alliance (CMA), and Robert P. Wilder, famed promoter of foreign missions among college and university students, anticipated the Pentecostal hermeneutical practice of utilizing narrative accounts in Acts for deriving doctrinal truth.[27]

It was from the pneumatological matrix of the holiness movement that Pentecostalism, as a new strain of restorationism, emerged.[28] Placing even greater confidence in the importance of the Spirit baptisms recorded in Acts, Pentecostals were convinced that believers could experience glossolalia in the "last days"—the very time in which they were living (Acts 2:17–18). Thomas G. Atteberry, an early Pentecostal editor in Los Angeles, wrote in January 1909 that "this supernatural manifestation was intended by its Founder to abide in the Church continually as a proof to the world that she had a commission that was divine and that her work was of God."[29] Reflecting on the discovery of this neglected biblical truth, and grateful as well for the insights that Luther, Wesley, Blumhardt, Trudel, and A. B. Simpson had recovered, Daniel W. Kerr, an early leader in the Assemblies of God, concluded:

> During the past few years God has enabled us to discover and recover this wonderful truth concerning the Baptism in the Spirit as it was given at the beginning. Thus we have all that the others got, and we got this too. We see all they see, but they don't see what we see.[30]

In his *Theological Roots of Pentecostalism* (1987, rprnt. 1991), historian Donald W. Dayton reports that "when Pentecostalism emerged in the next few years, leaders of the Holiness movement recognized that it was only the gift of tongues that set it apart from their own teachings."[31]

Predictably, therefore, most Pentecostals have supported the holiness notion of a second work of grace, albeit one of empowerment (for some there are two subsequent works: one for sanctification, the other for empowerment).[32] Glossolalia provides the earliest verification of Spirit baptism to the individual. Interestingly, however, the properties of this enduement of power closely resemble the marks of the sanctified life: greater sensitivity to the Spirit's guidance, more intense dedication to God, and an ever-increasing love for Christ and the lost.[33] In defending the pertinence of the doctrine for the church today, Assemblies of God historian William W. Menzies insists that "theology that has little or no relevance for life as it is lived in the kitchen or the market place may be a pleasant academic diversion, but it bears little resemblance to the theology of the biblical writers. Faith and life are intimately interwoven."[34] His remark echoes both the experiential concerns of pietism and the sentiments of restorationism. Not surprisingly, the earliest history of the Pentecostal movement, written by Bennett Freeman Lawrence, was appropriately titled *The Apostolic Faith Restored* (1916).

UNMISTAKABLE EVIDENCE?

Parham theorized that tongues as xenolalia or xenoglossa (unlearned human languages, a form of glossolalia) was a key component in the divine plan to expedite missionary evangelism at the end of human history. If his theory had been proven, the entire course of Pentecostalism would have been quite different. But, even as early as 1906, the first year of the influential Azusa Street revival in Los Angeles, Pentecostals did not uniformly accept his insistence on xenolalia or the ironclad connection of tongues as evidence. Notably, A. G. Garr, one of the earliest missionaries to travel abroad (expecting to preach in Bengali when he arrived in

Calcutta, India), reported in 1908: "I supposed God would let us talk to the natives of India in their own tongue; but He did not. So far I have not seen anyone who is able to preach to the natives in their own tongue with the languages given with the Holy Ghost."[35]

From this point, we will examine the perspectives of (1) some who perpetuated Parham's view, although modified it to be glossolalia (simply unknown tongues), and (2) others who were less restrictive. The dependence on the pattern in Acts by both camps will be reviewed.

PROPONENTS OF INITIAL EVIDENCE

While the opinions of Charles Parham (chapter 4) and the early views of William J. Seymour (chapter 5) became well known through their publications and preaching ministries, others also substantially contributed to the discussion concerning Spirit baptism. In what may have been the first book-length exposition of Pentecostal theology, *The Spirit and the Bride* (1907), George Floyd Taylor, an early leader in the Pentecostal Holiness Church, vigorously defended the new teaching (i.e., Spirit baptism must be accompanied by tongues). In answering the charge that other manifestations of the Spirit might be equal proof of Spirit baptism, Taylor appealed to the pattern in Acts: "Look up all the accounts given in Scripture of any receiving the Baptism, and you will not find any other manifestation mentioned on that occasion without the manifestation of tongues."[36] For many early Pentecostals, the force of the biblical data compelled them to believe that of all the Pentecostal phenomena, tongues alone was purposefully given to authenticate Spirit baptism. After wrestling with key passages in Acts, Joseph Hillery King, also a leader in the Pentecostal Holiness Church, said his misgivings "had nothing to stand upon. . . . The Book of Acts was against me."[37] He later wrote:

> The Book of Acts is the only one in the Bible that presents to us the Pentecostal baptism from an historic standpoint; and it gives the standard by which to determine the reality and fulness of the Spirit's outpouring, since in every instance where the Spirit was poured out for the first time this miraculous utterance accompanied the same, so we infer that its connection with the baptism is to be regarded as an evidence of its reception.[38]

Questions about tongues as evidence also arose in early 1907 among members of the Apostolic Faith movement in Texas, where it was stoutly defended by Warren F. Carothers, a lieutenant of Charles F. Parham. In an "open discussion of the Scriptures on this subject" at Waco, Howard

A. Goss remembered that Carothers appealed to the pattern in Acts, particularly Acts 10:45–46 ("*For*they heard them speak with tongues and magnify God" [Goss's emphasis]). "We could see that God was mightily helping him to unfold wise and logical deductions and . . . God came down upon all of us in great power and blessing, confirming this teaching in each one of our hearts as never before."[39] Further testimony came when several workers traveled to San Antonio to preach on the baptism in the Holy Spirit. Convinced that news about tongues had not arrived there, they agreed not to mention the phenomenon or even the word "evidence" in order to test the validity of the new doctrine. After preaching on Spirit baptism, everyone in the audience "spoke in tongues as the Spirit gave utterance when they received the Holy Ghost. This satisfied even the most skeptical among us."[40]

One of the most articulate spokespersons for the doctrine during the early years of the Assemblies of God was Daniel W. Kerr, a former CMA pastor. He strongly influenced the endorsement of the doctrine in 1918 when it was being seriously questioned within the ranks by another well-known minister, Fred F. Bosworth.[41] Sharing the fears of many Pentecostals since his time, Kerr believed that "whenever we . . . begin to let down on this particular point, the fire dies out, the ardor and fervor begin to wane, the glory departs."[42]

In his study of the New Testament, Kerr observed that the writers had "selected" their materials for inclusion from the available data, presaging the judicious use of redaction criticism employed by later Pentecostal exegetes.[43] The apostle John, for example, "made a SELECTION of just such materials as served his purpose, and that is, to confirm believers in the faith concerning Jesus Christ the Son of God" (Kerr's emphasis). Following a similar methodology, Kerr says that Luke chose

> from a voluminous mass of material just such facts and just such manifestations of the power of God as served his purpose. What is his purpose? No doubt, his purpose is to show that what Jesus promised He hath so fulfilled. He says, "they that believe shall speak in other tongues." The 120 believed and, therefore, they spake in other tongues as the Spirit gave them utterance. We also believe, and we speak in other tongues as the Spirit gives utterance.[44]

According to Kerr, "Is this not an altogether striking characteristic of the book of Acts?"[45] The plain sense of the biblical text clearly demonstrated that whether in Acts 2, 8 (by implication), 10, or 19, Spirit baptism was accompanied by glossolalia.

In a then novel attempt to substantiate the legitimacy of this hermeneutical approach, Stanley H. Frodsham, an editor of the *Pentecostal*

Evangel, found justification for it in George Mackinlay's *Recent Discoveries in St. Luke's Writings* (1921). The author claimed to have discovered "the law of threefold mention" ("triplication") in his study of the Lucan literature. To Frodsham (writing in 1926), the three specific references to glossolalia in Acts justifiably upheld the veracity of tongues as evidence, despite the fact that Mackinlay did not draw the same conclusion.[46]

In a parallel development among those who defended the evidential role of tongues, certain Oneness Pentecostals doubted that Spirit baptism was a post-conversionary experience (a second work of grace). While all Oneness believers pressed after 1914 for further restoration of the apostolic pattern by espousing water baptism in the name of Jesus according to Acts 2:38 (ironically another appeal to a paradigm), the soteriology of some linked repentance and water baptism in the name of Jesus with Spirit baptism (accompanied by tongues). Frank J. Ewart, an early adherent, emphasized that this New Testament insight "instantly brought our practices and precepts in line with those of the Apostles, and miracles again attended the use of the name [of Jesus]."[47] He also observed at a church revival in Belvedere, California, that "the vast majority of the new converts were filled with the Holy Ghost after coming up out of the water. They would leave the [baptismal] tank speaking in other tongues."[48] From this perspective, the words of Jesus in John 3:5 ("I tell you the truth, unless a man is born of water and the Spirit, he cannot enter the kingdom of God") align conversion with Spirit baptism.

But despite some divergences of opinion, Pentecostals who identified tongues with baptism in the Holy Spirit, frequently perceived the experience to be the gateway to the nine gifts mentioned by Paul in 1 Corinthians 12 (including the "gift of tongues," understood to be for public use in the congregation).[49] While the "gift of tongues" was not for all, evidential tongues could be had by everyone baptized in the Spirit. After all, Jesus had announced before his ascension: "And these signs will accompany those who believe . . . they will speak in new tongues" (Mark 16:17). The appeal to the disputed longer ending of Mark, always a vested concern among Pentecostals, seemed to corroborate their belief in the requirement of tongues.[50]

Regardless of the forceful claims about the spiritual effects of speaking in tongues, certainty as to their actual meaning declined after the general demise of Parham's xenolalic hypothesis. For example, Pentecostals often pointed to the predictive intent of Isaiah 28:11 ("For with stammering lips and another tongue will he [the Lord] speak to this people") that Paul quotes in 1 Corinthians 14:21. If one followed the interpretation of Frodsham (reflecting Parham's view), then Paul's subsequent remark in verse 22 ("tongues are for a sign . . . to them that believe not") could only have referred to the utility of xenolalia in gospel witness: the proclamation of the gospel by individuals unfamiliar with the language(s) of their hearers. In contrast to this opinion, however, glossolalia or "unknown tongues" has left believers with more questions than answers relative to Paul's intended meaning.[51]

For the most part, Pentecostal writers proved to be more adept at describing the effects of speaking in tongues than in defining its meaning within Christian spirituality.[52] The well-known missionary A. G. Garr said that glossolalia

> is the sweetest joy and the greatest pleasure to the soul when God comes upon one . . . and begins Himself to speak in His language. Oh! the blessedness of His presence when those foreign words flow from the Spirit of God through the soul and then are given back to Him in praise, in prophecy, or in worship.[53]

Another prominent Pentecostal and editor (*Triumphs of Faith*), Carrie Judd Montgomery, wrote in July 1908:

> The blessing and power abides and He prays and praises through me in tongues quite frequently. When His power is heavy upon me, nothing seems to give vent and expression to His fullness like speaking or singing in an unknown tongue.[54]

But, why would God have the Spirit pray through believers to him in such a fashion? How does this generate empowerment?

Regardless of the questions we wish they would have addressed at greater length, early adherents unmistakably tied their new-found understanding of Spirit baptism with holiness of character. Elmer Kirk Fisher, pastor of the Upper Room Mission in Los Angeles, remarked: "You cannot receive the baptism of the Holy Ghost unless you are cleansed by the blood, both from actual transgressions and inbred sin." The devil might have his counterfeits or people might fail in their testimonies, but Fisher, appealing to the veracity of the pattern in Acts, challenged his readers not to lower the standard of the word of God since "those who receive the full baptism of the Holy Ghost will speak in tongues as the Spirit gives utterance *always*" (my emphasis).[55]

In spite of the hermeneutical and theological arguments, baptism in the Holy Spirit was perceived to be more than a rational tenet of faith. Donald Gee, an influential British Pentecostal leader, wrote: "In the final analysis, the Baptism in the Spirit is not a doctrine, but an experience," with the ultimate proof being "whether I know the experience in burning *fact* in heart and life" (Gee's emphasis).[56] It was this tension between doctrinal standards and personal reception that occasionally generated crises in the faith of believers, even among those who warmly endorsed the teaching. For example, J. Roswell Flower, a founding father of the Assemblies of God, sought for the Pentecostal baptism with tongues for about two years until he realized that "I would seek several more years if I did not step out by faith and claim the promise." Although believing and testifying to having received, he still did not speak in tongues for several months.[57] Founder of the International Church of the Foursquare Gospel, Aimee Semple McPherson, held a more implacable position. Her view did not include "delays," which she described as the "take-it-by-faith-believe-you-have-it-and-go-on-experience."[58]

Even with the growing problem of "chronic seekers" in the churches (those who were unable to speak in tongues, for whatever reason),[59] belief in the evidential nature of tongues continued to gain credence.[60] Organizations which were formed, such as the Assemblies of God, International Church of the Foursquare Gospel, Church of God (Cleveland, Tenn.), Pentecostal Assemblies of Canada, and United Pentecostal Church, made the doctrine a cardinal point of belief. Recent documentation, however, suggests that even within some of these circles, uncertainties about the absolute claim of the doctrine or its hermeneutical underpinning have remained.[61]

VOICES OF DISSENT

While committed to the holiness view of a subsequent experience of grace for each believer, illustrated by the Spirit baptisms in Acts, some Pentecostals concluded that glossolalia in Acts and in 1 Corinthians were the same in nature and function. Luke's references do not depict, therefore, a different use from that which Paul explains as the "gift of tongues." Since the gifts are sovereignly dispensed by the Spirit (1 Cor. 12:7–11), one cannot insist that tongues alone determines the essential evidence. And concerned that believers were seeking them more than the fruits of the Spirit, particularly Christ-like love, these dissenting voices naturally exhibited less interest in the necessity of the outward sign. This reasoning, however, inclined them to interpret Luke through Pauline categories.

Among those dissenters, Minnie F. Abrams, a holiness missionary to India associated with the famed Pandita Ramabai's Mukti Mission, wrote in 1906: "We have not received the full Pentecostal baptism of the Holy Ghost until we are able not only to bear the fruit of the Spirit, but to exercise the gifts of the Spirit. I Cor. 12:4–11."[62] While not discounting the value of the pattern in Acts, she nevertheless remained more consistent with her Wesleyanism than Parham by emphasizing love as the primary evidence. Refusing to distinguish between the use of tongues in Acts and 1 Corinthians, she later wrote:

> Now I want to say that I believe it is God's rule to give speaking in tongues at the time or sometime after one's baptism, but I think I see from the Word of God that He has exceptions, and I do not like to strain a point to bring it to my ideas, and when I see anybody seeking to speak in tongues rather than seeking the power to save souls I am grieved.[63]

Ramabai, with whom she worked closely, apparently never spoke in tongues, but maintained that "the gift of tongues is certainly one of the signs of the baptism of the Holy Spirit. . . . Love, perfect divine love, is the only and most necessary sign of the baptism of the Holy Spirit." Tongues-speaking could be defended by Scripture, but there was no warrant to claim that it is "the only and most necessary sign."[64]

A unique Pentecostal ecumenicity functioned at the Mukti Mission since workers there held differing views on the evidential nature of tongues. Notwithstanding, Abrams reported: "this Baptism of the Holy Ghost with tongues and other gifts has so united the workers at Mukti in the love of the Spirit, that we are able to work in love and harmony, as one man, for the salvation of souls." It made little difference to her whether the workers were Calvinists or Arminians (both were present), because genuine spiritual maturity required love and humility, dependence on the Holy Spirit "to deepen the work of the Cross in each one of us," and shared concern to evangelize the unsaved with Pentecostal power. Magnanimous in her attitude toward other Christians who did not share her belief in Spirit baptism, she urged Pentecostals to open their doors to them, to listen patiently to their criticisms and ridicule, and to sit under their ministry because "the rivers of life will flow out, they cannot be dammed up by others. The fire in us will set others on fire." Through this means, Pentecostals could model to other Christians Paul's witness of the Spirit to the Ephesian disciples (Acts 19:1–7).[65]

Certain European Pentecostals also hesitated about asserting the necessity of tongues: George Jeffreys (England), Jonathan Paul (Germany), and Leonhard Steiner (Switzerland), among others.[66] Despite the diversity of opinion, the Pentecostal World Conference (organized in 1947) affirms the doctrine of initial evidence.

On the American scene, even Agnes N. Ozman, the first to speak in tongues at Parham's Bible school, considered the teaching of tongues as sole evidence of Spirit baptism to be an error (at least for a time, since she later received ministerial credentials from the Assemblies of God in 1917).[67] Others, such as William Hamner Piper (pastor of the Stone Church, Chicago, and the first editor of the *Latter Rain Evangel*) forthrightly condemned it as "false teaching"; and D. Wesley Myland (a prominent leader and former CMA pastor) did not expressly endorse the doctrine.[68]

At the Elim Tabernacle and the influential Rochester Bible Training School (Rochester, New York), both operated by the Duncan sisters, ambiguity about tongues prevailed. Elizabeth V. Baker, the eldest sister, who helped direct the ministry enterprises from the beginning, advised: "You who are waiting for the seal of your Pentecost, take it, count upon it. You who have not the Baptism at all as yet, take it, and say, 'Lord, I put in my claim for it by faith, for I know You want me to have it.' "[69] After Baker's death, Susan Duncan wrote that "she is one of those who died in faith, not having received the promise," probably indicating that she had never spoken in tongues.[70]

Confusion between tongues as evidence and tongues as a gift also arose within the Church of God (Cleveland, Tenn.) in 1909. Two ministers were consequently expelled.[71] On another front, Joel A. Wright, an early Pentecostal preacher and founder of the First Fruits Harvesters ministry in Rumney, New Hampshire (partially from which emerged the later New England Fellowship [1929], a forerunner of the National Association of Evangelicals [1942]), also hesitated about the doctrine. He stated in 1920 that the signs which follow the preaching of the gospel (Mark 16:17-18) confirm baptism in the Holy Spirit.

> What is the evidence to the world that I have the baptism of the Holy Ghost? The signs that will follow: the sick will be healed; demons will be cast out; I shall speak in tongues. But the evidence to my heart is faith. . . . tongues is not what you should seek but you should seek God in His mighty baptism. And then believe for tongues, a sign that should follow.[72]

By far the best-known leader to contest the doctrine of evidential tongues was the Assemblies of God minister, Fred F. Bosworth. Despite having been affiliated with the organization from its founding in 1914, Bosworth eventually concluded that the teaching was an error. For him, the manifestations of tongues both in Acts and 1 Corinthians represented the gift of tongues, the former not denoting a different usage—one that every believer should experience. He further challenged the hermeneutical presupposition of the pattern: (1) it was not supported by an explicit command in Scripture ("without a solitary 'Thus saith the Lord' "); and (2) it was simply "assumed from the fact that in three instances recorded in the Acts they spoke in tongues as a result of the baptism."[73] Although the phenomena in Acts should serve as a warning, reasoned Bosworth, to those who deny the possibility of gifts in the church today, it remains unscriptural to teach that everyone receives the same endowment of the Spirit. After all, Paul assumed a negative response when he asked rhetorically: "Do all speak in tongues?" (1 Cor. 12:30).

Bosworth warned that "not one of the inspired apostles or prophets ever taught it, and not one of the world's great soul winners ever taught it." Furthermore, it would divide equally devout Christians. With this in mind, he cautioned:

> When we, as a movement, will confine ourselves to what the Scriptures plainly teach upon this important subject of the baptism and ALL the manifestations of the Spirit, and preach to the world the great things about the baptism in the Holy Ghost our usefulness will be enhanced many fold (Bosworth's emphasis).[74]

Bosworth resigned from the Assemblies of God in 1918 when its General Council reaffirmed the teaching, following a stirring admonition by Daniel W. Kerr.[75]

A TEST OF ORTHODOXY

It is presently uncertain who first coined the term "*initial* evidence." The earliest Pentecostals who insisted that speaking in tongues must accompany Spirit baptism often referred to the phenomenon as "evidential tongues," the "evidence," the "sign of tongues," the "only evidence," and the "Bible evidence," among others. The earliest reference to it as being "initial" that I have located is in the "Statement of Fundamental Truths" of the Assemblies of God, written and adopted in 1916. Article 6, "The Full Consummation of the Baptism in the Holy Ghost," mentions "the initial sign of speaking in tongues."[76] When it was amended two years later in the controversy raised by Bosworth, the doctrine was identified as "our distinctive testimony" and the article was changed to read "the initial *physical* sign of speaking with other tongues" (my emphasis).[77] Before long, the expressions "initial evidence" and "initial physical evidence" became preferential terms among many proponents, serving to emphasize the value of tongues, but not to the exclusion of the fruit of the Spirit and the empowerment considered to lie at the heart of the experience.

Significantly, the amendment of the "Statement of Fundamental Truths" by the Assemblies of God also illustrates that at least by 1918, the Pentecostal movement had passed a theological milestone: the period of debate over the nature of tongues had ostensibly ended, signalled by controversy, schism, and the emergence of creedal formulations. For many Pentecostals, the line of orthodoxy on the evidential role of tongues in Spirit baptism had been clearly drawn.

FINAL REMARKS

Like other restorationists, Pentecostals scrutinized the picture of early Christian faith and practice painted by Luke. The precedent for building the initial evidence doctrine on a New Testament pattern can be traced directly back to the holiness interpretation of Spirit baptisms in Acts. Nonetheless, their dependence on the implied importance of glossolalic references for doctrine uniquely pressed the importance of the Acts narrative farther. Whereas most Pentecostals agreed on the post-conversionary character of the Spirit baptisms cited there (with the exception of many Oneness Pentecostals), nevertheless, from as early as 1906, they failed to achieve consensus on the evidential nature of tongues. Hence, they also differed in their understanding of glossolalic manifestations in Acts. Those who defined these occurrences with Pauline categories generally questioned their indispensableness, while advocates boldly defended the requirement by emphasizing the theological value of Lucan narrative. Pentecostals still remain divided over the issue, disclosing the vital role that glossolalia continues to play in their conception of the Spirit-filled life.

The interpretation of Acts by those who have supported the doctrine of initial evidence, however, has directly challenged the approach of scholars who have consistently given didactic literature (particularly Paul's epistles) a standing above narrative materials in theological formulation.[78] Regardless of the methodological disputes involved, this hallmark of Pentecostal belief has provided an important model for understanding and experiencing the Christian faith, characterized by high regard for the authority of Scripture, a vibrant life in the Spirit, and activism in ministry.[79] Hermeneutically, therefore, Pentecostals stand in a respected and historic line of evangelical Christians who have legitimately recognized the Acts of the Apostles to be a vital repository of theological truth.

Although the extent to which narrative should be utilized in establishing doctrine has not been germane to this study, it is significant that contemporary New Testament scholarship has become far more sympathetic to its theological value.[80] A growing regard for the diversity of literary genres in the New Testament has led to a fresh appreciation for the complementary theologies of Luke and Paul. Theologian Clark H. Pinnock adds that Pentecostalism "has not only restored joy and power to the church but a clearer reading of the Bible as well."[81] Pentecostals were more avant-garde in their hermeneutics than they realized.

NOTES

1. M. J. Erickson, *Christian Theology* (Grand Rapids: Baker, 1985), 79–80.

2. Ibid., 877–82; for other Reformed perspectives, see A. A. Hoekema, *Tongues and Spirit-Baptism* (Grand Rapids: Baker, 1981), 114; J. R. W. Stott, *The Baptism & Fullness of the Holy Spirit* (Downers Grove, Ill.: Inter-Varsity, 1964), 18; F. D. Bruner, *A Theology of the Holy Spirit* (Grand Rapids: Eerdmans, 1970), 155ff.

3. C. F. Parham, *A Voice Crying in the Wilderness*, 2d ed. (Baxter Springs, Kan.: Apostolic Faith Bible College, reprint of 1910 ed.), 36–38; S. M. Horton, *What the Bible Says About the Holy Spirit* (Springfield, Mo.: Gospel Publishing House, 1976), 142–44, 156–62; F. L. Arrington, *The Acts of the Apostles* (Peabody, Mass.: Hendrickson, 1988), 21–24, 117–18.

4. S. M. Burgess, "Montanist and Patristic Perfectionism," in *Reaching Beyond: Chapters in the History of Perfectionism*, ed. S. M. Burgess (Peabody, Mass.: Hendrickson, 1986), 119–25; J. Moorman, *A History of the Franciscan Order* (Oxford: Clarendon, 1968), 3–19.

5. *Luther's Works*, vol. 34. Career of the Reformer 4, ed. L. W. Spitz (Philadelphia: Fortress, 1960), 336–37.

6. *Calvin: Theological Treatises*, Library of Christian Classics 22, ed. J. K. S. Reid (London: SCM, 1954), 58–66.

7. For an abridged exposition of this belief, see P. Riedemann, *Account of Our Religion*, in *The Protestant Reformation*, ed. H. J. Hillerbrand (New York: Harper & Row, 1968), 143–46.

8. For two excellent treatments of the development of pietism, see F. E. Stoeffler, *The Rise of Evangelical Pietism* (Leiden: E. J. Brill, 1965); idem, *German Pietism During the Eighteenth Century* (Leiden: E. J. Brill, 1973).

9. J. Pelikan, *From Luther to Kierkegaard* (St. Louis: Concordia, 1950), 49–75.

10. D. Brown, *Understanding Pietism* (Grand Rapids: Eerdmans, 1978), 68.

11. Philipp Jakob Spener, *Pia Desideria*, trans. and ed. T. G. Tappert (Philadelphia: Fortress, 1964), 46.

12. A. J. Lewis, *Zinzendorf, The Ecumenical Pioneer* (Philadelphia: Westminster, 1962), 59.

13. Howard A. Synder, *The Radical Wesley* (Downers Grove, Ill.: Inter-Varsity, 1980), 125–42.

14. G. G. Hunter, III, *To Spread the Power* (Nashville: Abingdon, 1987), 40–41.

15. C. Welch, *Protestant Thought in the Nineteenth Century*, vol. 1 (1799–1870) (New Haven: Yale University Press, 1972), 1:28. For an excellent

discussion of restorationism on the American scene, see R. T. Hughes, ed., *The American Quest for the Primitive Church* (Urbana: University of Illinois Press, 1988).

16. G. D. Fee and D. Stuart, *How to Read the Bible for All Its Worth* (Grand Rapids: Zondervan, 1981), 88.

17. E. E. Dowling, *The Restoration Movement* (Cincinnati: Standard Publishing, 1964), 3; see also, A. Campbell, *The Christian System* (Cincinnati: H. S. Bosworth, 1866; reprint, New York: Arno Press and the *New York Times*, 1969), 5–6; J. D. Much, *Christians Only* (Cincinnati: Standard, 1962), 9; idem, *The Free Church*, 2d ed. (Louisville: Restoration, 1966), 18–21.

18. W. R. Estep, *The Anabaptist Story* (Grand Rapids: Eerdmans, 1975), 215–231.

19. T. Armitage, *A History of the Baptists* (New York: Bryan, Taylor, and Co., 1890; reprint, Watertown, Wis.: Maranatha Baptist, 1976), 114.

20. W. W. Stevens, *Doctrines of the Christian Religion* (Nashville: Broadman, 1967), 306–7.

21. For an example of this exegesis of Acts, see C. W. Carter, gen. ed., *Wesleyan Bible Commentary*, 7 vols. (Grand Rapids: Eerdmans, 1964), vol. 4, *Matthew, Mark, Luke, John, Acts*, by R. Earle, H. J. S. Blaney, C. W. Carter, 550.

22. W. T. Dayton, "The Divine Purification and Perfection of Man," in *A Contemporary Wesleyan Theology*, ed. C. W. Carter (Grand Rapids: Zondervan, 1983), vol. 1, 544.

23. L. W. Wood, *Pentecostal Grace* (Wilmore, Ky.: Francis Asbury, 1980), 264–73; A. R. G. Deasley, "Entire Sanctification and the Baptism with the Holy Spirit: Perspectives on the Biblical View of the Relationship," *WTJ* 14 (Spring 1979): 34–39.

24. For information on the evangelical healing movement, see P. G. Chappell, "The Divine Healing Movement in America" (Ph.D. diss., Drew University, 1983).

25. R. A. Torrey, *What the Bible Teaches* (New York: Fleming H. Revell Co., 1898), 271, 272; see also D. L. Moody, *Moody: His Word, Work, and Workers* (Cincinnati: Nelson & Phillips, 1877), 396–403.

26. A. J. Gordon, *The Ministry of the Spirit* (Philadelphia: American Baptist Publication Society, 1894), 79–80.

27. A. B. Simpson, *The Acts of the Holy Ghost. Christ in the Bible Series*, vol. 16 (Harrisburg: Christian Publications, n.d.), 23–25; R. P. Wilder, "Power from on High," in *Spiritual Awakening Among India's Students* (Madras: Addison & Co., 1896), 24–30; idem, *Studies on the Holy Spirit* (London: SCM, 1909), 11–13. See also C. Nienkirchen, "Albert B. Simpson: Fore-runner of the Modern Pentecostal Movement," paper presented at the 16th annual meeting of the Society for Pentecostal Studies, Costa Mesa, California, 13–15 November 1986.

28. This development has been documented in D. W. Dayton's *Theological Roots of Pentecostalism* (reprint, Peabody, Mass.: Hendrickson, 1991). See also E. L. Waldvogel [Blumhofer], "The 'Overcoming Life': A Study in the Reformed Evangelical Origins of Pentecostalism" (Ph.D. diss., Harvard University, 1977). For the pneumatological connection, also W. J. Hollenweger, *The Pentecostals* (reprint, Peabody, Mass.: Hendrickson, 1988), 336–38.

29. T. G. Atteberry, "Signs and Miracles," *Apostolic Truth*, January 1907, 4. E. W. Kenyon, an early observer of Pentecostalism who later had a marked influence on some sectors of the movement in the areas of positive confession and faith healing, wrote the following in 1907 about the revival of speaking in tongues:

"Now as to the value of this. Of course it is 'given to profit withal.' As far as I can see there is no profit except as it gives the outward proof of having received the Holy Spirit. Again it convinces foreigners that something beyond the natural has come into the Christian.

I cannot see that those with tongues have any more power in testimony or preaching than many Spirit-indwelt people I know. But the joy that comes into the soul and the ecstasy that thrills it is worth the effort that some seem to display to get the gift."

See E. W. Kenyon, "The Gift of Tongues," *Reality*, May 1907, 229; cf., D. R. McConnell, *A Different Gospel* (Peabody, Mass.: Hendrickson, 1988), 16.

30. D. W. Kerr, "The Basis for Our Distinctive Testimony," *Pentecostal Evangel*, 2 September 1922, 4. See also G. Wacker, "Playing for Keeps: The Primitivist Impulse in Early Pentecostalism," in Hughes, ed., *The American Quest*, 196–219.

31. Dayton, *Theological Roots*, 175.

32. A representative sampling of the literature includes:

E. C. Erickson (Fellowship of Christian Assemblies), "The Bible on Speaking in Tongues," (printed sermon) (Duluth: Duluth Gospel Tabernacle, 1935); H. Horton (Assemblies of God in Great Britain and Ireland), *What is the Good of Speaking with Tongues?* (Luton, Beds., England: Redemption Tidings, 1946); F. H. Squire (Full Gospel Testimony, England), *The Revelation of the Holy Spirit* (Leamington Spa, England: Full Gospel Publishing House, n.d.); M. Pearlman (Assemblies of God, U.S.A.), *Knowing the Doctrines of the Bible* (Springfield, Mo.: Gospel Publishing House, 1937); R. H. Hughes (Church of God [Cleveland, Tenn.]), *What is Pentecost?* (Cleveland, Tenn.: Pathway, 1963); G. P. Duffield and N. M. Van Cleave (International Church of the Foursquare Gospel), *Foundations of Pentecostal Theology* (Los Angeles: L.I.F.E. Bible College, 1983).

33. S. M. Horton, *What the Bible Says*, 261.

34. W. W. Menzies, "The Methodology of Pentecostal Theology: An Essay on Hermeneutics," in *Essays on Apostolic Themes*, ed. P. Elbert (Peabody, Mass.: Hendrickson, 1985), 13.

35. A. G. Garr cited in "The Modern Gift of Tongues," *The Dawn* 14 (September 15, 1937): 278 (quoted from the Supplement to *Confidence*, May 1908). Reports of xenolalia have continued to surface through the years; see R. W. Harris, *Spoken by the Spirit* (Springfield, Mo.: Gospel Publishing House, 1973).

36. G. F. Taylor, *The Spirit and the Bride* (Falcon, N.C.: Falcon Printing Co., 1907; reprinted with two other documents under the title *Three Early Pentecostal Tracts*), ed. D. W. Dayton (New York: Garland, 1985), 46.

37. J. H. King, "How I Obtained Pentecost," *A Cloud of Witnesses to Pentecost in India*, September 1907, 50.

38. J. H. King, *From Passover to Pentecost*, 4th ed. (Franklin Springs, Ga.: Advocate, 1976; originally published in 1911), 183.

39. E. E. Goss, *The Winds of God* (New York: Comet Press Books, 1958), 58–59.

40. Ibid., 60. Another "test case" was later conducted by Charles Hamilton Pridgeon in Pittsburgh, Pennsylvania; see W. W. Menzies, *Anointed to Serve* (Springfield, Mo.: Gospel Publishing House, 1971), 126, n. 9.

41. Carl Brumback, *Suddenly . . . from Heaven* (Springfield, Mo.: Gospel Publishing House, 1961), 216–25.

42. D. W. Kerr, "The Bible Evidence of the Baptism with the Holy Ghost," *Pentecostal Evangel*, 11 August 1923, 2.

43. R. N. Soulen defines redaction criticism as "a method of Biblical criticism which seeks to lay bare the theological perspectives of a Biblical writer by analyzing the editorial (redactional) and compositional techniques and interpretations employed by him in shaping and framing the written and/or oral traditions at hand (see Luke 1:1–4)," in *Handbook of Biblical Criticism*, 2d ed. (Atlanta: John Knox, 1981), 165. Examples of Pentecostal writers after Kerr include: D. Gee, "The Initial Evidence of the Baptism in the Holy Spirit," *Pentecostal Evangel*, 12 July 1959, 3, 23–24; Menzies, "The Methodology," 5–10; R. Stronstad, *The Charismatic Theology of St. Luke* (Peabody, Mass.: Hendrickson, 1984); and D. C. Stamps, gen. ed., *The Full Life Study Bible* (New Testament) (Grand Rapids: Zondervan, 1990), 228.

44. Kerr, "The Bible Evidence," 3.

45. Ibid., 2; see also D. W. Kerr, "The Basis for Our Distinctive Testimony," *Pentecostal Evangel*, 2 September 1922, 4.

46. S. H. Frodsham, *With Signs Following* (Springfield, Mo.: Gospel Publishing House, 1926), 240. For relevant passages, see G. Mackinlay, *Recent Discoveries in St. Luke's Writings* (London: Marshall Brothers, 1921), 54–58, 97–98, 156–60, 246–48; also Table IX ("Triplications in the Acts"). For another attempted hermeneutical defense (the "law of first occurrence"), see H. W. Steinberg, "Initial Evidence of the Baptism in the Holy Spirit," in *Conference on the Holy Spirit Digest*, ed. G. Jones (Springfield, Mo.: Gospel Publishing House, 1983), vol. 1, 40. An exposition of the law of first occurrence (first mention) may be found in J. E. Hartill, *Principles of Biblical Interpretation* (Grand Rapids: Zondervan, 1947), 70.

47. F. J. Ewart, *The Name and the Book* (Phoenix, Ariz.: Jesus Name Church, 1936), 79.

48. F. J. Ewart, *The Phenomenon of Pentecost*, rev. ed. (Hazelwood, Mo.: Word Aflame, 1975), 113.

49. A. G. Garr, "Tongues, The Bible Evidence," *A Cloud of Witnesses to Pentecost in India*, September 1907, 42–44.

50. For early defenses of the longer ending of Mark, see S. H. Frodsham, *With Signs*, 240–41; and A. W. Frodsham, "The Sixteenth Chapter of Mark: How God Vindicates His Word in the Last Days," *Pentecostal Evangel*, 28 April 1923, 9.

51. Ibid., 208–29; cf., S. M. Horton, *What the Bible Says*, 229.

52. For example, A. A. Boddy lists the following five benefits in his "Speaking in Tongues: What is It?" *Confidence*, May 1910, 100:

1. Wondrous joy that the Spirit has thus sealed the believer unto the day of redemption. It is something very real.

2. An increase in the believer's personal love of the Lord Jesus.

3. A new interest in the word of God. The Bible becomes very precious and its messages very real.
4. A love to the souls for whom Christ has died and a desire to bring them to Him.
5. The soon coming of the Lord is now often laid upon the believer's heart.

53. Garr, "Tongues," 43.

54. C. J. Montgomery, "The Promise of the Father," *Triumphs of Faith,* July 1908, 149. See also O. D. Gouty, "The Doctrine of Carrie Judd Montgomery on the Initial Evidence of Baptism in the Holy Spirit," 1990 (Typewritten).

55. E. K. Fisher, "Stand For the Bible Evidence," *Bridegroom's Messenger,* 15 June 1909, 2.

56. D. Gee, untitled article, *Pentecostal Evangel,* 11 August 1923, 3. Gee's later publications included *Pentecost* (Springfield, Mo.: Gospel Publishing House, 1932); *After Pentecost* (Springfield, Mo.: Gospel Publishing House, 1945); for his discussion on the pattern in Acts, see *The Phenomena of Pentecost* (Springfield, Mo.: Gospel Publishing House, 1931), ch. 1. See also, A. White, "Spirit-Baptism and Initial Evidence in the Writings of the 'Apostle of Balance': Donald Gee," 1990 (Typewritten).

57. J. R. Flower, "God Honors Faith," *Pentecost,* 1 February 1910, 1; cf., idem, "How I Received the Baptism in the Holy Spirit," (Part 1) *Pentecostal Evangel,* 7 September 1952, 5–7; idem, "How I Received the Baptism in the Holy Spirit" (Part 2), *Pentecostal Evangel,* 14 September 1952, 5, 12–13.

58. A. S. McPherson, "The Baptism of the Holy Spirit," *Bridal Call,* June 1921, 1.

59. Pentecostals occasionally published materials (books and articles in periodicals) discussing the necessary steps in preparing to receive Spirit baptism. An example can be found in J. W. Welch, "The Baptism in·the Holy Ghost," *Pentecostal Evangel,* 26 August 1939, 7.

60. Representative expositions include C. Brumback, *What Meaneth This?* (Springfield, Mo.: Gospel Publishing House, 1947); H. Carter, *Spiritual Gifts and Their Operation* (Springfield, Mo.: Gospel Publishing House, 1968); R. C. Dalton, *Tongues Like As of Fire* (Springfield, Mo.: Gospel Publishing House, 1945); W. H. Horton, ed., *The Glossolalia Phenomenon* (Cleveland, Tenn.: Pathway, 1966); W. G. MacDonald, *Glossolalia in the New Testament* (Springfield, Mo.: Gospel Publishing House, ca. 1964); A. Kitay, *The Baptism of the Holy Ghost* (Hazelwood, Mo.: Word Aflame, 1988); R. M. Riggs, *The Spirit Himself* (Springfield, Mo.: Gospel Publishing House, 1949); W. H. Turner, *Pentecost and Tongues,* 2d ed. (Franklin Springs, Ga.: Advocate, 1968).

61. See C. Verge, "Pentecostal Clergy and Higher Education," *Eastern Journal of Practical Theology* (Eastern Pentecostal Bible College, Peterborough, Ontario, Canada) 2 (Spring 1988): 44; idem, "A Comparison of the Present Day Beliefs and Practices of Pentecostal Assemblies of Canada Ministers, based on Education and Age" (Ph.D. diss., New York University, 1986). See also M. M. Poloma, *The Assemblies of God at the Crossroads* (Knoxville: University of Tennessee Press, 1989), 40, 43. Poloma believes that some ministers have redefined their understanding of the doctrine; cf., Menzies, *Anointed to Serve,* 320.

For questions about the proper hermeneutical use of the narrative literature in the book of Acts for building the doctrine of initial evidence, see G. D. Fee, "Baptism in the Holy Spirit: the Issue of Separability and Subsequence," *Pneuma: Journal of the Society for Pentecostal Studies*, 7 (Fall 1985): 87–99; cf., Menzies, "The Methodology."

62. M. F. Abrams, *The Baptism of the Holy Ghost & Fire*, 2d ed. (Kedgaon, India: Mukti Mission Press, 1906), 69–70. For information on Pandita Ramabai, see H. S. Dyer, *Pandita Ramabai*, 2d ed.(Glasgow: Pickering & Inglis, n.d.). Abrams and Ramabai heard about the events at the Azusa Street revival through reports from Los Angeles in 1906; see *Apostolic Faith*, September 1907, 4, cols. 2–3.

63. M. F. Abrams, "The Object of the Baptism in the Holy Spirit," *Latter Rain Evangel*, May 1911, 10; cf., the sentiments on tongues as initial evidence published in Max Wood Moorhead's *Cloud of Witnesses to Pentecost in India*, printed first in Colombo, Ceylon (Sri Lanka), and later in Bombay (in the same region as the Mukti Mission). Three copies of this periodical (September 1907, August 1909, July 1910) may be found at the Assemblies of God Archives, Springfield, Missouri.

64. S. M. Adhav, ed., *Pandita Ramabai*, Confessing the Faith in India Series—No. 13 (Madras, India: Christian Literature Society, 1979), 223.

65. M. F. Abrams, "A Message from Mukti," *Confidence*, 15 September 1908, 14. The length of time in which spiritual unity remained at Mukti among those who differed on the necessity of tongues is presently unknown. Yet, as an early observer of the acrimony among Pentecostals (as well as the hostile reactions of other Christians toward speaking in tongues), Pandita Ramabai lamented, "It is sad beyond all expression, that God's children, who have been praying for years for an outpouring of the Holy Spirit . . . should now, when God is beginning to answer their prayer, be so hasty in judging and picking their fellow-Christians to pieces." Cited in Adhav, *Pandita*, 224.

66. R. M. Anderson, *Vision of the Disinherited* (New York: Oxford University Press, 1979), 162; Hollenweger, *Pentecostals*, 334–35.

67. A. Ozman, "The First One to Speak in Tongues," *Latter Rain Evangel*, January 1909, 2; cf., Parham, *Life*, 67.

68. W. H. Piper, "Manifestations and 'Demonstrations' of the Spirit," *Latter Rain Evangel*, October 1908, 18. B. Lidbeck, "Spirit Baptism and the Initial Evidence in *Latter Rain Evangel*," 1990 (Typewritten); idem, "D. W. Myland's Doctrine of Spirit Baptism and the Initial Evidence," 1990 (Typewritten). See also Myland, *Latter Rain*, 92–94. Notice Myland's identification of tongues as the "gift of tongues" and the need for interpretation. Given his friendship with Piper, it is reasonable to conclude that Myland's failure to insist on tongues as evidence means that his position was ambiguous on the issue. This may explain his reluctance to join the Assemblies of God in 1914.

69. E. V. Baker, "The Possibilities of Faith," *Trust*, September 1916, 6.

70. S. A. Duncan, editorial note, *Trust*, September 1916, 6; see also, R. F. Land, "Initial Evidence in the Periodical *Trust*," 1990 (Typewritten).

71. A. J. Tomlinson, *The Diary of A. J. Tomlinson*, 3 vols., ed. H. A. Tomlinson (New York: The Church of God, World Headquarters, 1949), vol. 1, 120–56.

72. J. A. Wright, "The Old Paths," a reprint from *The Sheaf,* September 1920, 8. Joel A. Wright's son, J. Elwin Wright, founded the New England Fellowship (NEF) in 1929 and later became one of the founding fathers of the National Association of Evangelicals (NAE; 1942). When the First Fruits Harvesters organization did not require tongues as initial evidence for Spirit baptism, a large group eventually moved away from Pentecostalism and formed the New England Fellowship. J. Elwin Wright, however, strongly worked to include Pentecostals in the NAE. See C. M. Robeck, Jr., "Wright, James Elwin," *DPCM,* 905–6; also, telephone interview with Ruth Flokstra, Springfield, Missouri, 2 November 1990.

73. F. F. Bosworth, *"Do All Speak With Tongues?"* (New York: Christian Alliance Publishing Co., n.d.), 9. For a refutation of Bosworth's arguments by the Norwegian Pentecostal pioneer Thomas B. Barratt, see "The Baptism of the Holy Ghost and Fire, What Is the Scriptural Evidence?" Evangel Tract No. 953 (Springfield, Mo.: Gospel Publishing House, n.d.).

74. Bosworth, *Do All Speak,* 17–18.

75. Brumback, *Suddenly,* 216–225.

76. General Council Minutes (Assemblies of God), 1916, 11.

77. General Council Minutes (Assemblies of God), 1918, 10; see also Anderson, *Vision,* 161–64.

78. For significant hermeneutical discussions of the issue, see B. Aker, "New Directions in Lucan Theology: Reflections on Luke 3:21–22 and Some Implications," in *Faces of Renewal,* 108–27; R. P. Menzies, "The Development of Early Christian Pneumatology with special reference to Luke–Acts" (Ph.D. diss., University of Aberdeen, Scotland, 1989); Stronstad, *Charismatic Theology.*

79. See M. B. Dowd, "Countours of a Narrative Pentecostal Theology and Practice," paper presented to the 15th annual meeting of the Society for Pentecostal Studies, Gaithersburg, Maryland, 14–16 November 1985, E18.

80. For evangelicals, see I. H. Marshall, *Luke: Historian and Theologian* (Grand Rapids: Zondervan, 1971), and especially pertinent to the issue at hand is J. R. Michaels's "Luke–Acts," in *DPCM,* 544–61. Those outside evangelical circles include: J. A. Fitzmyer, S.J., *Luke the Theologian* (New York: Paulist, 1989); R. F. O'Toole, S.J., *The Unity of Luke's Theology,* Good News Studies 9 (Wilmington: Michael Glazier, 1984); and C. H. Talbert, *Literary Patterns, Theological Themes, and the Genre of Luke–Acts* (Missoula, Mont.: Society of Biblical Literature and Scholars Press, 1974).

81. C. H. Pinnock, foreword to *The Charismatic Theology of St. Luke,* by R. Stronstad (Peabody, Mass.: Hendrickson, 1984), viii.

7

POPULAR EXPOSITIONS OF
INITIAL EVIDENCE IN PENTECOSTALISM

Gary B. McGee

Pentecostals have always been avid publishers. The truth of the full gospel had to be proclaimed to the ends of the earth, not only through preaching, but by the written word as well.[1] Following the Bosworth/ Kerr debate over the doctrine of initial evidence within the Assemblies of God in 1918, Pentecostal advocates, representing a variety of organizations, proceeded to defend the doctrine through printed expositions.[2]

In book publishing, serious attempts to expound its biblical foundations gradually came to include *Pentecost* (1932), by Donald Gee; *The Baptism with the Holy Ghost and the Evidence* (ca. 1935), by Paul H. Walker; *Tongues Like as of Fire* (1945), by Robert Chandler Dalton; *What Meaneth This?* (1947), by Carl Brumback; *The Spirit Himself* (1949), by Ralph M. Riggs; and *The Baptism in the Holy Spirit* (1956), by Harold Horton.

Later books contributed significantly to the discussion: *Basic Bible Beliefs* (ca. 1961), by Milton A. Tomlinson; *The Holy Spirit* (1962), by L. Thomas Holdcroft; *Glossolalia in the New Testament* (ca. 1964), by William G. MacDonald; *The Glossolalia Phenomenon* (1966), edited by Wade H. Horton; *These Are Not Drunken, As Ye Suppose* (1968; issued in a revised edition in 1987 as *Spirit Baptism: A Biblical Investigation*), by

Howard M. Ervin (an American Baptist charismatic who is sympathetic to the doctrine); *The Spirit—God in Action* (1974), by Anthony D. Palma; *What the Bible Says About the Holy Spirit* (1976), by Stanley M. Horton; *Foundations of Pentecostal Theology* (1983), by Guy P. Duffield and Nathaniel M. Van Cleave; Alan Kitay, *The Baptism of the Holy Ghost* (1988); and *The Hallmarks of Pentecost* (1989), by George Canty.

Recent studies include *Spirit-Baptism* (1983), by Harold D. Hunter; *The Charismatic Theology of Saint Luke* (1984), by Roger Stronstad; *Conversion-Initiation and the Baptism in the Holy Spirit* (1984), by Howard M. Ervin; and *Renewal Theology*, volume 2 (1990), by J. Rodman Williams (a sympathetic Presbyterian charismatic). Important chapters in collections of essays also merit consideration: "The Methodology of Pentecostal Theology: An Essay on Hermeneutics," by William W. Menzies in *Essays on Apostolic Themes* (1985), and "New Directions in Lucan Theology: Reflections on Luke 3:21–22 and Some Implications" by Ben Aker in *Faces of Renewal* (1988), among many others.

These well-known publications, however, provide only part of the picture of Pentecostal exposition. Other printed materials (articles in church magazines, tracts, booklets, and lesser known books) also deserve review. For this purpose, I have selected several apologetic treatises on initial evidence that represent this sizable body of literature. While many other examples could be cited, the following quotations effectively demonstrate how Pentecostals articulated their understanding of the relationship of glossolalia to Spirit baptism through the print media.

POWER FOR SERVICE

Pentecostals have believed that the baptism in the Holy Spirit with speaking in tongues provides empowerment for Christian witness in the last days before the imminent return of Christ. The origin of the Pentecostal movement itself was closely linked to a vision of sending missionaries "to the regions beyond," their ministries to be characterized by the same "signs and wonders" which followed the preaching of the early Christians in the Acts of the Apostles. This restorationist perspective is demonstrated in the brief interpretation of church history and the significance of the coming of the Pentecostal movement found in *The Missionary Manual* (1931), published by the Foreign Missions Department of the Assemblies of God:

> The Lord's Pentecostal Missionary Fellowship and Movement began on the day of Pentecost nearly two thousand years ago. On that glorious and

memorable day, the Father in heaven, in answer to the prayer of the Son, Jesus Christ, gave the Holy Spirit, the third Person of the Trinity, and He descended upon the waiting disciples in the city of Jerusalem, baptizing them into one body and enduing them with power for the task of world-wide evangelization committed to them by the Master. All became witnesses and spoke in other languages as the Spirit gave them utterance. Peter preached to the multitude and before the day was over three thousand souls were added to their number.

The Holy Spirit assumed the entire control and leadership of the church, the body of Christ, and the Lord continued His mighty works through its members. Persecutions arose and believers were scattered abroad, preaching the Gospel everywhere they went. Thus the Good News was carried throughout Judea, to Samaria, the sea coast towns and farther afield. Believers returned to their homes in distant countries to preach the Gospel, and it was not long before the news was carried to Rome, the capital city of the Roman Empire. Local Assemblies of God's people sprang up everywhere, and in turn continued to propagate the Gospel. The complete story is contained in the book of Acts.

The Holy Spirit continued in control until the close of the first century, then He was largely rejected and His position as leader usurped by men. The results are written in history. The Lord's missionary movement halted. Local Assemblies died. The Dark Ages ensued.

The Reformation followed, but the Holy Spirit was not fully restored, and upon the ruins of the early church have grown up the great denominations. Today the professing church is largely in apostasy, neither cold nor hot, and is nearly ready to be spued [*sic*] out.

But God looks down in mercy. The Lord's missionary movement, begun on the day of Pentecost, must be completed. He must have a people, a remnant, a bride.

In these latter days, the last days of the age, God is again pouring out His Spirit in accordance with His promise. In the year 1901 the latter rain began to fall in different parts of the world. Again, waiting, hungry-hearted people were baptized in the Holy Spirit. *The Lord's Pentecostal missionary movement was resumed.* Believers went everywhere preaching the Gospel. Numerous local Assemblies sprang into existence in America, Europe, and other parts of the world.

In the years 1906, 1907, and 1908, the Pentecostal missionaries began pressing on to the regions beyond. Whole families volunteered for the work, sold their possessions, and started for the field. They were possessed with a passion to go to the ends of the earth for their Lord, and no sacrifice seemed too great to them that the Gospel might be proclaimed and the coming of the Lord might be hastened.

At the present time there are hundreds of missionaries on the fields—nearly every nation in the world has received a Pentecostal witness—and those who have received the Holy Spirit with the sign of speaking in tongues as the Spirit gives utterance are probably numbered by the hundreds of thousands. The local Assemblies are uncounted.

It is the Lord Himself who is continuing His works through those who are willing to yield their all to the Holy Spirit and receive this wonderful Baptism. God is looking for men and women to use. He has no other body, nor hands, nor feet for the earthly ministry. He gives gifts to men and gives men as gifts.[3]

THE VALUE OF TONGUES

Through the years, Pentecostals have devoted considerable attention to the effects of speaking in tongues on the spirituality and ministry of the believer. For example, Aimee Semple McPherson, flamboyant evangelist and founder of the International Church of the Foursquare Gospel, answered questions in catechistic form about the benefits of Spirit baptism and speaking in tongues in an article published in *Word and Work* magazine in 1917:

Q. What is the use of this sign of tongues which accompanies the incoming Spirit?

A. When you walk down the street looking for a barber, first you look for a *red and white pole*, the *sign*, in other words. When you are looking for dinner you look for a sign that says, *Restaurant*. The barber's pole can not shave you, neither can the wooden restaurant sign feed you, but they are just signs to indicate that behind those doors there is a barber who can serve you, or within the restaurant doors there is food that will satisfy your hunger. So it is with the Bible sign, the speaking in tongues. It indicates that the Comforter has come to abide within.

Q. Of what use is the speaking in tongues, outside of being the evidence of the indwelling Spirit?

A. 1 Cor. 14:21, Tongues are a sign to them that believe not, also he that speaketh in an unknown tongue edifieth himself, verse 4. My spirit prayeth, verse 14, Verily thou giveth thanks well, verse 17, also he speaks of Jesus and His soon coming.[4]

The close connection of Spirit baptism and holiness of character is clearly evident in Stanley H. Frodsham's *Rivers of Living Water* (1934):

Purified lips! A cleansed tongue! A holy tongue! Is that not the need of every child of God? Is there not a need of coming to this greater Baptizer to be baptized into the Holy Ghost and into this holy fire which will cleanse our lips and cleanse our whole being, making us fit instruments to go forth with His message?

Is there such a thing as a substitute for the fire of God? Yes. We read that two of the sons of Aaron offered strange fire before the Lord. It was not acceptable, and they were destroyed. Many are kindling fires which are not the fires of the Holy Ghost, and judgment will come upon such attempted substitutes for the true fire which God sent down from heaven on the Day of Pentecost. The outstanding symbol of Pentecost was the tongue of fire. The fire of God came down upon the acceptable sacrifice, and those hundred and twenty waiting ones became firebrands for God. Their tongues were tongues of fire. Their utterance was that of the Spirit. That last unruly member was brought into captivity, and they spoke with other tongues as the Spirit of God gave utterance. God had full possession, and they were filled with the true fire from heaven.

The fires of human enthusiasm will not take the place of this blessed fire from heaven. The cold and lukewarm church of today needs to be awakened to see the need of the Baptism in the Holy Ghost and fire that they had on the Day of Pentecost. . . .[5]

An early leader and executive in the Assemblies of God, John W. Welch preached a sermon to the student body at Central Bible Institute (College after 1965) entitled "What the Baptism Really Is" shortly before his death in 1939. In asserting the importance of tongues as initial evidence, he declared:

Some people question tongues as the evidence of the Baptism. Here is the philosophy of tongues: The Baptism is the submerging of the whole being, including the mind, and tongues proves the submerging of the mind. Speaking a language unknown to the mind shows that the mind and the whole being are, at that moment, subjected to God. What physical phenomenon would better prove the submerging of the mind than tongues?

Without the baptism in the Holy Spirit our ministry is limited. We are limited to preaching things we have learned from books of men or testifying of past experiences. But with the Spirit's indwelling, our minds are illuminated, giving us a fresh revelation of Jesus and His Word and enabling us to bring forth the thoughts of God with expedience and power. Besides illuminating the mind for service, the Spirit's indwelling helps one surrender his will and emotions to God. This, in turn, facilitates spiritual introspection and cleansing.[6]

That Spirit baptism with glossolalia minimized distinctions between clergy and laity by empowering every believer for Christian witness is illustrated in *The Holy Ghost and Fire* (1956), written by the well-known Canadian Pentecostal pioneer leader, Daniel N. Buntain:

Tongues of fire sat upon not only the twelve or the seventy chosen evangelists, but upon the ordinary believers as well, including the women. Instantly all became active witnesses for Christ. The fire did not fall on the twelve to be communicated by them to others. It did not leave the ordinary men to be mere spectators, while the work of the Lord was committed to the selected ministry. It swept away the priesthood and made a way whereby every man and woman might enter into the heavenlies. True, all were not apostles or evangelists, but all were priests and had equal access to the throne of God. From now on no man was to be a depository or storehouse wherein spiritual favors might be stored for the use of those who might purchase or otherwise secure them.[7]

Former General Superintendent of Open Bible Standard Churches Frank W. Smith commented on the therapeutic values of tongues in the *Message of the Open Bible* through an article titled "What Value Tongues?" (1963):

> Another great value is the relaxation of tension. There is a refreshing of spirit for the initiated. We live in times of tension that this world has never previously experienced. The wrong move could trigger an explosion that would blow this planet to bits. The nervous system is strained to the breaking point. Minds are ready to snap. The burdens of life are pyramiding daily. "Hurry up!" is the key note of the time. And what is the rush? We are hastening to the day of destruction. Where can one find relief or release? Isaiah has the answer. "For with stammering lips and an [*sic*] another tongue will he speak to this people. To whom he said, this is the rest with which ye can cause the weary to rest; and this is the refreshing." Isa. 28:11, 12.

> The therapeutic value of praying in an unknown tongue should never be underestimated. In Romans 8:28 [*sic*] the Apostle said, "Likewise the Spirit also helpeth our infirmities: for we know not what to pray for as we ought: but the Spirit itself maketh intercession for us with groanings which cannot be uttered." The groanings may not be intelligible to man, but they reach the heart of God. The Apostle said, "he that searcheth the hearts knoweth what is the mind of the Spirit, because he maketh intercession for the sins according to the will of God." Who could ever evaluate such prayer? It is prayer with a divine intelligence, "for he that searcheth the hearts knoweth what is the mind of the Spirit." It is prayer "according to the will of God." It is prayer with a divine dimension.[8]

THE PATTERN OF INITIAL EVIDENCE IN ACTS

Several writers responded to Fred Bosworth's contentions in *Do All Speak with Tongues?* (n.d.) that the teaching on initial evidence lacks explicit statements from Scripture to support it. Among them, the famed Norwegian Pentecostal pioneer, Thomas Ball Barratt, replied in the tract "The Baptism of the Holy Ghost and Fire: What is the Scriptural Evidence?" and stated:

> The writer [Bosworth] . . . says that, "we have no 'Thus saith the Lord' in the Scriptures that all are to speak in tongues, but the very opposite [is true]. We have many 'Thus saith the Lord's' as to *other* evidences or rather results

of the Baptism in the Spirit. For instance: 'They SHALL prophesy' etc., etc." Now is this statement true to the Word?

In Mark 16:16–18 the Lord says, "He that believeth and is baptized SHALL be saved; (Is that true?) but he that believeth not SHALL be damned. (Is that true?) "And these signs SHALL follow them that BELIEVE." (Is that true?) "In my name SHALL they cast out devils." (Is that true?) "They SHALL speak with *new tongues.*" (Is *that* true?) The writer possibly will say, "with some reservations." But the Bible does not give any. If there are reservations in this case, then there are reservations to be made in each of the others. The only reservation the Bible makes is UNBELIEF. "These signs SHALL follow them that BELIEVE." It goes on to say, "They SHALL take up serpents; and if they drink any deadly thing, it SHALL NOT hurt them; they SHALL lay hands on the sick, and they SHALL recover." I have read a book of the writer [Bosworth] concerning *healing by faith*, an excellent book!—but if reservations are to be made, then we are at liberty to do so in the statement here concerning *healing* as well as in that concerning *tongues.*

He [Bosworth] cites, as seen above, Peter's statement on the Day of Pentecost, when he explains the great miracle that was being enacted before their eyes, and quotes the prophecy of the prophet Joel, "And it shall come to pass in the LAST days, saith God, I WILL pour out of My Spirit upon ALL flesh: and your sons and your daughters SHALL prophesy (Is that true?), and your young men SHALL see visions, and your old men SHALL dream dreams: and on My servants and on My handmaidens I will pour out in THOSE days of My Spirit; and they SHALL prophesy." (Is that true?) Now notice please that this was the interpretation Peter gave of TONGUES. He is explaining the miracle of TONGUES, and states that THEY were PROPHETIC in their kind. This explains also Acts 19:6, "and they spake with tongues, and prophesied." Prophecy is not merely the foretelling of coming events, but "he that prophesieth *speaketh unto men to edification and exhortation and comfort.*" 1 Cor. 14:3. On the Day of Pentecost, the NEW tongues were used in that way. The speakers spoke of "the WONDERFUL WORKS OF GOD." Tongues then when understood, that is, when the language spoken is understood, either directly, or by interpretation, may be prophetic, and influence the people directly, in the same way as words of prophecy without the tongues. As the apostle Peter is here speaking of TONGUES, and explaining their nature, we may state that we have, even in this case, *another of the Lord's SHALL's* concerning tongues: They SHALL speak in TONGUES—prophetically, that is—*proclaim the wonderful works of God in new tongues,* and that is what takes place when the tongues are heard, as people receive their Baptism—CHRIST IS GLORIFIED!—the wonderful works of God are proclaimed by the fire-baptized souls.

The statement therefore, that "*there is not a solitary passage of Scripture,*" concerning tongues as a proof or sign of the Baptism of the Holy Ghost, is *FALSE.* Acts 10:46 is furthermore a very decisive passage in favor of this teaching. Peter and his six friends had evidently been in doubt as to the advisability of visiting the heathen, but the Lord prepared him, and when the gospel was preached to Cornelius and the company met together in his house, the HOLY GHOST FELL ON ALL them which heard the word." How did Peter and his friends know it? The Bible gives the answer, "FOR THEY HEARD THEM SPEAK WITH TONGUES, AND MAGNIFY GOD!" As already seen, tongues accompanied invariably the outpouring of the Holy Ghost in the cases mentioned in the book of Acts. It was the NEW sign of the Christian church! Concerning the two cases, as we have seen, where they are not mentioned, in one, the recipient states later, that he spoke *"more in tongues than they all,"* and in the case of the believers at Samaria, we may rest assured that Peter who at Caesarea later on, *claimed tongues to be the proof of the Baptism,* would have been *unsatisfied with anything less at Samaria.* It is scriptural therefore to state that TONGUES, given by the Holy Spirit are a real proof of His presence, and that they may be expected by all Spirit-filled believers.

The writer [Bosworth] asks, "If Luke was so careful to record it when only these few (on the Day of Pentecost) spoke in tongues, why did he not record it when all the multiplied thousands since Pentecost spoke in tongues, if they all did?" The simple answer to this is, that Luke did *not* record *when* and *how* all these multiplied thousands received the Baptism, and therefore he did not say anything about their speaking in tongues. The cases he does mention leaves us in no doubt as to whether they spoke in tongues or no.[9]

A similar view appears in the printed sermon "The Bible on Speaking in Tongues" (1935) by the Scandinavian—American Pentecostal leader Elmer C. Erickson:

Speaking in tongues occurred at the time of the outpouring or infilling of the Holy Spirit; and this was true not only in one isolated instance. Out of the four recorded instances in the book of Acts where people received the infilling of the Holy Spirit, in three it is definitely stated that they spake in tongues: Acts 2:1–4; 10:44–46; 19:1–6. There is no record of anyone ever speaking in tongues before he was baptized in the Holy Ghost.

This speaking in tongues on the day of Pentecost is not only a fulfillment of Isa. 28:11 and Mark 16:17, but also a fulfillment of Joel 2. The speaking in tongues on the day of Pentecost was Joel's prophecy in action. . . .

Speaking in tongues accompanied the outpouring of the spirit [*sic*] in the house of Cornelius. See Acts 10:44– 46. Some years ago I was invited to the home of a Presbyterian minister in our city. This minister had a friend visiting in his home who was connected with Paul Rader's tabernacle in Chicago. As we talked together on the subject of the spirit-filled [*sic*] life, this friend said, "There is no verse in the Bible that says speaking in tongues was ever an evidence to anyone that a person had received the infilling of the Holy Ghost." I asked him to read Acts 10:44–46. "While Peter yet spake these words, the Holy Ghost fell on all them that heard the word. And they of the circumcision which believed were astonished, as many as came with

Peter, because that on the Gentiles also was poured out the gift of the Holy Ghost. For they heard them speak with tongues and magnify God." Was not the speaking in tongues an evidence to these believing Jews that these Gentiles had received the infilling of the Holy Ghost? What else could the conjunction "for" mean? Our friend said, "I never noticed that before."

Let us look at Acts 19:1–6. Here the speaking in tongues accompanied the outpouring of the Holy Spirit again. Fighters of the truth of the Baptism in the Holy Spirit say that the twelve disciples at Ephesus were not saved men. They would have us believe that what they received in Paul's prayer meeting was salvation. If Paul was in doubt about their salvation, would he ask them such a question as, "have ye received the Holy Ghost since ye believed?" Why doesn't he ask them if they are saved? I have never heard a scripturally enlightened person ask the unsaved one whether or not he has received the Holy Ghost, because the scripturally enlightened one knows that the world, the unconverted, cannot receive the Holy Ghost. Jesus said, speaking of the Holy Ghost, "whom the world cannot receive, because it seeth him not, neither knoweth him, but ye know him, for he dwelleth with you and shall be in you."[10]

Aimee Semple McPherson added her support for tongues as initial evidence by writing:

Q. Has the Lord a new fashioned twentieth century method of baptizing believers with the Holy Ghost? Or does He still fill them, and accompany the infilling with the same Bible evidence, speaking in tongues as He did in the days of old?

A. No, the Lord has not changed, just as there is only one way to be saved and that is through Jesus' precious blood, even so there is just one way to receive the Holy Ghost, and that is as they did on the day of Pentecost. The way Peter received, and Mary and all the saints is good enough for me. Why should we be an exception to the rule?[11]

TONGUES AS EVIDENCE OR GIFT OF TONGUES?

Although he had hesitated on the necessity of tongues as proof of Spirit baptism in the controversy within the Assemblies of God in 1918, W. T. Gaston, a later General Superintendent, made his position clear in the tract "The Sign and the Gift of Tongues" (n.d.). On the important differentiation between the function of tongues in the book of Acts and the gift of tongues in 1 Corinthians 12 and 14 for the stance on initial evidence, Gaston remarks:

In Mark 16 new tongues is mentioned as one of the signs that shall follow them that believe the Gospel. Three concrete examples are recorded in the book of Acts. In 1 Corinthians 12, we read that the gift of tongues was set in the Church. Its use is regulated in Chapter 14. Is "the sign" promised in Mark and fulfilled in Acts, and "the gift" defined and regulated in Corinthians always the same in essence and use? This is a live question today; as no honest, well-informed soul will deny that there are multiplied thousands of genuine cases of new tongues following the preaching of the Gospel today.

Many dear brethren contend that every genuine example is the gift of tongues; that the Baptism in the Spirit is for all believers, and that each believer so anointed, will receive one or more of the nine gifts—as He will; while an increasingly large number of Spirit-filled saints see a distinction in the province and use of tongues, in that initial experience in the outpouring of the Spirit as in the Acts, where the manifestation seems included and inherent in the larger experience of the Spirit Baptism. The yielded human vessel is controlled entirely by the divine Spirit—hence unlimited and unrestrained. And as a gift in the established assembly as at Corinth, where the manifestation is under the control of the anointed human mind, its exercise is limited and prescribed. This distinction in use is clearly marked in the Scriptures. . . .

Another reason why I cannot see that all speaking in tongues is the gift, in the limited and prescribed sense of 1 Corinthians 14, is because that apostolic instruction that governed the use of the gift in the assemblies, is in conflict with the practice of the apostles relative to the tongues phenomenon in the Pentecostal outpouring. First, observe, those who have the gift in the assembly, are to keep silence unless there is an interpreter; only speak to themselves and to God; and where there is an interpreter, they are to "speak by two, and at the most by three, and that by course; and let one interpret." That is, not more than three ought to speak in any one service, and one at a time; while one is to interpret. I repeat, these instructions are in open conflict with the practice of the apostles in the Acts. At Caesarea, the whole crowd magnified God in tongues without any effort on Peter's part to maintain order, and have the languages interpreted. And too, when we consider that they broke right in on the preacher's sermon, and the speaker an apostle, and no doubt mightily anointed, for Peter was not through his message—he said he had only fairly "began"; when these Gentiles began to speak in tongues, not once at a time in Bible order, but all at once. They surely spoiled a good sermon at Caesarea. But assuredly the Holy Spirit has a right to supersede even an apostle; and this is the simple but glowing account of the Holy Spirit falling upon, and taking possession of them. Peter might well forbear to speak to them, while God is condescending to speak through them.

. . . when by the Spirit Himself, using their yielded, enraptured faculties, they [the believers in Acts 2] began to magnify God, all at once, and in divers languages. Could anything be more in flagrant violation of the general understanding of "decency and order" in religious services? Yet the apostles did not attempt to call these assemblies to order. In fact they did it themselves, at Jerusalem (Acts 2:4).

I close with this remark, that to avoid making the Scriptures dealing with this subject contradict themselves, and Paul's teachings seriously disagree with his practice, we must see a distinction between the use of tongues, under the control of the mind and regulated by apostolic instruction, and that initial speaking in tongues which accompanied the outpouring of the Spirit in the Acts, where the candidate—mind, tongue and all— is controlled by the Spirit, without any attempt at regulation by any apostle at any time.[12]

IS THE DOCTRINE BIBLICAL?

In several articles in the *Pentecostal Evangel* following the debate over the doctrine of initial evidence, Daniel W. Kerr, the most influential theological spokesperson of the Assemblies of God in its earlier years, continued to explain and defend the teaching. In "Not Ashamed" he summed up the apology for the doctrine, declaring:

We are not ashamed of the Gospel of Christ. Neither are we ashamed of its initial physical sign in the baptism of the Holy Ghost. For on the face of the question, there is as much reason to believe that the great mass of Pentecostal people, who from the beginning, believed that the speaking in other tongues as the Spirit gives utterance, were right in their conclusions on this point, as to believe that those who oppose this distinctive testimony, were right in their conclusion. We admit this much. But we are not convinced that the Pentecostal people have been in error all these years of blessed fellowship with the Father and with His Son Jesus Christ in speaking in other tongues. A person that has eaten an apple or even just tasted it, is better qualified to speak on the question of the kind and quality of the apple, than one who only speaks from hearsay. Just so, those who have received the fullness of the baptism in the Holy Spirit, are better qualified to testify [to] that which they have experienced. Or is this experience limited to a few favorites in the family of God? Some say it is, while others say it is for all! Who is right? To the law and the testimony of the New Testament Scriptures. By it, and by it alone, we will stand or fall.[13]

FINAL REMARKS

Despite the temptation to defend the veracity of tongues as initial evidence on the basis of personal testimonies to the experience by many Pentecostals, proponents of the doctrine, like Kerr, diligently searched the Scriptures. It is quite apparent that along with other conservative Protestants, Pentecostals have used the "sola scriptura" principle, dating from the sixteenth-century Reformation, as the ideal in their praxis of theological formulation.

NOTES

1. For a discussion and survey of Pentecostal publications, see W. E. Warner, "Publications," *DPCM*, pp. 742–52.

2. For information on the Bosworth/Kerr debate within the Assemblies of God, see Carl Brumback, *Suddenly . . . From Heaven* (Springfield, Mo.: Gospel Publishing House, 1961), 216–25. The position of the Assemblies of God on the evidential necessity of tongues for Spirit baptism was decided at the General Council meeting in Springfield, Missouri, in September 1918. In essence, Bosworth proposed that glossolalia is but one of the gifts of the Spirit that God might choose to give to a believer as evidence of receiving the Spirit. Kerr, however, maintained that glossolalia was initial evidence for every recipient of Spirit baptism.

3. *Missionary Manual* (Springfield, Mo.: Foreign Missions Department, 1931), 6–7.

4. Aimee Semple McPherson, "Questions and Answers Concerning the Baptism of the Holy Ghost," *Word and Work*, "The Bridal Call Number," 8 September 1917, 487.

5. Stanley H. Frodsham, *Rivers of Living Water* (Springfield, Mo.: Gospel Publishing House, 1934), 21, 23–24.

6. John W. Welch, "What the Baptism Really Is," *Advance*, August 26, 1939, 6.

7. D. N. Buntain, *The Holy Ghost and Fire* (Springfield, Mo.: Gospel Publishing House, 1956), 33.

8. Frank W. Smith, "What Value Tongues?" *Message of the Open Bible*, June 1963, 5.

9. Thomas B. Barratt, "The Baptism of the Holy Ghost and Fire. What is the Scriptural Evidence?" Evangel Tract No. 953 (Springfield, Mo.: Gospel Publishing House, n.d.), 20–24.

10. E. C. Erickson, "The Bible on Speaking in Tongues," (Duluth, Minn.: Duluth Gospel Tabernacle; sermon preached on September 22, 1935), 8–9.

11. McPherson, "Questions and Answers," 487–88.

12. W. T. Gaston, "The Sign and the Gift of Tongues," Tract No. 4664 (Springfield, Mo.: Gospel Publishing House, n.d.), 3–4, 9–10, 11, 12.

13. D. W. Kerr, "Not Ashamed," *Pentecostal Evangel*, 2 April 1921, 5.

8

INITIAL EVIDENCE AND THE CHARISMATIC MOVEMENT: AN ECUMENICAL APPRAISAL

Henry I. Lederle

"The kingdom of Heaven is like treasure lying buried in a field. The man who found it, buried it again; and for sheer joy went and sold everything he had, and bought that field. Here is another picture of the kingdom of Heaven. A merchant looking out for fine pearls found one of very special value; so he went and sold everything he had, and bought it" (Matt. 13:44–46 NEB).

A contemporary symbolic reinterpretation (with no claim to exegetical value—even of the allegorical kind) of these brief parables of the King-dom may help to illustrate the basic contention of this essay. There is a valuable treasure hidden in a run-of-the-mill or—more poetically phrased—a pearl within the encasement of an oyster. The charismatic movement's approach to "initial evidence" is, simply stated, making a clearer distinction between the treasure (the pearl of great price) and its surroundings (the oyster). It would be hoped that the analogy will be-come sharper as we proceed.

The position of the charismatic movement regarding the American Pentecostal teaching that glossolalia constitutes the "initial (physical) evidence" of the baptism in the Holy Spirit can be succinctly stated: Most charismatics associate (renewal in or) being baptized in the Spirit with the manifestation of the charismata, which regularly include speaking in tongues—usually in a prominent position. Few charismatics accept that glossolalia is the condition *sine qua non* for Spirit baptism.

This latter position, where the validity of Spirit baptism hinges on glossolalia as a precondition, has even been derisively dubbed "the so-called law of tongues."[1] Phillip Wiebe points out that even where it is conceded that the classical cases in Acts, traditionally used by Pentecostals, do all contain references to glossolalia (and some charismatic scholars would contest this), there is no assertion anywhere in the New Testament claiming it as the *only* evidence.[2] Neither can it be convincingly established that glossolalia is the *first* effect of Spirit baptism. Speaking in tongues, so most charismatics would maintain, does constitute evidence that one has been baptized in the Spirit, but such evidence is not *conclusive*. The reason for this is simply that glossolalia as a religious phenomenon also occurs in spiritist circles and in non-Christian religions. It is even attested in totally secular contexts.[3]

The issue of "initial evidence" has been contentious within Pentecostalism from the beginning. It is historically unassailable that it was the novel linking of Spirit baptism with tongues as evidence that constituted the radically new point of departure in the teaching of the fledgling movement that spread like wildfire across the United States.[4] The history of the controversy about tongues as the exclusive evidence of Spirit baptism, embroiling prominent figures like F. F. Bosworth, A. B. Simpson, Jonathan Paul, and Leonhard Steiner (the organizer of the first Pentecostal World Conference in 1947), does not fall within the ambit of this essay. Nevertheless, the international Pentecostal community includes many in Germany, England, and Chile, for example, whose views on initial evidence resemble those of charismatics rather than those of American Pentecostals.[5]

Nevertheless, despite pressures to ameliorate this viewpoint, there have continued to be eloquent advocates of tongues as an essential sign. The British Assemblies of God theologian Donald Gee (1891–1966) considered this as a sacred trust never to be abandoned. He refuses to give in to the temptation to minimize the role of glossolalia:

> Experience has proved that wherever there has been a weakening on this point fewer and fewer believers have in actual fact been baptized in the Holy Spirit and the Testimony has tended to lose the fire that gave it birth and keeps it living.[6]

For these reasons, there is today a new restorationist trend within classical Pentecostalism seeking the fire and the vibrant freedom of the

Spirit experienced in the early days. At the same time, a counter-movement continues, which seeks higher levels of societal acceptance and integration into the mainstream of evangelical Christianity and even further afield in ecumenical dialogue. In this study, however, I believe a fresh look at the experience of Spirit baptism in those "good old days" of power and glory may be helpful.

THE PEARL

From the myriad of testimonies from the early days of Pentecost, I have chosen the following description of the "baptism in the Holy Spirit" from the year 1907. It is the testimony of that great pioneer of the healing ministry, John G. Lake, the Pentecostal "Apostle to Africa."[7] Gordon Lindsay gives the following description of Lake's "special anointing" of the Spirit:

> Shortly after my entrance into the ministry of healing, while attending a service where the necessity for the Baptism of the Spirit was presented, as I knelt in prayer and reconsecration to God, an anointing of the Spirit came upon me. Waves of Holy Glory passed through my being, and I was lifted into a new realm of God's presence and power. After this, answers to prayer were frequent and miracles of healing occurred from time to time. I felt myself on the borderland of a great spiritual realm, but was unable to enter in fully, so my nature was not satisfied with the attainment.[8]

Thereafter for nine months, Lake continued to pray for Spirit baptism, and then in the context of a night of prayer, the light of God shone around him and a voice spoke to him.

> I found myself in a center of an arc of light ten feet in diameter—the whitest light in all the universe. So white! O how it spoke of purity. The remembrance of that whiteness, that wonderful whiteness, has been the ideal that has stood before my soul, of the purity of the nature of God ever since.[9]

Soon afterwards, while preparing to pray for a woman who was sick, Lake had another experience which he compared to passing under a shower of warm tropical rain, which fell not upon him, but through him. In the ensuing calm, the Spirit spoke to him:

> "I have heard your prayers, I have seen your tears. You are now baptized in the Holy Spirit." Then currents of power began to rush through my being from the crown of my head to the soles of my feet. The shocks of power increased in rapidity and voltage. As these currents of power would pass through me, they seemed to come upon my head, rush through my body and through my feet into the floor. The power was so great that my body

began to vibrate intensely so that I believe if I had not been sitting in such a deep low chair I might have fallen upon the floor.[10]

The woman was healed, and Lake was filled with inexpressible joy and awe at the presence of God. This series of physical experiences represented to Lake a touch of God on his life. It also resulted in a deep love and compassion for all people, a desire to witness to the gospel of Christ, and a concern to "demonstrate His power to save and bless."[11]

Who would deny that this testimony illustrates the essence of Pentecost? We have here an illustration of the empowering dimension of "life in the Spirit," of the dynamic experiential quality of Christian life in which the charisms of the Spirit flow freely. This quality of "Pentecostal lifestyle" contrasted strongly with the sub-normal standards of Christian life and witness found among many nominal Christians of the time. Within the parameters of the present discussion, the remarkable feature is that nowhere in this whole testimony of Spirit baptism do we find any reference to glossolalia! (I am not suggesting, however, that Lake's testimony is at all typical of testimonies of this period with regard to the absence of a reference to tongues, but the mere fact that *one* such major figure makes no mention of glossolalia is in itself very significant.)

THE OYSTER

The "pearl of great price" has been identified above as "life in the Spirit." This dimension of dynamic Christian experience and openness to the presence and power of the Spirit in human lives is *elusive*—it cannot be pinned down. The wind blows where it wills (John 3:8). No formal structure can contain it. This frustrates the efficient "can do" mind-set of modernity. The children of the Enlightenment wish to work with empirical verification, intellectual guarantees, and linear causality. This tendency to formalize may be seen throughout the history of the church. Biblical thinking has never meshed well with this rationalistic proof-mentality, and as a result biblical ideas have sometimes been externalized, solidified, or domesticated in our theology. Donald Gelpi would speak of "reification."[12]

The deep-seated ideal for the church to remain in living contact with its apostolic heritage is the case in point. Where this linkage, which is a pneumatological reality, has become formalized, we are dealing with the husk instead of the kernel, with the encapsulating oyster rather than the pearl.

The pearl represents the living contact with our New Testament heritage, our bond with the faith of the *apostle*. It is significant that Bishop William J. Seymour, perhaps the father of modern Pentecostalism, after initially using another name, specifically selected the name "Apostolic Faith Mission" for the Azusa Street ministry. The largest Pentecostal church in South Africa still goes by this name. It can be noted in passing that the Faith and Order Commission of the World Council of Churches recently chose the same designation for their project to further the doctrinal unity of the church universal, namely, "Towards the Common Expression of the Apostolic Faith Today" (strange bedfellows?).[13]

Three major illustrations of this tendency to formalize our link with the apostolic faith of the early Christian church come to mind. The first of these *theologoumena* (rationalistic theological constructs according to A. A. Van Ruler) is the doctrine of apostolic succession.[14] I am taking this to mean the notion in sacramental churches (Orthodox, Roman Catholic, and Anglican) that the validity of episcopal ordination is somehow formally guaranteed by the external continuity which is seen as stretching back to the original apostolic eyewitnesses of the resurrection of Christ. The supposedly unbroken tactile ("hands on heads") sequence of ordinations is seen as certifying the continuation of apostolic authority and power. Where this description pertains, the doctrine of apostolic succession could function as a dangerous (magical?) substitute for the dynamic nature of the apostolic heritage as "life in the Spirit" linking with the witness, teaching, fellowship, and service of the original apostles.

The second temptation to formalize or reify our apostolic faith is found mostly among Protestants. The Scriptures, as the living word of God, are described in rationalistic categories such as "propositional truth" and "inerrant." Criteria based on Scottish common sense philosophy are anachronistically applied to the Bible—the book of faith and life, "a lamp to guide my feet and a light on my path" (Psa. 119:105). This Christian rationalism denies the dual authorship of the Bible (God and humankind), substituting in its place a docetic view of the Scriptures which is then bolstered by rationalistic apologetics attempting "to prove the credibility of Scripture by arguments and evidences."[15]

Another Protestant example of formalizing the apostolic faith is the largely Lutheran and Reformed tradition of *confessionalism*. In certain circles the written creeds and confessions of the Reformation era have in actuality greater doctrinal authority than the Bible. The living faith of the Reformers is hypostasized and elevated to become an absolute norm (in practice if not in theory). In both these instances, some Protestants have domesticated and externalized the apostolic life in the Spirit.

The third temptation to formalize or to try and pin down the apostolic heritage may be found among the "Third Force" (to use Henry P. Van Dusen's term), the Pentecostals.[16] G. J. Pillay speaks of glossolalia being regarded "as proof of apostolic experience."[17] Could not the doctrine of "initial evidence" function as an external empirical guarantee for the dynamic life in the Spirit, thereby providing a formalized structure which attempts to "domesticate" the Spirit? Surely an encounter with God should serve as the *gateway* to life in the Spirit, rather than as the *goal* which can always be formally verified *once* it has been reached![18]

It should be noted that the above critique is *not* directed against the historic succession of ordination in the church; neither is the unquestionable authority of the Bible as the unfailing and God-breathed word of God being contested. Similarly, there is no attempt here to challenge the validity of glossolalia as an inspirational and joyous charism of God's Spirit, either in the gathered assembly or as a private prayer language. But, the oyster is mistaken for the pearl when legitimate aspects of our apostolic faith (glossolalia) become formalized ("initial evidence"). Where this happens, the vulnerability of being continually dependent on the Spirit is circumvented by an external guarantee of life in the Spirit based on a single empirical event. I believe that the hesitancy among charismatics to embrace a full-fledged doctrine of initial evidence as sole condition for Spirit baptism rests not only on the lack of explicit or conclusive support for it in Scripture, but also on a general uneasiness about the "proof mentality" which it may harbor and which may lead to triumphalism and elitism.

One may also wonder if this hesitancy and uneasiness is limited to charismatics. David Barrett makes the following surprising statement in his statistical survey of Pentecostalism: "Most Pentecostal denominations teach that tongues-speaking is mandatory for all members, but in practice today only 35% of all members have practiced this gift either initially or as an ongoing experience."[19]

CLASSIFYING THE CHARISMATICS

After a theological analysis of initial evidence, we turn now to the term "charismatic." Up to now it has been used without making any distinctions. Although the movement is by no means homogeneous, I believe the generalizations made with respect to initial evidence do hold true. Charismatics broadly link tongues to Spirit baptism, but very few consider it as a necessary condition to validate the experience. To add some contours to the charismatic landscape, a taxonomy will now be attempted and the positions vis-à-vis initial evidence plotted on a sliding scale from 1 to 5. The following five positions are distinguished:

Value 1 represents a clear tendency to underplay the relevance and importance of tongues, denying initial evidence and sometimes even questioning the desirability of glossolalia as a charism.

Value 2 represents accepting tongues as a valid and desirable charism but denying any direct link to Spirit baptism.

Value 3 represents acknowledging that glossolalia provides a good basis for concluding that Spirit baptism has been experienced.

Value 4 represents the "package deal" view that, technically speaking, you do not *have to* speak in tongues but that you will (provided you are in the least open to it).

Value 5 represents the so-called *law* of tongues, i.e., everyone validly baptized in the Spirit has spoken in tongues (as a "sign") at least once. Glossolalia is the sole and necessary condition for Spirit baptism.

For the classification of *denominational* charismatics (those working for renewal in the Holy Spirit within denominational structures), the following three major categories developed in my study *Treasures Old and New* (1988) will be used.[20]

(A) The *neo-Pentecostals* differ from Pentecostals more in degree than in theological principle. In terms of Frederick Dale Bruner's "three pillars," they accept a "theology of subsequence" (two-stage pattern for Christian life), reject "conditions" to qualify for Spirit baptism, and feel uneasy about any Spirit baptism without glossolalia. They are spread over values 4 to 5.[21]

(B) The *sacramentalists* see Spirit baptism as the experiential "release" of the Spirit. This is the flowering of (infant) baptismal grace or the renewal of the sacrament of confirmation. They are spread over values 2 to 3.

(C) The *integrationists* seek to integrate charismatic experience into (for the most part) evangelical Christianity. Spirit baptism is viewed either as the final stage of Christian initiation; as tantamount to being filled with the Spirit; as renewal in the Spirit for the whole parish; or as a fresh "coming" of the Spirit, a spiritual breakthrough or growth experience. This position is represented by values 1 to 2. (Not dissimilar is the viewpoint that defines Spirit baptism as the charismatic dimension of normal Christian living. This would fall under value 2.)

Apart from the denominational renewal charismatics, attention has to be given to the independent or non-denominational groupings of charismatics. There are at least four theologically distinct streams:

(D) The *Faith movement* has been recently characterized as having "a specific emphasis on faith as a mechanism at the disposal of the believer to make him or her victorious."[22] This "creative" faith is applied especially in areas of health and prosperity.[23] With respect to glossolalia, I would identify their position as values 4 and 5.

(E) The *Shepherding* or *Discipleship movement* rejects denominational "tradition," wishing to restore the Kingdom ministry of the New Testament, to reestablish the fivefold pattern of ministry (Eph. 4:11) and to emphasize relationships rather than structures.[24] They fall under values 3 to 4.

(F) The *Signs and Wonders movement* (the "Third Wave") is characterized by employing spiritual power as a means of evangelism.[25] Their perspective on power healing involves the "equipping of the saints" in an every member ministry. They also underscore the importance of insight into worldviews. Their position on initial evidence would approximate to values 1 to 2.

(G) The *Dominion movement* is focused on reestablishing godly rule in the world and is influenced by theonomist and Christian reconstructionist thinking.[26] Revelatory prophecy is crucial and the Church is seen as the Tabernacle of David—a "Kingdom Now" perspective which challenges the traditional Pentecostal brand of dispensational premillennialism. Their position on tongues seems to straddle values 2 to 4.

THE CHARISMATIC CHALLENGE TO INITIAL EVIDENCE

In this essay a polemical or apologetical tone has been avoided, but in post-modern and post-positivistic scholarship, it is generally acknowledged that academic analysis is never neutral, never free of presuppositions, and a degree of advocacy is inevitable. In the choice of the symbols: the pearl and the oyster, I have placed my cards on the table. The Pentecostal pearl of great price is the dynamic life in the Spirit, i.e., being open to the supernatural reality of God and the full range of charisms as a present-day reality as one seeks to walk by the Spirit. This ongoing experience of Christ's power and presence cannot be guaranteed by the external requirement that all need to speak in tongues (on at least one occasion). It is for the pearl, or the treasure in the field, that we should sell everything we have and not for the oyster or the packaging in which the pearl often (but not always) comes (glossolalia). I believe that behind the insistence of Pentecostals like Donald Gee lies the fear that the pearl itself may be lost. This is to be respected. With the light presently at my disposal, I would submit that one should distinguish more clearly between the pearl and the oyster.

In the final analysis, the challenge of charismatics to those who teach initial evidence is to reflect on its validity afresh. It is probably not realistic to advocate the abandoning of this most distinctive teaching of American Pentecostalism. That may not even be necessary. It seems as if the call is for *a critical reinterpretation and reappropriation*. The history of recent ecumenical dialogue may shed some light on this complex issue.

There has been much progress made in the multilateral dialogues of the World Council of Churches and the bilateral dialogues of the major confessional communions of Christianity in the last thirty years. In the rigor of ongoing ecumenical scrutiny, many misunderstandings have been cleared up, many outdated concepts—influenced by philosophical categories no longer adhered to—discarded, and many new ways of looking at old insights discovered. A more accurate assessment into remaining differences has also been achieved. Three examples will suffice to illustrate the process: papal infallibility, "the great baptismal divide," and, a choice from my background, Calvinistic double predestination.

(1) It was discovered by Protestants that even behind the totally unacceptable doctrine of papal infallibility there is a "gospel intention," namely, the teaching that the Spirit will unfailingly guide the Church in all truth and that the gates of hell will not prevail against it. This evangelical promise to the church became individualized and centralized in the papacy as late as 1870. This is a tough nut to crack. In the Anglican and Roman Catholic dialogues, some "progress" was made in defining a Petrine office of central unity to which Anglicans were open.[27] The Fries-Rahner plan suggested a form of ecclesiastical unity in which Protestants acknowledge the value of a centralized administrative office, while Catholics continue to accept infallibility.[28] Neither of these interim compromises seems to have amounted to much.

(2) The Lima document of 1982 achieved a measure of convergence with regard to water baptism.[29] Both sides accepted the continuing character of Christian nurture. This led to the realization that the one tradition— infant baptism, followed by the expressing of personal commitment at confirmation or a public profession of faith—was somewhat paralleled by the other tradition of a presentation and blessing in infancy followed by the explicit act of believer's baptism. The existing differences also became less sharp when all acknowledged that baptism was to be seen both as God's gift and our human response to that gift.

(3) The vast majority of Reformed churches in Europe (the continent with the highest number of Calvinists) has accepted the Agreement of Leuenberg (1973).[30] This involved the drastic reinterpretation of John Calvin's "horrible decree" of the equal ultimacy of the elect and the reprobate. Election through free grace is maintained and linked to the call to salvation in Christ. That specific individuals have been eternally decreed for final condemnation by God is no longer accepted by those who had previously taught it. Even the condemnations of Lutherans in Reformed confessions were seen as being no longer applicable to present-day European churches. This consensus was not merely the result of the process of official ecumenical dialogue. It had been prepared by several decades of theological discussions and the publications of leading Reformed scholars such as G. C. Berkouwer. A small remnant of traditionalists who still espouse *double* predestination remain in some conservative "splinter" churches.

These examples highlight the difficulty as well as the positive results of the endeavor of dialogue. An official *dialogue between classical Pentecostals and denominational and independent charismatics* should be much easier than the cases referred to above, because the extent of existing consensus is so much greater between them. At such a dialogue, the gospel intention behind the initial evidence teaching could be probed and reassessed. Perhaps the influence of a collection of essays such as this might become a catalyst in the whole process.

> Here is another picture of the kingdom of Heaven. A merchant looking out for fine pearls found one of very special value; so he went and sold everything he had, and bought it (Matt. 13:45–46, NEB).

NOTES

1. T. A. Smail, *Reflected Glory: The Spirit in Christ and Christians* (London: Hodder and Stoughton, 1975), 40.
2. P. H. Wiebe, "The Pentecostal Initial Evidence Doctrine," *JETS* 27 (December 1984): 465–72.
3. L. C. May, "A Survey of Glossolalia and Related Phenomena in Non-Christian Religions," in *Speaking in Tongues: A Guide to Research on Glossolalia*, ed. Watson E. Mills (Grand Rapids: Eerdmans, 1986), 53–82.
4. J. R. Goff, Jr., *Fields White Unto Harvest: Charles F. Parham and the Missionary Origins of Pentecostalism* (Fayetteville: University of Arkansas Press, 1988), 62–86; H. Vinson Synan, *The Holiness-Pentecostal Movement in the United States* (Grand Rapids: Eerdmans, 1971), 95–116; Henry I. Lederle, *Treasures Old and New: Interpretations of "Spirit-Baptism" in the Charismatic Renewal Movement* (Peabody, Mass.: Hendrickson, 1988), 15–32.
5. W. J. Hollenweger, *The Pentecostals* (London: SCM Press, 1972; reprint, Peabody, Mass.: Hendrickson, 1988), 335.
6. Donald Gee cited in J. J. McNamee, "The Role of the Spirit in Pentecostalism. A Comparative Study" (Ph.D. diss., Eberhard Karls University, Tübingen, 1974), 50–51.
7. For information on Lake, see J. R. Zeigler, "Lake, John Graham," *DPCM*, 531.
8. G. Lindsay, *John G. Lake—Apostle to Africa* (Dallas: Christ for the Nations, 1972), 16.
9. Ibid., 17.
10. Ibid., 18.
11. Ibid., 19–20.
12. D. L. Gelpi, *Pentecostalism: A Theological Viewpoint* (New York: Paulist Press, 1971).
13. H.-G. Link, ed., *Apostolic Faith Today* (Geneva: World Council of Churches, 1985).
14. Cf., A. A. Van Ruler, *Calvinist Trinitarianism and Theocentric Politics*, trans. John Bolt (Lewiston, N.Y.: Edwin Mellen Press, 1989).

15. D. G. Bloesch, *Essentials of Evangelical Theology,* vol. 2, *God, Authority, and Salvation* (New York: Harper & Row, 1982), 76.

16. H. P. Van Dusen, "The Third Force," *Life* (9 June 1958): 122–24.

17. G. J. Pillay, "Text, Paradigms and Context: An Examination of David Bosch's Use of Paradigms in the Reading of Christian History," *Missionalia* 18 (April 1990): 120–21.

18. Cf., the title of the paper by a South African Pentecostal, G. R. Wessels, "The Baptism with the Holy Spirit—not a Goal, but a Gateway," read at the Pentecostal World Conference at Stockholm, Sweden, in 1955. See W. J. Hollenweger, ed., *Die Pfingstkirchen: Selbstdarstellungen, Dokumente, Kommentare* (Stuttgart: Evangelisches Verlagswerk, 1971), 177–78.

19. D. B. Barrett, "Statistics, Global," *DPCM,* 820.

20. Lederle, *Treasures,* chs. 2–4.

21. F. D. Bruner, *A Theology of the Holy Spirit: The Pentecostal Experience and the New Testament* (Grand Rapids: Eerdmans, 1970), ch. 3.

22. J. N. Horn, *From Rags to Riches* (Pretoria: UNISA, 1990), 117.

23. For the Faith or Positive Confession movement, see D. R. McConnell, *A Different Gospel: A Historical and Biblical Analysis of the Modern Faith Movement* (Peabody, Mass.: Hendrickson, 1988); also P. G. Chappell, "Healing Movements," *DPCM,* 353–74.

24. For the Shepherding or Discipleship Movement, see K. McDonnell, ed., *Presence, Power, Praise: Documents on the Charismatic Renewal,* 3 vols. (Collegeville, Minn.: Liturgical Press, 1980), vol. 2, 116–47; A. Walker, *Restoring the Kingdom: The Radical Christianity of the House Church Movement,* rev. ed. (London: Hodder and Stoughton, 1988); also H. D. Hunter, "Shepherding Movement," *DPCM,* 783–85.

25. For the Signs and Wonders Movement, see C. P. Wagner, *The Third Wave of the Holy Spirit* (Ann Arbor, Mich.: Servant Publications, 1988); John Wimber with Kevin Springer, *Power Evangelism* (San Francisco: Harper & Row, 1987).

26. For the Dominion Movement, see W. A. Griffin, "Kingdom Now: New Hope or New Heresy," a paper presented to the 17th annual meeting of the Society for Pentecostal Studies, Virginia Beach, Virginia, 12–14 November 1987.

27. For information on the Anglican and Roman Catholic Dialogue, see H. Meyer and L. Vischer, eds., *Growth in Agreement: Reports and Agreed Statements of Ecumenical Conversations on a World Level* (Geneva: World Council of Churches, 1984).

28. For information on the Fries-Rahner plan, see H. Fries and K. Rahner, *Unity of the Churches—An Actual Possibility* (Philadelphia: Fortress, 1985).

29. For the Lima document, see *Baptism, Eucharist and Ministry* (Geneva: World Council of Churches, 1982), Faith and Order paper No. 111.

30. For the Agreement of Leuenberg, see Link, *Apostolic Faith Today,* 168–74.

II

INITIAL EVIDENCE
AND THE BIBLICAL TEXT:
FOUR PERSPECTIVES

9

SOME NEW DIRECTIONS IN THE HERMENEUTICS OF CLASSICAL PENTECOSTALISM'S DOCTRINE OF INITIAL EVIDENCE

Donald A. Johns

I write this essay as a "classical Pentecostal." First, that means that I hold that there is a distinct experience of the believer with the Spirit of God that can be separated from conversion, an experience in which the believer enters a new phase in relationship with the Spirit. Classical Pentecostals call this experience "being baptized in the Holy Spirit,"[1] and for the purposes of this essay, we may use the term "separability" to refer to the characteristic of this experience as separate from conversion. Second, as a classical Pentecostal, I believe that this experience is accompanied by a particular activity known as "speaking in tongues" (i.e., speaking in a language[2] that is unknown to the speaker, the Spirit giving the words to say); moreover, I contend that these "tongues" can be used as evidence that a believer has been baptized in the Spirit. There are other, later kinds of evidence of being baptized in the Spirit; so to allow for these my tradition has generally adopted the phrase "initial physical evidence" to denote the "evidential value" of speaking in tongues (again, terms to which we will refer later). These two beliefs—"separability" and "evidential value" of speaking in tongues—are the two distinctive tenets of classical Pentecostalism.

I have pictured my primary audience as being classical Pentecostals, people who already hold these two tenets to be true. With this audience in mind, I do not intend this essay to be a full exposition or defense of these principal doctrines. Rather, this essay will suggest how past hermeneutical models may be inadequate for explicating the doctrine of initial evidence, and it will indicate how recent tools of biblical scholarship can show that there is a solid exegetical base for the doctrines of separability and evidential value.

I adopt this approach because traditional classical Pentecostal hermeneutics[3] has been faulted for failing to provide an adequate exegetical foundation for Pentecostalism's two distinctive tenets. To suggest that there has been a failure in any sense may upset some classical Pentecostals. But this truth has been demonstrated in a very pragmatic way by the number of people who are now ex-Pentecostals. Many of these I went to Bible college with or later taught. To be sure they are a minority, but they are a significant minority. Their classical Pentecostal doctrinal framework collapsed when it was overloaded by the tough questions of non-Pentecostal scholars. But I have become firmly convinced that constructive application of the tools of biblical scholarship need not undermine Pentecostalism's doctrines; rather, their proper use can greatly strengthen the exegetical and hermeneutical bases for the two distinctively classical Pentecostal tenets of separability and the evidential value of tongues. In this sense, then, my observations may be able to contribute toward a full exposition of those tenets, or even toward a defense.

Often special training is required to use the tools of biblical scholarship properly. But all classical Pentecostals can make use of the generally accepted results of the scholarly specialists in biblical studies. With this in mind, I consciously address my remarks not only to classical Pentecostal biblical scholars, but also to the rest of the classical Pentecostals who rely on their work.

THE INADEQUACY OF PAST FRAMEWORKS

The inadequacy of past frameworks for arguing the validity of separability and evidential value is visible in three areas: (1) Pentecostals have not responded to arguments that read Luke's Acts in light of Paul's understanding of the Spirit, which associates the Spirit more with conversion than empowerment and does not lend itself to viewing the coming of the Spirit as an experience separate from conversion. Pentecostalism's weakness here lies in our lack of an adequate means for dealing, on the one hand, with Pauline statements about every believer having received the Spirit; and, on the other hand, we have neglected to deal soundly with passages in Luke–Acts that describe post–Easter disciples as people who needed to receive the Spirit. Pentecostals can address this problem by adopting and refining accepted interpretive methods.

(2) Concerning the issue of the value of tongues as evidence of being baptized in the Spirit, Pentecostals have been faulted also for their inductive "pattern approach" to proving that doctrine. That is, on the three occasions where people receive the Spirit in the Lucan sense for the first time, and where there is any description of the event, speaking in tongues is mentioned in close connection with receiving the Spirit. These texts are Acts 2:1–12; 10:44–48 (see also 11:15–18); and 19:1–7. Two other passages are sometimes included, but these have questionable value.[4] Of the three, the most compelling text is Acts 10:44–48, which explains how Peter and his associates knew that Cornelius and his family and friends had received the Spirit: "for" (Greek: *gar*) they heard them speaking in tongues and praising God; they received the Spirit in the same way that the Jerusalem disciples had. The inadequacy of the pattern approach is that it is simple inductive reasoning. For inductive reasoning, the more cases observed the better, but there are only three valid supporting cases (although there are no cases which actually contradict the pattern). Establishing a pattern by means of inductive reasoning was the best way classical Pentecostals had of dealing with narrative biblical texts. But this approach is vulnerable on several fronts: for example, there are only a relatively few cases to observe; moreover, the method is inconsistent. After all, there are other patterns in Acts that classical Pentecostals do not use doctrinally. Here again classical Pentecostalism may find an ally in the resources of biblical scholarship, particularly in the recent contributions of literary and narrative criticism and theology. With these tools they can meet the challenge of showing how historical narrative indeed teaches normative theology.

(3) Pentecostal hermeneutical formulations can also be served by investigating the nature of language and meaning. For example, in what sense does "baptized in the Spirit" name the experience Pentecostals claim? This problem too is related to the Luke/Paul question, but it also involves the range of and nature of the language that Luke uses to describe the relationship of the Spirit to the believer.

We might note that classical Pentecostals have often associated any techniques that have "criticism" or "critical" in their names with attacks on the truthfulness or authority of Scripture, so again I mention that I am calling for a constructive application of these techniques.

It may seem to some that I am calling for a complete revision of classical Pentecostal hermeneutics. But this is not really so. In some cases we will discover that classical Pentecostal hermeneutics intuitively adopted techniques that are present in contemporary biblical scholarship in a more developed and polished form. In such cases, I simply call for a conscious adoption and refinement of principles that are not so far from what we are already tacitly using. In other cases, the suggested techniques will be new to most classical Pentecostals, but their constructive use can and should be integrated into Pentecostalism's current overall hermeneutical approach.

I should note at this point that I did not adopt any of these techniques in order to deal with the inadequacies of current classical Pentecostal hermeneutics. Rather, I adopted a constructive use of these techniques because of the nature of the Bible and its individual writings. There are other tools as well, but they are not as central to classical Pentecostal issues, and so they are not appropriate for inclusion in an essay like this.

In the next section of this essay I will explore those three areas that I have briefly identified above and will examine how the tools of biblical scholarship can prove useful for explicating the chief doctrines of Pentecostalism. Finally, I will explicitly comment on the two issues that define one as a classical Pentecostal: separability and the evidential value of tongues.

BIBLICAL THEOLOGY AND
THE SPIRIT IN LUKE AND PAUL

The contributions of biblical scholarship significant for our purposes concern the nature of biblical theology. The success of the classical Pentecostal tenet of the separability of being baptized in the Spirit depends on whether it is appropriate hermeneutically to read Luke on his own terms instead of viewing Luke through the lens of Paul.

To understand the nature of biblical theology, one must first distinguish it from systematic theology. Systematic theology builds a unified description of God's truth from particular philosophical and theological perspectives. Unfortunately, the emphasis on unity has often led to systematic theology's building doctrines by taking individual verses from all over Scripture and using them as if they were all written by the same human author at the same time, to the same audience. But the New Testament as well as the Old is a collection of documents, many or even most of which were written to different people in specific but different situations. The nature of the biblical texts makes it impossible to immediately jump from an individual verse to a doctrine of systematic theology. We must rather take a somewhat longer route and consider the unique self-revelation of God to each author of Scripture, the experiences and background of each author, and the needs of the community addressed. All of these factors affect the way that each author perceives what I call the structures of theological truth: what the theological themes are, how they are related to each other, and how they are applied to human lives, as well as the different ways each author uses words and larger language-forms.

Now, I am aware that there is no single universally accepted definition of biblical theology, but as a working definition we might say that biblical theology will first set forth the theology of a New Testament author in his own terms, categories, and thought forms.[5] Once this is done for each New Testament author, the resulting presentations can be related to each other, networks of connections established, and points of contrast also established. But no one author should be given primacy over the others; especially the interpreter should not use one writer's theological structures as an outline into which all the other writers' theologies are made to fit. Neither should the interpreter force one author's meaning for a term on all the other authors.

A sensitivity to these principles of sound biblical theology is vital because one significant challenge to the Pentecostal view of separability has come from trying to make Luke fit the Pauline mold in terminology and theological structure. That is, according to the more systematic approach, the Spirit is received at conversion (which Paul actually says), and only at conversion (which Paul does *not* say, but that is how the argument goes). The principles of a biblical theology expose the flaw in such an approach and in turn offer a firmer basis for the classical Pentecostal tenet of separability. If Luke's presentation of receiving the Spirit is fully developed within his own theological structures, it should be evident that Luke and Paul will not always write about the same aspects of the relationship between the believer and the Spirit.[6] The relationship between the believer and the Holy Spirit is a complex one, and no single New Testament author discusses the totality of it. Luke emphasizes Spirit-empowered ministry, but largely ignores both the ethical aspects of the Spirit in the believer and the role of the Spirit in conversion. Paul discusses all three. But that is okay—a biblical theological approach lets each New Testament author be himself and say what he wants to say, even if it differs in perspective from another writer, and whether or not one wrote a letter and the other told a story.

Another implication of developing a biblical theology rather than a systematic theology is that Pentecost is not the "birthday of the church." What is at stake here? If the church comes into existence as such at Pentecost, then it can be (and is) argued that the baptism in the Spirit and the associated phenomena that Luke describes involve a one-time giving of the Spirit to the church as a whole. Pentecost did initiate a new phase in the relationship of the Holy Spirit and the church, and therefore the individual believers who made up the church, but Pentecost was not the beginning of that relationship. Pentecost as described in Acts must be interpreted primarily within Luke's theological structures, not Paul's, and for Luke, the church is in direct continuity with the people of God of the old covenant. Any notion of Pentecost as "birthday of the church" is thus foreign to his understanding. Moreover, for Luke, if any shift to the church as a new, identifiable group is to be made, it must begin with John the Baptist's call, which began the process of the distillation of the people of God into an identifiable group that would ultimately result in the church as we know it today.[7] Thus, the pre-Pentecost church can be described in the Pauline terms of Romans 8:9–11, i.e., they "had the Spirit of Christ," they were "in the Spirit," and the Spirit was "living in them." But Luke can still record the coming of the Spirit as a *coming* and have little or nothing to say about the role of the Spirit in conversion,[8] because he is interested in the role of the Spirit in spreading the Good News.

The contribution of biblical theology also comes into play with Acts 8:4–24, cautioning us not to mistrust Luke's judgment when he states that the Samaritans "believed." They were now members of God's people. Not having received the Spirit in the Lucan sense had nothing to do with whether or not they were members of God's people. Still, it was a matter of concern to the apostles and called for their attention.

In a similar text in Acts 19, the people were already "disciples," members of God's people, although they have been left behind by developments in salvation history. Paul,[9] perhaps suspecting that such was the case, found out that they did not receive the Spirit when they believed.[10] He inquires further and learns that these disciples were located in the John-the-Baptist stage of salvation history. Their response is *not* a statement that they have not even heard that there was such a thing as the Spirit. Their almost certain familiarity with John's message and the Old Testament should preclude such a translation. Rather, taking a cue from the similar construction in John 7:39, I understand their statement to mean that they had not heard that the Baptist's prophecy of the Coming Baptizer had been fulfilled, that people were being baptized in the Spirit.

In any case, these disciples are brought up to date; they respond in faith and are baptized. Then the Holy Spirit comes upon them, providing a fitting closure to Luke's treatment of receiving the Spirit. As the message concerning the Spirit began with John the Baptist, so now at last a group of his own disciples finally receive the Spirit.

In Acts 10, we should first note that Luke again shows continuity between the old and the new. This Gentile household worshiped the one true God. In the metaphorical vision to Peter in verse 15, God indicates that he has cleansed Cornelius and his household, and they are not to be called common or secular, which is to say that they should be treated as members of God's people. In 10:35, Peter concludes that Cornelius and his household are already acceptable to God. In 10:36–38, it seems that these Gentiles are already aware of the message that Jesus preached, although perhaps not of the final outcome of Jesus' ministry: his death and resurrection. A strong case can be made that Cornelius and company were already members of the people of God as defined by Luke. The case is quite a bit stronger than a case built from 11:14, 18, that Cornelius was not yet a member of God's people. My view of the status of Cornelius and his household is certainly in line with Luke's theme of the universality of the offer of salvation.

Looking at the actual event, the believers from among the circumcised[11] who came with Peter were amazed, not that the Gentiles could be saved, but that they too could receive the gift of the Spirit. The amazement at salvation comes later, and is on the part of the larger church at Jerusalem.

THEOLOGY AND NARRATIVE WORD OF GOD

People use different language forms and genres to accomplish different goals. The Bible contains many of these forms and genres. The whole Bible is the message of God to humanity ("word of God"), i.e., God is behind its production, and it communicates what he wants it to communicate. If so, then the *set of goals* that our hermeneutics must adopt in general is one that is inductively dictated by the forms and genres and their uses, not by a single goal of doctrine. The specific set of goals adopted will vary with the specific kind of text. Luke chose to write narrative, not expository discourse, and so the hermeneutical goals we adopt must be appropriate. These will include doctrine, but they should not be limited to it.

Most biblical scholars today agree that biblical narratives express the theological views of their authors. This used to be a point of contention between classical Pentecostals, who claimed narrative could teach theology and could therefore be used as a base for doctrine, and many non-Pentecostals, who claimed it could not.

This is not to say that most biblical scholars necessarily view the theology taught by narrative (or any other kind of biblical text, for that matter) as binding on modern believers. That depends on the particular scholar's views on the authority of Scripture. The point I want to make is that biblical scholarship has developed tools to mine the theology that the authors of biblical narrative express through their works.

To understand what this means for dealing with narrative texts, we first must determine what narrative texts do in human communication. Narrative can teach directly: biblical authors often include speeches of their characters to get their own points across, and the comments of the narrator often evaluate or explain an event narrated. This is significant for the classical Pentecostal, because the narrator in Acts 10:46 explicitly assigns evidential value to speaking in tongues and states that this was the view of Peter and his associates. Then Peter, in Acts 10:47 and 11:15–17, states that the Gentiles received the gift of the Spirit in the same way as the disciples did on the day of Pentecost.

Redaction Criticism

Apart from these author-approved speeches, however, the exegete needs a special set of tools to get at the message that the author wanted to teach. One of the best tool kits for that purpose is redaction or composition criticism.[12] Redaction criticism looks at how a New Testament author uses his sources: certain things are chosen, others are left out, and if selection of material shows a theologically motivated pattern, then the author's (inspired) theological perspective can be established. A description of theological perspectives that the biblical author incorporated into the narrative is primary source material for establishing a biblical theology, in our case, a Lucan theology. Given my conservative view of the inspiration and authority of Scripture and of the theology that each author teaches, this description will also affect doctrine. Authors also arrange material in different ways, and this too can show theological perspectives. In addition, authors modify material, e.g., summarizing, paraphrasing, clarifying, and changing perspective. Finally, authors write their own material, which should not be taken to mean they were writing fiction; they could compose accounts without falsifying the information that the accounts contain.[13]

It is also true that the best results here can be obtained when a source is available for comparison to the work under study (e.g., Mark as a source for Luke, or Samuel-Kings as a source for Chronicles). If the source is available, it is beyond doubt where selection, arrangement, and modification have occurred. But even when working with other materials, redaction critics pay attention to specific points of detail when looking for the theological concerns of the author. These points of detail are objectively present in the text, and the redaction critics' observations often prove valuable. Further, if practiced properly, there are controls that prevent trying to make the text say what it does not say.

Redaction criticism is one of the areas that is similar to what classical Pentecostals have been doing all along, drawing out the theology expressed by narrative texts, specifically those of Acts. But using an actual discipline would make the results of our exegesis much more precise and stronger. One example from the work of redaction critic Robert F. O'Toole is that in Acts, "the disciples continue the work of Jesus."[14] O'Toole cannot be said to be a Pentecostal, but his insights, especially concerning the prophetic ministries of both Jesus and his post-Pentecost followers,[15] parallel several of the findings of Pentecostal author Roger Stronstad in his *Charismatic Theology of Saint Luke* (1984). Moreover, O'Toole provides a larger Lucan theology framework into which Stronstad's conclusion, that Pentecost involves the transferral of charismatic ministry from Jesus to his disciples, can fit.

The main area, though, where I see redaction criticism helping classical Pentecostals is in exegeting the main Pentecostal texts in Acts. It can contribute much toward a firmer base for both separability and the evidential value of speaking in tongues, by helping to expose Luke's motives behind choosing to report speaking in tongues and choosing to report that some believers had not received the Spirit, and so on.

Narrative Theology

Narrative theology, a relatively new discipline within hermeneutics, asserts that the story-form itself has significance for theology. This discipline is aimed not so much at translating biblical stories into doctrines as in helping us understand how people use stories, and therefore what effect biblical stories should have on us.[16] These effects are not doctrine, but they are significant both for doctrine and for living one's life in the world in relation to God and other people.

One way that people use stories is cohesively, to give a group an identity, to tell a group about itself, to promote bonding of the whole, and to promote behavior and experience consistent with the group's identity. We especially recount stories of the beginnings of a group, or pivotal points in the group's history, or stories that reveal the genius, the essential qualities of that group.[17] "How can the church preach the Good News about Jesus so powerfully?" I can hear Theophilus asking. "Well," Luke says, "let me tell you a story. On the day of Pentecost. . . ." This function of stories is relevant because the stories of Acts tell the church about itself, about its essential qualities, and concerning Pentecost itself, about a pivotal point that inaugurates a new essential quality, being filled with the Spirit, which has as a goal effective, powerful, God-directed service. Although it is possible to abstract this theological point into propositional terms as I have just done, the theological point can be perceived directly through the story.

Narrative theology also shows how stories help me to structure my "world." This statement calls for a little explanation. The objective world, the total of reality, even that part of the total that I come in contact with, is too complex, unorganized, and perhaps too frightening for me to live in. So I reduce objective reality into a somewhat simplified understanding of it, something I can handle, namely, my "world."[18] Here I can find order. I understand how my "world" works, and that provides me with a sense of security. Then I superimpose my "world" on *the* world: I superimpose my version on objective reality. My version filters external data and experiences. Most people cannot tell the difference between their own "world" and the real objective world because the one is superimposed on the other and because anything that does not fit their own version is filtered out, discarded as untrue, or simply ignored. But back to the point: the real world is a world of movement and life, and stories provide the principles that do the structuring of one's own "world," not in static abstraction, but in vital action.[19]

Amos N. Wilder believes that the overarching biblical story provides order to the believer's "world," although it is shown to be an order that is always threatened by chaos or anarchy or false images of reality. According to Wilder, biblical stories provide a "house of being," a place where we can find order, security, and meaning. Further, these stories form the basic patterns for our own personal stories.[20] If I treat this characteristic seriously, then biblical stories, including those of immediate interest in Acts, should provide an ordering of my own "world" and a paradigm or pattern of how to live my life, what kind of experiences to expect with God, etc.

Now, any given story might really provide only one small room in the "house of being." But the better the story, the better it matches my already existing "world," and the more importance I attach to the story, the more I will use it to live in the real world. Conversely, a good story that does not match my already existing "world" may have the effect of leading me to change my "world."

Part of the power of a story to strengthen, shape, or change my "world" comes from the ability of a story to captivate the imagination of the reader. A story builds a small replica of the real world in the imagination of the reader, but it is a replica governed by its own rules. As the reader's imagination is drawn into the story, the world of the story becomes the reader's own "world," to a certain depth, and for a period of time. Sooner or later the reader must reemerge from the story world. But the way in which we perceive the real objective world will probably have changed somewhat. Sometimes the change is almost imperceptible—perhaps we become a little more hardened to violence after watching a TV show. Other times the change may be more dramatic, as when we find our "world" shattered by one of Jesus' parables, finding out that God does not play by our rules.

Biblical stories not only help to provide structure for my "world," they provide an inspired sample of someone else's "world," a sample that God wants me to experience by entering the story world of the biblical text. It is easy to respond intuitively to a contemporary story—what is hard is an interpretation that consciously reproduces and sets forth the mechanics of that intuitive response. But the "otherness" of the world of the Bible makes this kind of analysis even more necessary to mold our intuitive responses and help us to respond to the biblical story correctly. We have to understand the kind of response a story would have evoked from the various kinds of readers to whom that story was first told, and then reread the story with that response in mind.

Moreover, God has revealed himself, which includes revealing truth about himself—more or less the idea of "doctrine." But revealing himself is more than just revealing data: it is also encounter. The record of these encounters is now preserved for all of God's people in the stories of Scripture. As I encounter truth about God in the Bible, it becomes revelation of God's truth to me. However, biblical narrative also records the encounter itself, not just truth about God. As I read biblical narrative and enter the biblical story world, I can through reading experience these encounters with God, and this experience should include a personal encounter with God, as the Spirit uses the narrative word of God to address me. These experiences inside the biblical story world are intended to shape and guide my experiences *outside* the biblical story world. And one of the primary encounters of God with his people in the book of Acts is the receiving of the Spirit.

Thus, interpreting a biblical narrative text is not merely reconstructing a historical account, although that is one valid use of a biblical historical narrative like Acts. Rather, the inspired author believed that a story had a continuing significance to the community of faith. Luke maintained the story form in Acts because the significance of what he wanted to communicate is more directly perceived through story than through expository prose, and probably because he wanted to affect the reader in ways that could not be done by any form other than story.

Biblical narrative as word of God, then, calls for a hermeneutics that first of all pays serious attention to the world that a biblical story builds. Such a hermeneutics must assist the reader to enter the world of the story and *experience* the rules or principles by which the biblical story world operates. In Acts, these will include the stories of receiving the Spirit. After all, these stories are word of God, whereas our doctrine based on Scripture is not. The patterning or paradigmatic effect of stories is automatic when stories are told in settings that invoke the cohesive use of language within a community. But given our distance in time and culture from the biblical world, our hermeneutics should explicitly help the reader reflect on the patterning or paradigmatic effect that each story should have.

Second, entering the biblical story world in Acts will also involve vicariously receiving the Spirit, and this should lead to a real personal experience of being baptized in the Spirit, one that can then be evaluated against the stories Luke told. Here, then, is another area where classical Pentecostals intuitively adopted a similar approach. Classical Pentecostals explicitly evaluate their experience against the biblical stories. Many times I have filled out forms from my own denominational institutions where the question was asked, "have you been baptized in the Holy Spirit according to Acts 2:1–4?"

Third, hermeneutics must retain doctrine as a major goal. Thus, the hermeneutics I would propose must also be able to examine the house of being that a story creates and recognize the significance of the structures, principles, forces, relationships, and dynamics that are involved. Where these are theological, they must be incorporated into both biblical and systematic theology. Thus, Luke tells stories of Pentecost and of other occasions when people were baptized in the Spirit. In so doing, he constructs a story world that effectively claims that the real world operates by the same principles. This is very close to what the term "normative" means in the ongoing "normal versus normative"[21] discussion regarding speaking in tongues. That is, Luke seems to be claiming that one of these principles by which the real world operates is that a person speaks in tongues as vital evidence of the overall experience of being baptized in the Spirit.

THE NATURE OF LANGUAGE AND
MEANING AND HERMENEUTICS

Literary Criticism: Metaphor

Biblical theology involves understanding the individual author's use of theological terminology and using it in setting forth the author's theological structures. When we examine Luke's terminology for receiving the Spirit, we find that much of it is metaphorical.[22]

In recent literary-critical studies, the understanding of metaphor has exploded beyond the familiar bounds of "a comparison that does not use 'like' or 'as.' " Today, metaphor is seen not as illustrating an already known meaning. Rather, a metaphor *creates* meaning by putting an image on top of the real world. Metaphor then asks the hearer to visualize the real world through the image as if the image were a window that shapes and colors the view. There comes a moment of insight as we use our imaginations to understand reality by using the window of the image.

Using a metaphor is one of the few ways people can stretch human language to apply to new situations. It should not be surprising that much of Luke's terminology involving the reception of the Spirit is metaphorical, since Pentecost inaugurated a new phase in the relationship of God to his people. But after metaphors have been in circulation for a while, they no longer stimulate the imagination to create meaning. They become "dead" (note the metaphorical term), and when used they are heard simply as literal language, not figurative. It takes a conscious effort to bring a metaphor back to life, to restore its power to once again create meaning for the hearer or reader. Many of Luke's metaphorical terms now need this restorative work.

Whenever an exegete studies theological terms in Scripture, there is a risk of confusing lexicography with doing theology. Still, if it is the business of a New Testament theologian to set forth the theology of a New Testament writer in his own terms, categories, and thought forms, a study of the writer's theological terminology can be significant. In addition, since metaphor creates meaning in the imagination of the reader, it can be the bearer of more theological insight than a similar amount of nonmetaphorical language. The significance of metaphor for this essay, then, is that by analyzing the meaning generated by the metaphors both individually and collectively, we classical Pentecostals could better understand the Lucan view of the relationship of the Spirit to the believer.

Luke chose metaphorical terms that asked the original readers to use several mental pictures to understand receiving the Spirit. Some of these metaphors are new, others may have been somewhat conventional, having an Old Testament derivation. However, even a familiar Old Testament image can have power restored to it when it is applied to such a perplexing and unfamiliar event as the church speaking in tongues and praising God on the day of Pentecost. But since there are several metaphors that describe receiving the Spirit in Acts, we should initially conclude that the image produced by any of the metaphors cannot be ultimate. No one term, even a metaphorical one, can adequately cover even this rather narrow range of the human experience of the Spirit of God.

These metaphor-generated images are necessary, but they are not yet the end for the person whose task it is to discuss the experience in terms of systematic theology. In the systematic area, we must ask why each metaphor was used to depict the underlying spiritual reality, and how these metaphors complement each other and work together to build a fuller impression of that reality. Behind these metaphors is another person, a divine person, the Holy Spirit, who is not a thing or a liquid. Yet, because the Spirit is so "other," the images are necessary to grasp some understanding of what the relationship between Spirit and believer involves. Finally, while systematic theology requires us to translate these metaphors to expository theological speech, biblical theology requires us to retain them and use them in presenting Luke's theological themes and structures. Since this essay is mostly concerned with being baptized in the Spirit, we can briefly examine that metaphor. We will find that it is significant especially with regard to separability.

In the extant recorded memories of John the Baptist's message there are several images of the Coming One. These are to a great extent visual icons, metaphors: John himself was a baptizer, and he prepared the way for an eschatological baptizer. John becomes the "picture-half" of a metaphor describing the Coming One. But the baptizing of the Coming One would be of a different order, not using a physical liquid for immersion but rather the divine power, the Spirit of the Lord viewed in Old Testament terms. John also uses metaphors himself, looking to agricultural practices for the images of burning unproductive fruit trees and of separating the wheat from the chaff and burning the chaff. (It is probable that the reuse of the fire image for destruction of the chaff and the unproductive fruit trees should caution the reader about wanting to be baptized in the Holy Spirit *and fire*, a phrase that has some currency among classical Pentecostals.) The role of the Coming One would be to bring the kingdom of God, which brings blessings for those who surrender to it, and destruction to those who will not submit.[23] The blessings are here particularized as being baptized in the Spirit.

The reader may not remember John's imaging of Jesus after Jesus has appeared on the scene and constructed his own definition of himself as the Son of Man (however that phrase really ought to be understood). Although they are dormant, these images are still in place, and they are reactivated at the end of Luke (24:49) and the beginning of Acts (1:5–8) by Jesus himself. He tells his disciples that their great task will soon begin, but they must wait for the actualization in their lives of the image used by John the Baptist: they would be baptized in the Holy Spirit.

The wait is significant because it lets Jesus physically exit the stage. Whatever being baptized in the Spirit involves, it does not require the physical presence of the eschatological Baptizer.[24]

But back to the end of Luke and the beginning of Acts. The metaphoric structures are reactivated, but also enriched by the addition of other images. One significant difference is that Jesus does not call attention to himself as the Baptizer; rather, he focuses attention on the activity of the Father. In Acts 2:33 Peter will, however, reaffirm Jesus' role of receiving the promised Spirit from the Father and pouring out that Spirit on the disciples.

In the opening of Acts, we are justified in contrasting 1:5 with 1:8. In v. 8, Jesus points to a worldwide mission of his disciples and promises that they would receive power for that mission "when the Holy Spirit comes upon them." Will this power be one that will come and persist? Or will it come as needed? The latter seems correct since Acts reports that Peter and Paul were "filled with the Spirit" on three distinct occasions each.[25] The aorist participle in 1:8 could easily be rendered "whenever [the Holy Spirit] comes upon [you]." On the other hand, v. 5 with its baptizing terminology appears to point to a single specific event in these disciples' lives: "In a few days you will be baptized in the Holy Spirit."

This event would also, of course, be the first "coming upon," "receiving power," and "being filled" as well. Thus, it seems probable that, while all these metaphors are interconnected, Luke has Jesus hinting at a distinction of the baptizing term from the others. That is, for any given person, the baptizing image is used concerning initiatory aspects and is not repeated with each "filling" or "coming upon."

All of the non-Pauline usages of being baptized in the Spirit are placed in contrast with John's baptism, and since John's baptism was initiatory, the change effected by being baptized in the Spirit should be viewed as in some sense initiatory. But this initiatory sense is not that of inclusion in the people of God, i.e., salvation; that is precluded by Lucan theology.

But Lucan theology does suggest that being baptized in the Spirit is an initiation into powerful, effective service, a service that especially involves inspired prophetic speech.[26]

Semantics: Syntagmatic Relationships

Analysis of syntagmatic relations and their contribution to meaning is especially helpful in discussing being baptized in the Spirit, since so many of the terms that describe the experience are actually phrases, and of course all occur within sentence syntax. Syntagmatic relationships (also called "collocational relationships") are the relationships that words can enter into with each other within sentence syntax as a result of their interacting meanings. Some combinations of words are appropriate, while others are not.[27] For example, we use words like "drink" and "strong" with "coffee," but we do not use "eat" or "powerful." So, "drink" and "strong" can form syntagmatic relationships with "coffee," but "eat" and "powerful" cannot. Analysis of syntagmatic relationships attempts to understand the reasons why certain combinations are appropriate, and what the interaction of the words' meanings contributes to understanding the combined whole.

The study of syntagmatic relations of words in nonmetaphorical speech should be the key in figuring out what the syntagmatic relations expressed in metaphorical speech mean. Keep in mind that the syntagmatic relations that are possible for a word are primarily a matter of unwritten usage rules of a language, rules that are the private property of no individual. They will tend to be consistent between authors, although they will not be completely so. It is not possible to analyze each term in depth here, but we can show the relevance of the analysis of syntagmatic relations to the issue of separability.

Considerations involving the syntagmatic relationships of *baptizō* have led me to identify 1 Corinthians 12:13 as a text relating directly to being baptized in the Holy Spirit.

> *kai gar en heni pneumati hēmeis pantes eis hen sōma ebaptisthēmen, eite Ioudaioi eite Hellēnes eite douloi eite eleutheroi, kai pantes hen pneuma epotisthēmen*

> For by one Spirit we were all baptized into one body—Jews or Greeks, slaves or free—and all were made to drink of one Spirit (RSV).

Non-Pentecostals have held this interpretation, too. But their view defines being baptized in the Spirit as receiving the Spirit at the moment of salvation, becoming part of the body of Christ. This meaning for being baptized in the Spirit is then transferred to the non-Pauline occurrences of the term. But a syntagmatic analysis of *baptizō* in the New Testament precludes this interpretation. Instead, the classical Pentecostal tenet of separability is strengthened, because (1) Paul does not use the "baptized in the Spirit" to refer to the complex event of conversion, and (2) Paul does talk about being baptized in the Spirit in a way that partially parallels Luke. The details of such analysis are far too lengthy to be included here, but I will set forth my own conclusions. As is standard usage, the *en* specifies the metaphorical "liquid" in which the baptizing is done, i.e., the Spirit. The *eis* (often incorrectly translated "into" in this text), as is usual in connection with *baptizō*, gives the purpose for the baptizing: it was done with a view toward the "one body." Verse 13 is in the middle of a discussion of the unity of the body, the local church, no matter which charismatic function each individual believer has. Each charismatic function contributes toward the overall healthy function of the entire body, and all of these powerful gifts come from the same Father, Son, and Spirit (although the Spirit is emphasized more strongly). As charismatic ministry is directed toward the body, it promotes the "one body," i.e., the healthy function and unity of the body. The nonstandard "one" in the phrase "in *one* Spirit" is a reiteration of the unity of the source of all charismatic ministries (cf. verses 4, 8, 9, 11). So, in Pauline usage, to be baptized in the Spirit does not cause one to become a part of the body of Christ. The meaning that arises from the syntagmatic relationship of *baptizō* plus *eis* does not specify that the thing being baptized becomes part of the object introduced by the preposition *eis*. Rather, to be baptized in the Spirit is the initiation into charismatic ministry[28] that is directed toward the body, the local church, promoting healthy function and unity. On the one hand, Paul thus addresses a purpose for being baptized in the Spirit that is not covered by Luke, which should not be surprising in view of New Testament theological principles discussed above. On the other hand, just as in Luke–Acts, being baptized in the Spirit initiates the believer into charismatic ministry, not salvation, and this strengthens the tenet of separability.

CONCLUSIONS

Two issues have run beneath the surface throughout this essay: separability and evidential value. Three areas of current biblical scholarship were more often on the surface, but the issues would appear from time to time as the significance of each area of scholarship was shown.

Of the three areas, the first two, biblical theology and narrative theology, are the most significant; the third is important, but is more related to specific issues within the broader tasks defined by the first two.

New Testament theological and biblical narrative considerations suggest that Luke–Acts can and should be a source of doctrine. Acts tells stories that teach as well as provide a pattern or paradigm for our own experiences and relationship with God, and this can become a standard for evaluating our own stories, our own lives and experiences with God. By this I mean that these stories are intended by God to provide glimpses into the way things are, or should be, or should not be. These stories are narrative word of God. We will be negligent if we do not let them function as such.

While it is true that Luke was written not merely to answer the two questions regarding being baptized in the Spirit and the use of tongues as evidence, we have seen that the narratives and speeches do contain theological materials that are relevant. It is now time to draw some specific conclusions on these two issues.

Separability

Can the expression "being baptized in the Spirit" be legitimately used as it is today by classical Pentecostals? The answer, I think, is *yes*. Christians through the ages have used biblical terms to name systematic theological doctrines. But the same caveat applies as always does: do not confuse the doctrine of systematic theology with the biblical term. In this area, for example, the classical Pentecostal doctrine really encompasses most of the terms Luke uses for receiving the Spirit, and it therefore draws from texts where *baptizō* is not even used. But the "being baptized" terminology is the most appropriate of all Luke's terms for systematic theological discussion of the initiatory experience of receiving the Spirit.

The application of accepted principles and methods of biblical criticism—including establishing a biblical theology rather than a systematic theology, recognizing the nature of genre, and implementing the tools of redaction and literary criticism—to the traditional texts of the doctrine of initial evidence, will support the idea that being baptized in the Holy Spirit is something distinct from conversion. It can occur within the same time frame as conversion, but it is distinct. Conversion involves the establishing of relationship with God; being baptized in the Spirit involves initiation into powerful, charismatic ministry.

The Evidential Value of Tongues

What is the relationship between being baptized in the Spirit and speaking in tongues? It is difficult to deny that speaking in tongues *did* accompany being baptized in the Spirit in three texts in Acts. It is a common storytelling technique the world over to tell things in groups of threes: three times should be enough to tell anything. The paradigmatic effect of these stories should lead us to expect the same things in our own experience with the Spirit. Actually, as we are drawn into the story, we should experience the Spirit along with Peter, Cornelius, and all the rest. By telling these stories, Luke shows that this is the way his world works. As the word of God to us, Luke's version of the world deserves our serious consideration.

Then, there is one text where speaking in tongues is explicitly used as evidence that believers had received the Spirit in the Lucan sense, namely, Acts 10:45–47. Peter concludes that Cornelius and his household had received the Spirit in the same way that he and his associates had, and Peter's explanation is subsequently accepted by "the apostles and the brothers" in the Jerusalem church. We must note that speaking in tongues in this text is really a second-level sign or evidence, since the reception of the Spirit is itself a sign that these Gentiles have in fact been admitted to this new group that acknowledges Jesus as Lord. However, the function of the first-level sign can give a clue to follow in stating the value of tongues as evidence for reception of the Spirit. Peter argues that reception of the Spirit showed that these Gentiles were indeed members of the people of God: reception of the Spirit had evidential value. But the primary purpose of receiving the Spirit is not merely to prove that one is saved. There is a connection between being saved and receiving the Spirit. Receiving the Spirit does provide evidence that one is saved, but providing such evidence is not the primary God-intended purpose of giving the Spirit in the Lucan sense.

Correspondingly, Luke presents tongues as a natural result of being baptized in the Holy Spirit. In this text, Luke as narrator evaluates the reasoning of Peter and his associates by stating that they knew that the Gentiles had received the Holy Spirit because they heard the Gentiles speaking in other tongues and praising God. But a valid use of a natural result is not the same as saying that the God-intended purpose of tongues is evidential. The primary "purpose" of fire is not to produce smoke, but that natural result has made possible both the old proverb "where there's smoke, there's fire," and the new technology of smoke-detecting fire alarms. Much of Pentecostal thought on this problem has chosen to see *two* kinds of speaking in tongues, or even *three*: tongues as "initial phys-ical evidence" of being baptized in the Spirit, the gift of tongues à la 1 Corinthians 12–14, and a private "prayer language," again with refer-ence to 1 Corinthians 14. The distinction between the last two especially is in my opinion impossible to justify exegetically.[29]

It seems to me that speaking in tongues is essentially one kind of experience, produced by a certain kind of contact with the divine Spirit. The first time this kind of contact occurs is the initiatory event of being baptized in the Spirit, but the same kind of inspired speech can be the result of subsequent contacts as well. Whether *baptizō* means "immerse" or "flood," there is an overwhelming of the human psyche by the person and power of the Spirit of God. As to why God chose to produce tongues as a manifestation of this divine "coming upon," I use a hint supplied by Robert Capon in his *Parables of Grace* that "[Jesus] (and the Spirit as well) *prays in us*. Prayer is not really our work at all."[30] If so, then to initiate a believer into a charismatic ministry that is completely powered and di-rected by the Spirit, the Spirit must do all the work, at least in the speech content. The result is prayer and praise that is itself the total work of the Holy Spirit.

In sum, we might say that Luke is concerned with believers being "baptized" in the Spirit, initiated into powerful charismatic service, but Luke is even more concerned with the service itself. Subsequent "fillings" are to direct and empower believers to serve in specific settings to spread the gospel. Similarly, Paul in 1 Corinthians 12:13 is interested not in mere initiation but in the powerful impact of the manifestation of the Spirit in the ministry to the local body of Christ. So, I conclude that tongues can be used as the initial physical evidence that a believer has been baptized in the Spirit, initiated into powerful service, but even more important is that the believer actually continue in Spirit-empowered and Spirit-directed service. "Have you been initiated into Spirit-empowered, Spirit-directed charismatic service for your Lord?" is a valid question, and I consider it the rough equivalent of "Have you been baptized in the Holy Spirit?" Speaking in tongues as "initial physical evidence" can help answer those two equivalent questions. But even more important is the question, "Are you continuing in Spirit-empowered, Spirit-directed service?"

NOTES

1. As part of my use of New Testament theological methodology, I have chosen to try to use a verbal form fairly consistently, since a corresponding

nominal form such as "Spirit baptism" or "baptism in the Spirit" does not occur in the New Testament. While I do not reject the validity of these nominal forms, I suspect that their use can encourage a shift of focus from the two persons, the believer and the Spirit, to the believer and the experience, as in "Have you received the baptism?"

2. Not all classical Pentecostals would agree that "other tongues" would have to be an actual language. Further, it should be evident that this essay can deal only with speaking in tongues as understood by classical Pentecostals, and cannot, for example, even mention non-Christian varieties. For a full discussion of these, see Russell Spittler's article "Glossolalia," in *Dictionary of Pentecostal and Charismatic Movements*, ed. Stanley M. Burgess and Gary B. McGee (Grand Rapids: Zondervan, 1988).

3. I will be using the term "classical Pentecostal hermeneutics" to refer: (1) in general to the hermeneutical principles used by classical Pentecostals for all of Scripture, and (2) more specifically to the hermeneutical principles used by classical Pentecostals in exegeting the texts that are directly relevant to being baptized in the Spirit. I believe that the second set of principles should be a subset of the first, not a different set.

4. These two other texts are as follows: Simon was willing to pay the apostles for the ability to confer the Spirit, Acts 8:14–19. Something he saw was impressive enough to make him offer the money for this ability, and he had already seen great miracles done by Stephen. This something is conjectured to be speaking in tongues. This may well be the case, but such a conjecture cannot be used in a circular way to establish the pattern. The other case is a combination of Acts 8:17, where Ananias says Paul is going to receive the Spirit, and 1 Corinthians 14:18, where Paul states that he speaks in tongues more than any member of the Corinthian church. Here, Luke has used good storytelling technique in letting a speaker say what is going to happen, but that happening is never actually reported. To be sure, Paul did receive the Spirit, and he did speak in tongues, but there is no connection between the two in the texts, and thus this combination of texts has little help to offer in establishing a pattern for evidential value of speaking in tongues. One further text, although not from Acts, is Mark 16:17. On the one hand, there are two major problems with using this text to establish the classical Pentecostal view of being baptized in the Spirit. First, the passage Mark 16:9–20 is almost certainly not part of the original text of Mark. For discussion of the manuscript evidence, see Bruce M. Metzger, *A Textual Commentary on the Greek New Testament*, corrected edition (Stuttgart, Germany: United Bible Societies, 1975), 122–28. Second, v. 17 does not connect speaking in tongues with being baptized in the Spirit, but with being a believer. On the other hand, the text is very early and it explicitly gives evidential value to tongues, probably in connection with the commission given in v. 15 as a sign of the truth of the good news that is being preached. Thus, the author of this passage and probably the wider circle of the author's associates gave an evidential value to tongues, though not with reference to being baptized in the Spirit as did Luke.

5. Adapted from G. E. Ladd, *A Theology of the New Testament* (Grand Rapids: Eerdmans, 1974), 25.

6. For an example of this kind of published work on Luke, see Roger Stronstad, *The Charismatic Theology of Saint Luke* (Peabody, Mass.: Hendrick-

son, 1984). A forthcoming (as of this writing) work that I suspect holds promise is Robert P. Menzies's *The Development of Early Christian Pneumatology with Special Reference to Luke–Acts,* a Ph.D. dissertation done at the University of Aberdeen, Scotland, that will be published in the *JSNT* Supplement Series.

7. Cf. R. F. O'Toole, S.J., *Unity of Luke's Theology* (Wilmington, Del.: Michael Glazier, 1984), 21.

8. And John can add yet another dimension or phase to the reception of the Spirit, John 20:21–23. It is also poor methodology to arbitrarily force this text in John's Gospel into either the Lucan or Pauline theological structure.

9. Here we must note that the statements of Paul in Acts are *not* primarily to be interpreted within the structures of Pauline theology, but within those of Lucan theology. Paul in Acts can say only what Luke allows him to say. That is not to suggest that Luke invented the speeches of Acts out of thin air. But they have all been filtered through the Lucan theological grid, and they all serve Luke's theological objectives.

10. For this expression, cf. the corresponding one in 11:17. The point is not that the believing and receiving must take place at the same time, although in Luke's paradigm the two should be within the same general time frame. It is rather that receiving the Spirit in the Lucan sense is a natural sequel to believing Jesus, and when it was not so, there was cause for concern. Also cf. Paul's conversion and receiving of the Spirit in Acts 9, which were separated by three days.

11. Perhaps so designated to distinguish them from the believers who were not from among the circumcised, i.e., Cornelius and his household.

12. An excellent example of the constructive use of redaction criticism in the study of relevant texts is the paper by Robert P. Menzies presented at the November, 1990 meeting of the Society for Pentecostal Studies: "The Baptist's Prophecy in Lucan Perspective: A Redactional Analysis of Luke 3:16."

13. Some redaction critics take the last two points and go too far with them, concluding that the evangelist made up certain stories or parts of stories about Jesus. That kind of redaction criticism I cannot endorse, but the problem is more with the views of the person using the method than with the method itself.

14. O'Toole, *Luke's Theology,* 62. This is the title of chapter 3, pp. 62–94.

15. O'Toole, *Luke's Theology,* 81–82.

16. For an introduction to the concerns of several forms of this discipline, see G. Fackre, "Narrative Theology: An Overview," *Int* 37 (October 1983): 340–52.

17. S. Hauerwas, "Casuistry and Narrative Art," *Int* 37 (October 1983): 377–88; M. Goldberg, "Exodus 1:13–14," *Int* 37 (October 1983): 389–91.

18. I have consistently enclosed "world" in quotation marks in this section wherever it refers to this perceived world as opposed to the real world.

19. Cf. A. N. Wilder, "Story and Story-World," *Int* 37 (October 1983): 359–61.

20. A. N. Wilder, *Jesus' Parables and the War of Myths* (Philadelphia: Fortress, 1982), 51.

21. "Normal" usually stands for the view that speaking in tongues is a normal and beneficial Christian activity, as seen in Acts and 1 Corinthians.

But not every Christian should expect to speak in tongues, whether or not he or she is baptized in the Spirit by any definition. "Normative" means that the stories in Acts teach that all Christians who are baptized in the Holy Spirit *will* speak in tongues.

22. The following list summarizes Luke's terms. Note that most of these are metaphors: *pouring out:* Acts 2:17, 18; 10:45; *gift:* Acts 2:38; 10:45; 11:17; *baptized:* Acts 1:5; 11:16; *come upon:* Acts 1:8; 19:6; *filled with:* Acts 2:4; 4:8, 31; 9:17; 13:9, 52; Luke 1:15, 41, 67; *fall upon:* Acts 8:16; 10:44; 11:15; *receive:* Acts 2:38; 8:15; 10:47; 19:2; *promise:* Acts 2:39; Luke 24:49; *clothed with power:* Luke 24:49.

23. For a thorough treatment and a somewhat different interpretation, see Robert P. Menzies's paper noted above, "The Baptist's Prophecy." He makes the baptizing metaphor subordinate to the winnowing metaphor that immediately follows.

24. W. G. Kümmel, *The Theology of the New Testament* (Nashville: Abingdon, 1973), 313. Contrast, then, the image produced by John the Evangelist with Jesus' actions toward the ten disciples in John 20:21–23. There, a physical action was involved, and no outward actions are present in those who received the Spirit in that way on that occasion. I follow Kümmel somewhat for reading this Johannine text: he observes that John links the coming of the Spirit in the Johannine text not with charismatic supernatural activities but rather with spiritual authority. This is, in a sense, a Johannine equivalent of the Great Commission. It may well be an apostolic commission, the bestowing of "apostolic authority."

25. Peter: 2:4; 4:8; 4:31; Paul: 9:17; 13:9; 13:52.

26. See, e.g., Stronstad, *Charismatic Theology*, 51–52.

27. For more information on syntagmatic relationships, see P. Cotterell and M. Turner, *Linguistics and Biblical Interpretation* (Downers Grove: InterVarsity Press, 1989), 155–56; M. Silva, *Biblical Words and Their Meaning: An Introduction to Lexical Semantics* (Grand Rapids: Zondervan, 1983), 119, 141–43.

28. The initiatory aspects come from the meaning of *baptizō* and the specialized usage of "being baptized in the Spirit" by John the Baptist, Jesus, and the early church. The "charismatic ministry" is a strong contextual factor here in 1 Corinthians 12, as well as being a factor in the words of Jesus reported in Acts 1:5–8.

29. The usual reference to 1 Corinthians 14:5b to establish that tongues plus interpretation equals prophecy overlooks two points. First, in 14:2 and again in 28, Paul views tongues as directed to God; interpretation merely makes the content understandable to people. Second, while Paul does equate the *value* of prophecy and tongues plus interpretation in v. 5b, he does not equate their *function.*

30. Robert Farrar Capon, *The Parables of Grace* (Grand Rapids: Eerdmans, 1988), 70. The statement is part of his discussion of the Lord's Prayer.

10

A ONENESS PENTECOSTAL
LOOKS AT INITIAL EVIDENCE

J. L. Hall

A ONENESS PENTECOSTAL VIEW
OF THE SALVATION EXPERIENCE

The introduction of the "finished work of Calvary" doctrine in 1910–1911 by William Durham precipitated the first doctrinal division among Pentecostals, with at least half of the churches and ministers following his teaching against sanctification as a second work of grace.[1] Although most Pentecostal organizations that had originally formed as holiness groups retained a Wesleyan perspective of sanctification, most of the unaffiliated ministers adopted the baptistic "finished work" doctrine.[2] The "finished work" ministers, including those who formed the Assemblies of God in 1914, taught a two-stage experience, that of salvation and Spirit baptism, while the holiness Pentecostal groups continued to teach a three-stage experience consisting of salvation, sanctification, and Spirit baptism.[3]

The next doctrinal controversy that caused a division began in 1914 when Pentecostals began baptizing in the name of Jesus Christ and associating this practice with the doctrine of the Oneness of God. Known initially as the "new issue," the doctrine swept across the Pentecostal fellowship, being embraced by many of the leaders in the "finished work" group.[4] A division came in the Assemblies of God in 1916 when, in an atmosphere of confrontation, the organization adopted a trinitarian statement and rejected water baptism administered solely in the name of Jesus Christ or Lord Jesus.[5] About one-fourth of the ministers in the Assemblies of God withdrew to form a Oneness Pentecostal organization.[6]

Most Oneness Pentecostals also differed with their brethren who remained in the Assemblies of God on the doctrine of salvation. Just as Durham's "finished work" message reduced the earlier three-stage experience to two stages, Oneness Pentecostals reduced the two-stage experience to one stage; that is, they viewed the infilling of the Holy Ghost as the completion of the salvation process rather than as a subsequent enduement of power for service. Perhaps without conscious thought, they made a remarkable leap over the issues debated by the Reformers to embrace the doctrinal focus and practices of the New Testament church. Instead of arguing the issues of justification, sanctification, adoption, and regeneration, they simply followed the biblical emphasis on faith, obedience to God's word, repentance, water baptism, and the infilling of the Spirit as the normal salvation experience of all Christians.

Since most Oneness Pentecostals view the baptism of the Holy Ghost with the evidence of speaking in tongues as the completion of the salvation experience, the first part of this chapter explores the biblical basis of the Oneness perspective of salvation as it relates to repentance, water baptism in the name of Jesus Christ, and the reception of the Spirit. The second part focuses upon speaking in tongues as the initial physical evidence of Spirit baptism.

The Salvation Experience

The New Testament does not present Christians who are not Spirit-filled, but rather it assumes that in order to become a Christian a person believes in Jesus Christ, repents of his or her sins, is baptized in the name of Jesus Christ, and is filled with the Holy Ghost (Acts 2:38).[7] Although repentance, water baptism, and the reception of the Spirit are distinct "steps"[8] in the salvation process, together they constitute the "full"[9] experience of salvation, the new birth of water and the Spirit, which Jesus stated was necessary in order to enter into the kingdom of God (John 3:3, 5).[10] Repentance and water baptism are not considered to be works of the law or works that earn salvation, for salvation is a free gift of God bestowed upon all by grace through faith. Repentance and water baptism, however, are the scriptural faith-responses that a sinner makes to the preaching of the gospel.

Since Peter outlined these steps in the salvation process to the gathered crowds on the day of Pentecost who asked, "What shall we do?" the church today should give the same answer to sinners wanting to be saved.[11] While the instructions "Believe on Jesus Christ" and "Accept Jesus as your Savior" are true, they are incomplete without further explanation.

We should note that Jesus (Luke 13:1–3), Peter (Acts 2:38; 3:19; 8:22), Paul (Acts 17:30; 26:20), and the other apostles and leaders (Acts 11:18) viewed repentance as necessary for salvation. Likewise, Jesus (Matt. 28:19; Mark 16:16; John 3:3, 5), Peter (Acts 2:38; 10:48; 1 Pet. 3:21), and Paul (Acts 19:5; 22:16; Rom. 6:3–5; Gal. 3:27) placed water baptism in the plan of salvation. Moreover, Jesus (John 7:37–39; 14:16–20, 26; 15:26; 16:7; Luke 24:49; Acts 1:5, 8), Peter (Acts 2:14–40; 8:14–17; 15:7–8), and Paul (Acts 19:1–6; Rom. 8:9–16; 1 Cor. 3:16; 6:19; 12:13; Gal. 3:14; Eph. 1:13–14) viewed the infilling of the Holy Ghost as the normal and essential experience of believers.

Repentance, water baptism in the name of Jesus Christ, and the infilling of the Spirit are linked in the conversion experience of believers in the book of Acts.[12] For example, in Acts 8, when the Samaritans believed Philip concerning the kingdom of God, they were baptized in the name of Jesus Christ and later were filled with the Holy Ghost. Although the text does not state that the Samaritans repented, it can be safely assumed. Peter told Simon the Sorcerer, "Repent therefore of this thy wickedness, and pray God, if perhaps the thought of thine heart may be forgiven thee" (Acts 8:22 [all Scripture quotes in this chapter are from the AV]). If Peter taught that repentance was the way to forgiveness, it is reasonable to assume that Philip preached repentance to the Samaritans before he baptized them.

Paul repented on the road to Damascus as he surrendered his life to Jesus. He asked, "Lord, what wilt thou have me to do?" (Acts 9:6). After he fasted and prayed three days in Damascus, God sent Ananias to baptize Paul and to lay hands on him that he might receive both his sight and the Holy Ghost (Acts 9:17–18).

Although the sequence of water baptism and Spirit baptism was reversed in the conversion of the Gentiles, the three steps are still identifiable.[13] The record in Acts 10 does not mention repentance, but the church leaders recognized that the infilling of the Spirit came out of a repentant condition, for they "glorified God, saying, 'Then hath God also to the Gentiles granted repentance unto life' " (Acts 11:18).

The twelve disciples of John the Baptist (Acts 19) also completed the three steps. Since they had been baptized "unto repentance" by John the Baptist, they only needed Christian baptism and the infilling of the Holy

Ghost. After Paul explained about Christ, he baptized the twelve disciples in the name of Jesus Christ and laid hands on them, and they received the Holy Ghost (Acts 19:1–7).

In the book of Acts, then, we can identify the steps of repentance, water baptism in the name of Jesus Christ, and the infilling of the Holy Ghost (Acts 2:38; 8:12–22; 9:6–18 and 22:16; 10:43–48 and 11:18; 19:1–6). Since these constitute the preaching and practice of the early church, it is reasonable to contend that the church today should follow this biblical pattern.

Water Baptism in the Name of Jesus

It is interesting to note that in each of the events used by Pentecostals to establish speaking in tongues as the initial physical evidence of receiving the Holy Ghost, water baptism is specifically said to be in the name of Jesus (Acts 2:38; 8:16; 22:16; 10:48; 19:5), and this formula is implied in three others events (Acts 8:36–39; 16:31–33; Acts 18:8 and 1 Cor. 1:13–15). Moreover, this formula in Acts finds strength and support in the references to baptism in the epistles, for these state that we are baptized into Christ and buried with him in baptism (Rom. 6:3–5; 1 Cor. 6:11; Gal. 3:27; Col. 2:12).'

Although all the references in Acts and the Epistles indicate that water baptism was administered in the name of Jesus Christ, it should not be supposed that this apostolic formula contradicts the command of Christ in Matthew 28:19, or that it was a further revelation given to Peter on the day of Pentecost. Rather, baptism in the name of Jesus Christ is the biblical fulfillment of the command to baptize in the name (singular) of the Father, and of the Son, and of the Holy Ghost.

In the New Testament, water baptism is closely linked with Spirit baptism. Even the use of the word *baptize* to designate the reception of the Spirit originated when John the Baptist compared water baptism with the experience of the Spirit that would come through Christ. Apparently John viewed his baptism of repentance for the remission of sins as preparatory for the Spirit baptism by Christ, and the church similarly administered water baptism in preparation for Spirit baptism (Acts 2:38; 8:12–17; 19:1–6).

In his discussion with Nicodemus, Jesus linked water and the Spirit in the new birth, stating that unless a person is born of water and of the Spirit, he cannot enter into the kingdom of God (John 3:5). The new birth is one, but it involves two elements, water and the Spirit.[14]

On the day of Pentecost, Peter preached water baptism in the name of Jesus Christ as one preparation for receiving the Holy Ghost (Acts 2:38), and this was the pattern reflected in the revival at Samaria (Acts 8:12–17) and at Ephesus (Acts 19:1–6). As preparation for Spirit baptism, water baptism does not complete the conversion experience, but it reflects the death of Jesus Christ for the remission of sins and anticipates the infilling of the Spirit. Acts 8:16 implies that water baptism alone is not sufficient for salvation but that it must be complemented by Spirit baptism: "For as yet he [the Holy Ghost] was fallen upon none of them: only they were baptized in the name of the Lord Jesus."

This same perception is reflected in Paul's question to the men at Ephesus. When he discovered that they had not received the Holy Ghost, he asked, "Unto what then were you baptized?" (Acts 19:3). Just as John's baptism was preparatory to the coming of Christ, Paul viewed Christian baptism as preparatory for the reception of the Holy Ghost.

In Paul's own conversion, this same pattern was apparently followed. Although Ananias's primary mission was for Paul to receive the Holy Ghost, he told him to "arise, and be baptized, and wash away thy sins, calling on the name of the Lord" (Acts 9:17–18; 22:16).

The Gentiles in Acts 10 received the Holy Ghost before being baptized in water, but the link between the water baptism and Spirit baptism is still present. Peter asked, "Can any man forbid water, that these should not be baptized, which have received the Holy Ghost as well as we? And he commanded them to be baptized in the name of the Lord" (Acts 10:47–48). Peter contended that the reception of the Holy Ghost did not negate the need for water baptism, and the others apparently agreed.

The integrated and complementary relation of water baptism and the infilling of the Spirit in the conversion experience finds support in the analogy of recapitulating the death, burial, and resurrection of Christ. Water baptism is compared to Christ's death and burial from which the convert is to rise in the likeness of Christ's resurrection (receiving new life in the Spirit) to "walk in newness of life" (Rom. 6:1–6; 7:6). The Old Testament rite of circumcision also serves as a type of initiation into the church. Instead of circumcision, New Testament converts are "buried with him [Christ] in baptism, wherein also ye are risen with him through the faith of the operation of God, who hath raised him from the dead" Col. 2:11–12).

In Romans 6 and Colossians 2, water baptism is presented as the rite by which sins are buried or purged from the convert's life in preparation for the reception of life in Christ, and this life comes by receiving the Spirit of Christ, the Holy Ghost (Rom. 8:2, 9–10). Thus these references in Romans and Colossians inseparably link water baptism and Spirit reception in the salvation experience.

Galatians 3:27–28 does not specifically identify whether the term *baptized* there refers to water baptism or Spirit baptism or both, but 1 Corinthians 12:13 refers particularly to Spirit baptism. Stressing the regenerative role of Spirit baptism, the verse explicitly states that "by one Spirit" a person is baptized into the body of Christ. Since the New Testament presents only one Spirit baptism, it is safe to assume that Spirit baptism here is the same Spirit baptism experience in Acts.

The baptism in Galatians 3:27 may refer to water baptism, or perhaps it means that both water baptism and Spirit baptism form the initiatory experience that brings a convert into Christ. This interpretation would correspond to the "one baptism" in Ephesians 4:5 and the implication in Titus 3:5–6 that water baptism and the outpouring of the Spirit are both involved in the salvation experience.

The Baptism of the Holy Ghost

In the Old Testament era the Spirit of God moved upon, filled, and anointed people to accomplish God's plan and purpose, but the experience was either less than that made available on this side of Calvary or it was limited to those individuals chosen for special service (Heb. 11:39–40; 1 Pet. 1:10–12). In Jeremiah, God promised to establish a new covenant in which he would put his "law in their inward parts, and write it in their hearts. . . . For they shall all know me, from the least of them unto the greatest of them" (Jer. 31:31–34; Heb. 8:7–13; 10:16–20). That this prophecy, as well as Joel 2:28–32, refers to the new covenant instituted by the outpouring of the Spirit on the day of Pentecost appears conclusive.

Under both the old and new covenants, salvation comes from God's grace through faith, but the salvation experience under the new covenant is so much more glorious that the experience of the first covenant appears as not having had glory and is compared to living in bondage (2 Cor. 3:7–11; Gal. 4:21–31). In other words, the new covenant made the old covenant obsolete, for the old served only as a teacher pointing us to Christ. While the commandments of the old covenant revealed sin, they did not give a person power over the sinfulness of human nature. In contrast, the reception of the Holy Ghost under the new covenant dethrones sin in a person's life, setting that one free to live after the righteousness of God (Rom. 6–8).

The new covenant began only after the death, resurrection, and ascension of Jesus Christ, (Heb. 9:14–17), but in his ministry Jesus anticipated the blessings of the new covenant. He spoke of a new birth of water and the Spirit (John 3:3, 5), abundant life (John 10:10), remission of sins (Luke 24:47), freedom from the power of sin (John 8:32–36), and the coming of the Holy Ghost (John 7:37–39; 14:16–19, 26; 15:26; 16:7–11; 20:22; Luke 24:49; Acts 1:4–8). From the Gospel of John it appears that Jesus promised the gift of the Spirit to a Samaritan woman (John 4:10–14) and to all believers during a Feast of Tabernacles (John 7:37–39), but the Holy Ghost was not given until Jesus was glorified (John 7:39). In other words, Spirit baptism became available only after Jesus went to the cross (Heb. 9:15–17) and ascended (John 16:7; Luke 24:49; Acts 1:5–8).

Although Jesus appeared after his resurrection to the assembled disciples, breathed upon them, and commanded, "Receive ye the Holy Ghost" (John 20:22), it must not be assumed that he gave the Holy Ghost to them at this time. Such an interpretation conflicts with John 7:39 and 16:7 as well as the entire narrative in the Gospels and Acts. Later, immediately prior to his ascension, Jesus instructed the disciples to wait in Jerusalem for the coming of the Spirit. This injunction would be meaningless if the disciples had already received the Holy Ghost.[15]

To interpret Jesus' breathing upon the disciples as an impartation of a portion of the Holy Spirit and not his full nature creates another problem, for it implies that the Spirit can be divided. Similarly, to separate the Holy Spirit from the Spirit of Christ or Christ leads to tritheism and clearly contradicts the language of such passages as Romans 8:9–15 in which the Holy Ghost is called the Spirit of Christ and simply Christ.[16] It seems that Jesus breathed upon the disciples for two reasons: (1) to emphasize their need to receive the Holy Ghost and (2) to illustrate how the Spirit would come to them.

The outpouring of the Spirit on the day of Pentecost began the new covenant: it fulfilled the prophecy of Jeremiah, Joel, and John the Baptist, the promised blessing of Abraham (Gal. 3:13), and the promise of Jesus (John 7:37–39; 14:16–19; 16:7; Luke 24:49; Acts 1:4–8). Although the disciples had experienced salvation as provided under the old covenant, at Pentecost they experienced New Testament salvation with its greater blessing of transforming power.

At least eight verbs are used in the Gospels and Acts to indicate the experience of the Holy Ghost—*baptize* (Matt. 3:11; Mark 1:8; Luke 3:16; John 1:33; Acts 1:5; 11:16), *fill* (Acts 2:4; 9:17), *receive* (John 7:39; 20:22; Acts 2:38; 8:15, 17, 19; 10:47; 19:2) *fall on* (Acts 8:16; 10:44; 11:15), *come upon* (Acts 1:8; 19:6), *pour out* (Acts 2:17; 10:45), *give* (Acts 8:18; 11:17), and *endue* (Luke 24:49). Although these terms describe various perspectives of the outpouring of the Spirit, they refer to the same experience and are used interchangeably.

Of the seven terms that appear in Acts, six describe the outpouring of the Spirit on the day of Pentecost: *baptize, come upon, fill, pour out, fall on,* and *receive.* In the outpouring upon the Gentiles, five terms appear: *fall on, pour out, receive, baptize,* and *give.* Three terms describe the reception of the Spirit by the Samaritans: *fall on, receive,* and *give.* Only two terms denote the Spirit baptism of the disciples of John the Baptist: *receive* and *come on.* In Paul's case, only the term *fill* is used.

Although the majority of Pentecostals and charismatics teach that being baptized or filled with the Holy Ghost is an experience subsequent to salvation,[17] their position on this subject is scripturally questionable.[18] First, to infer that because a person believes he or she has received the Spirit is to contradict the clear language of Scripture (Acts 8 and 19), and it would imply that Simon the Sorcerer had received the Spirit of Christ, although his heart was not right in the sight of God, and he was still "in the gall of bitterness, and in the bond of iniquity" (Acts 8:13, 20–23). Second, 1 Corinthians 12:13 clearly states, "By one Spirit are we all baptized into one body." If the baptism of the Spirit puts a person into the church, then it is a part of the salvation experience.[19]

In Acts and the Epistles, Christians are not divided into those "baptized with the Spirit" and those not so baptized; on the contrary, the assumption is that all Christians are Spirit-filled. Romans 8:9 is explicit: "If any man have not the Spirit of Christ, he is none of his." 1 Corinthians 3:16 and 6:19 state that Christians are temples of the Holy Spirit, and Ephesians 1:13–14 says that they are sealed with the Spirit and that the Spirit is the earnest of their inheritance. Christians are commanded to walk in the Spirit (Rom. 8:4; Gal. 5:16, 25), to be led by the Spirit (Rom. 8:14; Gal. 5:18), to mortify the deeds of the body through the Spirit (Rom. 8:13), and to bear the fruit of the Spirit (Gal. 5:22)—all of which require the presence of the Spirit in their lives.

In one remarkable promise of Spirit baptism, Jesus identified himself as the Comforter who would come to abide in the disciples:

> And I will pray the Father, and he shall give you another Comforter, that he may abide with you for ever; even the Spirit of truth; whom the world cannot receive, because it seeth him not, neither knoweth him: but ye know him; for he dwelleth with you, and shall be in you. I will not leave you comfortless: I will come to you (John 14:16–18; see also Matt. 18:20; 28:20).

When a person receives the Holy Ghost, that person receives Christ, the hope of glory (Col. 1:27). The terms *Spirit, Spirit of the Lord, Holy Ghost, Spirit of God, Spirit of Christ,* and *Christ* are used interchangeably in the New Testament to identify the indwelling Spirit. (See Rom. 8:9–

15.) Thus Jesus Christ lives within us by the Holy Ghost. In 2 Corinthians 3:17, Paul identified the Spirit as being the Lord: "Now the Lord is that Spirit: and where the Spirit of the Lord is, there is liberty." (See also Gal. 4:6; Phil. 1:19.)

SPEAKING IN TONGUES AS THE INITIAL EVIDENCE

Although history records sporadic occurrences of speaking in tongues among such groups as the Jansenists, Camisards, Huguenots, early Quakers, early Methodists, Irvingites, and holiness groups, the doctrine of speaking in tongues as the initial evidence of the reception of the Holy Ghost was unknown. It was this teaching, however, that sparked the Pentecostal revival of this century.[20]

Under the guidance of Charles Fox Parham, students at Bethel Bible School in Topeka, Kansas, concluded from a Bible study that the one consistent sign of the infilling of the Spirit is speaking in tongues. On January 1, 1901, one of the students, Agnes Ozman, spoke in tongues when Parham laid hands on her in prayer.[21] Two nights later on January 3, other students and Parham himself received the Holy Ghost with the evidence of speaking in tongues.[22]

During the next few years, Parham and his workers ignited Pentecostal revivals in cities and towns in Kansas, Missouri, Oklahoma, Texas, and Illinois. From Houston, Texas, William J. Seymour took Parham's teaching to Los Angeles, where he became the leader of the revival in the famous Apostolic Faith Mission on Azusa Street. From Los Angeles, the Pentecostal message and experience soon reached nations around the world.

Although Pentecostals and other Christians have discussed, debated, and challenged the teaching that speaking in tongues is the only initial physical evidence of the baptism of the Holy Ghost, most of the early Pentecostals in this century accepted the doctrine.[23] All major classical Pentecostal organizations, including those holding the Oneness view, adopted the initial evidence of speaking in tongues as a part of their statement of beliefs.

In establishing that speaking in tongues is the outward evidence of receiving the Holy Ghost, Pentecostals rely primarily upon the historical pattern in the book of Acts. Other supporting passages include Mark 16:17, 1 Corinthians 12 and 14, and Isaiah 28:11–12.

This section first examines the four crucial passages in the book of Acts that support the doctrine: (1) the coming of the Spirit on the day of

Pentecost in Acts 2; (2) the revival in Samaria in Acts 8; (3) the outpouring of the Spirit on the Gentiles in Caesarea in Acts 10; and (4) the
reception of the Holy Ghost by the disciples of John the Baptist at
Ephesus in Acts 19. Then it briefly looks at Paul's experience and the
prophecy in Isaiah 28 before it answers why God chose tongues. Finally,
it discusses the inner witness of the Spirit.

The Day of Pentecost

Three miraculous signs accompanied the outpouring of the Holy Ghost
on the day of Pentecost, but neither the sound from heaven that filled the
room nor the "cloven tongues like as of fire" that appeared to the disciples
was repeated in later Spirit outpourings. The miracle of speaking in
tongues—not the sound or appearance of fiery tongues, or even the
ecstatic behavior of the disciples—commanded the attention and curiosity of the multitude that gathered around the disciples. The crowd's
question, "What meaneth this?" referred to the disciples' speaking in
languages unknown to them but understood by those who heard them.[24]

While the sound that filled the house was of God, it was not directly
associated with the inner experience of the disciples. Rather, it announced the imminence of the promised outpouring of the Spirit upon
the waiting disciples. In like manner, the fiery tongues provided a corporate manifestation. The cloven tongues "sat upon each of them" to signify
the availability of the outpouring for each individual. Since both the
sound and the cloven tongues happened immediately prior to the reception of the Holy Ghost, they served as a prelude and then vanished from
the scene when the disciples were filled with the Spirit. On the other
hand, speaking in tongues happened to each person at the moment the
Holy Ghost was received.

The miracle of speaking in tongues required cooperation between the
indwelling Spirit and the disciples, for they spoke "as the Spirit gave them
utterance." The Spirit within each person gave the utterance—the expression and the form of what was spoken—and the person spoke the words
the Spirit inspired.

When the multitude that was in Jerusalem to celebrate the Feast of
Pentecost heard Galileans speaking in languages of their native countries,
they were puzzled. Some in the crowd attributed the entire scene to
drunkenness, but the majority acknowledged the miracle and asked for
an explanation.

The apostle Peter answered that they were witnessing the outpouring
of the Spirit prophesied by Joel. In his explanation, he linked speaking in

tongues with the Holy Ghost: "Therefore being by the right hand of God exalted, and having received of the Father the promise of the Holy Ghost, he [Jesus Christ] hath shed forth this, which ye now see and hear" (Acts 2:33). In other words, after his exaltation Jesus "shed forth" the Holy Ghost, the evidence of which was speaking in tongues—what they saw and heard.

Among the Samaritans

While the biblical record does not specifically state that the people in Samaria spoke in tongues when they received the Holy Ghost, it implies that a miraculous sign occurred. Several significant observations can be made: (1) the Samaritans believed the message Philip preached about Jesus Christ, but they did not receive the Holy Ghost at the moment of their initial faith; (2) the Samaritans did not receive the Holy Ghost when they were baptized in water; (3) the miracles of deliverance and healing brought great joy to the people, but joy was not the sign of the outpouring of the Holy Ghost; (4) Philip and the apostles knew that the Holy Ghost had not fallen on the Samaritans; (5) Peter and John came from Jerusalem to help the Samaritans receive the Holy Ghost; (6) Philip and the apostles expected a definite miraculous sign to accompany the reception of the Spirit; and (7) the apostles and others witnessed the outward sign when the Samaritans received the Holy Ghost.

We conclude that the anticipated and manifested initial evidence in Samaria was not faith, deliverance from demons, healings, miracles, water baptism, or joy. Although the Holy Ghost was given when the apostles laid hands on the Samaritan believers, this act was neither the gift of the Holy Ghost nor the evidence. (Significantly, laying on of hands did not accompany the outpouring of the Spirit in either Acts 2 or Acts 10.) Laying on of hands aided the recipients, but giving the Holy Ghost is the work of God and not of man, for only Jesus baptizes with the Holy Ghost. Moreover, giving the Holy Ghost was beyond the anointed prayers of the apostles, for from the recipients themselves came the evidence of the infilling Spirit.

The passage reveals that the evidence was outwardly observed by the apostles and others. Even Simon the Sorcerer witnessed the sign: (Acts 8:18–19). Since the evidence was observed by both believers and a wicked person, it was an outward sign. Moreover, its miraculous nature is evident in that it impressed a magician who desired the power to bestow this supernatural sign at will.

While Acts 8 names no specific evidence, a comparison of the Samaritan event with the outpourings of the Spirit in Acts 2, 10, and 19 strongly indicates that the Samaritans spoke in tongues.[25]

Among the Gentiles

Through a vision of animals forbidden as food, God revealed to Peter that Gentiles were included in the plan of salvation. Following the instruction of the Spirit, Peter went to Caesarea with three men sent from Cornelius, a Gentile who prayed to God. Six Jewish Christians accompanied Peter as witnesses of this mission to Gentiles.

In his message to Cornelius and his relatives and friends, Peter stated that God had shown him that he accepts anyone, whether Jew or Gentile, who turns to him, for "through his [Jesus'] name whosoever believeth in him shall receive remission of sins" (Acts 10:43). At this point, "the Holy Ghost fell on all them which heard the word" (Acts 10:44).

The outpouring of the Spirit here explicitly demonstrates that speaking in tongues is the initial outward evidence of receiving the Holy Ghost, for that alone convinced Peter and the Jewish believers who accompanied him that Gentiles had received the Holy Ghost:

> And they of the circumcision which believed were astonished . . . because that on the Gentiles also was poured out the gift of the Holy Ghost. For they heard them speak with tongues, and magnify God (Acts 10:45–46).

Significantly, when Peter later explained to the church leaders what had happened in Caesarea, he compared it to the outpouring on the day of Pentecost: the "Holy Ghost fell on them, as on us at the beginning" (Acts 11:15). Moreover, he stated that the Gentiles' experience was a fulfillment of Christ's promise to baptize with the Holy Ghost (Acts 11:16). This reveals that at this early date in the history of the church the leaders considered the outpouring at Pentecost as the pattern by which people were to receive Spirit baptism. Since speaking in tongues was the only sign present in Caesarea, this alone caused the church to equate this event with the outpouring on the day of Pentecost.

We must remember that the early Jewish Christians neither expected nor easily accepted that Gentiles could be incorporated into the church, but the evidence of speaking in tongues persuaded the leaders that God had granted salvation to them. Peter stated not only the basis of his acceptance of Gentiles, but the basis upon which the church in general had to alter its doctrine toward Gentiles: "Forasmuch then as God gave them the like gift as he did unto us, who believed on the Lord Jesus Christ, what was I, that I could withstand God?" (Acts 11:17).

We can conclude that without the evidence of speaking in tongues neither Peter, the six Jewish Christians, nor the church leaders would have acknowledged that Gentiles had received the Holy Ghost and were therefore included in God's plan of salvation. The leaders, therefore, recognized speaking in tongues as the initial evidence of Spirit baptism, causing them to glorify God and acknowledge, "Then hath God also to the Gentiles granted repentance unto life" (Acts 11:18).

The Disciples of John the Baptist

Paul's ministry to the twelve disciples of John the Baptist reveals that he agreed with the other apostles that speaking in tongues is the initial evidence of the Holy Ghost. His question, "Have ye received the Holy Ghost since ye believed?" (Acts 19:2) did not deny their faith, although Paul may have discerned that it was flawed by incomplete knowledge and lack of understanding. His immediate concern was their experience with the Spirit, about which they lacked knowledge.

Beginning at the point of their spiritual attainment, Paul informed them of Christ and then baptized them in the name of Jesus Christ, after which he laid hands on them and they received the Holy Ghost and began speaking in tongues.

Obviously Paul expected and acknowledged the same initial sign that Peter and John expected and witnessed in Samaria. In both places, a confession of faith and water baptism were not the evidential sign, for the apostles laid hands on those who had already professed faith and had already submitted to water baptism. In Acts 19, Luke recorded the sign: "the Holy Ghost came on them; and they spake with tongues, and prophesied" (Acts 19:6).

We should not suppose that the phrase "and prophesied" indicates an additional or optional sign, for it appears only here in connection with Spirit baptism and it parallels the phrase "and magnify God" in Acts 10:46. The phrases merely indicate that the people spoke words of inspiration and praise in their own language after receiving the Spirit.

Since the order of the conversion event in Ephesus closely follows the pattern recorded in Acts 8, it is evident that Paul, Peter, John, Philip, and other church leaders agreed that Spirit baptism is accompanied by speaking in tongues. Moreover, they also recognized that while faith, confession, repentance, water baptism, deliverance from demons, miracles of healing, and great joy describe authentic encounters with the Spirit, none serves as the evidence of Spirit infilling.

The Experience of Paul

The account of Paul's conversion in Acts 9 does not mention speaking in tongues, but in his first letter to the Corinthians he affirmed that he spoke in tongues, an experience that he attributed to the Spirit of God (1 Cor. 12:10–11; 14:18).

The Prophecy of Isaiah

Paul lifted the prophetic words in Isaiah 28:11–12 from their historical setting to associate them with speaking in tongues in the New Testament: "In the law it is written, 'With men of other tongues and other lips will I speak unto this people; and yet for all that will they not hear me, saith the Lord.' Wherefore tongues are for a sign, not to them that believe, but to them that believe not" (1 Cor. 14:21–22). In other words, speaking in tongues is a sign of God's speaking to his people. Yet even with this miracle, God acknowledged that as a whole the people would not hear or believe him.

This prophecy also associates speaking in tongues with rest and refreshing. Jesus spoke of rest for those who "labour and are heavy laden" (Matt. 11:28). Likewise the writer of Hebrews referred to a rest that comes not from observing the Sabbath under the law of Moses, but from a spiritual experience entered by faith (Heb. 4:9–11). Apparently, the prophetic rest in Isaiah (Isa. 28:12), the rest given by Jesus, and the rest believers enter by faith refer to the same experience. In this case, the spiritual rest of the new covenant is communicated by God through the experience of speaking in tongues.

We note, moreover, that Peter may have referred to Isaiah's prophecy in his instructive exhortation to the crowd that gathered after the healing of the lame man: "Repent ye therefore, and be converted, that your sins may be blotted out, when the times of refreshing shall come from the presence of the Lord" (Acts 3:19). The parallel construction and elements in this verse and in Acts 2:38—repentance, blotting or remission of sins, and God sending a refreshing or giving the gift of the Holy Ghost—may again identify the refreshing as the Spirit baptism and consequently support the doctrine of initial evidence.

Why Speaking in Tongues?

Although the Bible does not state explicitly why God chose speaking in tongues as the evidence of the Holy Ghost, one reason may be the power of speech itself. The power to express thought is the power of personality and reveals character. Jesus said, "Out of the abundance of the heart the mouth speaketh" (Matt. 12:34). Since the ability of speech sets humanity apart from other creatures, how a person uses this gift of words identifies that person's moral and religious character.

The Bible states that the tongue is "a fire, a world of iniquity . . . that . . . defileth the whole body" (James 3:6). Moreover, an unregenerated person cannot tame the tongue, for "it is an unruly evil, full of deadly poison" (James 3:8). In order for a person to be saved, therefore, that person must submit his or her mind (by believing) and tongue (by confessing Jesus Christ) to God, thus putting the total self under the lordship of Jesus. In order to speak in another language as the Spirit gives the utterance, one must relinquish control of the tongue to the promptings of the Spirit. Therefore, speaking in tongues by the Spirit reveals that the Holy Ghost has "sealed" the individual—both identifying the person with Christ and signifying that the person now belongs to Christ (1 Cor. 6:19–20; Eph. 1:13–14; 4:30).[26]

A second possible reason why God chose speaking in tongues is that it may be the only universal initial evidence possible. Since the sign is to bear witness to the moment God fills a person's being, then the sign must reveal the supernatural presence of God moving within the person and in cooperation with the person. If a person merely speaks in a known language, no supernatural evidence is present, but if a person speaks in an unknown language, then this miraculous happening testifies to the inner presence and work of the Spirit.

Although it is difficult to conceive of another evidence that would universally reveal the integral link between the person being filled with the Spirit and the Spirit himself, speaking in tongues may be the only possible initial evidence of Spirit baptism.

Inner Witness

Three major accounts of the reception of the Holy Ghost specifically mention speaking in tongues (Acts 2:1–4; Acts 10:44–48; Acts 19:1–6). Nevertheless, while speaking in tongues is the initial physical evidence of Spirit baptism, this outward sign does not diminish the reality of the inner witness of this experience.

Acts 2:4 indicates the inner witness of the Spirit by stating that the disciples spoke in tongues "as the Spirit gave them utterance." In other words, the physical evidence emerged from the inspiration or prompting of the infilling Spirit. It is therefore inconceivable that the disciples did not inwardly discern the infilling presence of the Spirit, since the Spirit both inspired and formed the words they spoke.

On the one hand, if speaking in tongues was psychologically induced or merely human effort, it would be gibberish and therefore not a witness of the Spirit. On the other hand, when the Spirit gives the utterance, a person speaks in a language, although it is unknown to him and perhaps to anyone else present. What is spoken emerges from the believer's regenerated spirit and soul, thus reflecting and projecting a new relationship with God. In explaining the gift of tongues, Paul wrote that speaking in "unknown tongues" is a communication between a person's spirit and God in which the person speaking receives spiritual edification (1 Cor. 14:2). To call speaking in tongues mere gibberish denigrates the inner communication by which a person's spirit interacts with God's indwelling Spirit. (See 1 Cor. 14:2, 4, 13–14, 19, 27.)

On the day of Pentecost, people in the audience understood the "tongues," but the speakers themselves did not understand what they spoke. If no one present had understand the languages spoken, the miracle would have remained and the evidence would still have been effective, for the evidence is not only outward to others but both outward and inward to the person receiving the Spirit.

Although the discussion of speaking in tongues in 1 Corinthians 12 and 14 does not address the issue of the initial evidence of Spirit baptism, the essence of speaking as the Spirit gives the utterance is the same. All biblical speaking in tongues emerges from the indwelling Spirit and not merely from human will.

Paul wrote that the Spirit of God witnesses to our spirit that we are his children: "The Spirit itself beareth witness with our spirit, that we are the children of God" (Rom. 8:16). Spirit baptism unites a person with God as Father, causing that person to cry, "Abba, Father" (Rom. 8:15). Even Paul's dramatic experience near Damascus would have been insufficient without the culminating salvational experience of Spirit baptism. Indeed, Christianity would be reduced to a philosophy or a theological system of thought if its adherents did not encounter Christ within their being, for Christ within the believer is the only living witness of his resurrection.

This inner witness is therefore beyond theory and human understanding; it is more than a profession of faith, for it resides not in theological abstractions but in the reality of the union of God's Spirit with a person's spirit, a union in which the Holy Spirit is dominant yet without coercion or absorption (1 Cor. 6:17). Paul expressed this inner witness in paradoxical language: "I am crucified with Christ: nevertheless I live; yet not I, but Christ liveth in me: and the life which I now live in the flesh I live by the faith of the Son of God, who loved me, and gave himself for me" (Gal. 2:20). John likewise referred to the inner witness of the Spirit: "And hereby we know that he abideth in us, by the Spirit which he hath given us" (1 John 3:24; see also 1 John 4:13.)

Although the fruit of the Spirit—love, joy, peace, longsuffering, gentleness, goodness, faith, meekness, and temperance—speaks of an inner work of the Spirit that produces outward patterns of attitude and behavior, non-Christians can experience and to a degree exhibit similar attitudes and behavior. However, while non-Christians may reflect human character of a lofty kind, perhaps surpassing many professing Christians in charity, dedication, and sacrifice, without the indwelling Spirit whatever they achieve will still be tainted by their unregenerated carnal impulses. Only the Holy Ghost within a person sanctifies and purifies the inner spirit and soul.

The kingdom of God is "righteousness, and peace, and joy in the Holy Ghost" (Rom. 14:17). Since humans can know a measure of righteousness, peace, and joy without the gift of the Holy Ghost, the distinction is that the righteousness resident by the Spirit has no condemnation (Rom. 8:1). The peace that Jesus gives is "not as the world giveth" (John 14:27), but it a "peace [that] . . . passeth all understanding" (Phil. 4:7). Human joy is experienced relative to a person's circumstances, but the joy of the Holy Ghost is "joy unspeakable and full of glory" even in times of burdens, temptations, and trials of fire (1 Pet. 1:6–8). To experience righteousness without condemnation, peace beyond understanding, and joy unspeakable and full of glory does not negate the need for the initial physical evidence of Spirit baptism, but it focuses upon the wellspring of the indwelling Spirit from whom comes speaking in tongues.

If God were merely an abstract idea and not a personal being, then the person who possesses the idea of God would possess him. But God is more than an idea. He is a personal spirit-being, and when an individual receives him, God personally enters that one's life. Such a moment cannot pass unnoticed either by that person or by others. God gives both an inner witness and an outward physical expression of Spirit baptism.

CONCLUSION

Most Oneness Pentecostals view Spirit baptism as completing the salvational experience that is initiated by faith in Jesus Christ, repentance, and water baptism in the name of Jesus Christ. With other classical

Pentecostals, Oneness Pentecostals hold that the indispensable initial physical evidence of the baptism of the Holy Ghost is speaking in tongues as the Spirit gives the utterance.

NOTES

1. F. J. Ewart, *The Phenomenon of Pentecost* (St. Louis, Mo.: Pentecostal Publishing House, 1947), 73–75. H. V. Synan, *The Holiness-Pentecostal Movement in the United States* (Grand Rapids: Eerdmans, 1971), 162–63.

2. W. W. Menzies, *Anointed to Serve: The Story of the Assemblies of God* (Springfield, Mo.: Gospel Publishing House, 1971), 76–77.

3. W. J. Hollenweger, *The Pentecostals* (Minneapolis: Augsburg, 1977; repr. Peabody, Mass.: Hendrickson, 1988), 24–25.

4. Menzies, *Anointed to Serve*, 115.

5. Ewart, *Phenomenon*, 54–55.

6. Menzies, *Anointed to Serve*, 118–20. Menzies reports that the ministerial roll of the Assemblies of God dropped from 585 to 429.

7. The fundamental doctrine statement of the United Pentecostal Church reads: "The basic and fundamental doctrine of this organization shall be the Bible standard of full salvation, which is repentance, baptism in water by immersion in the name of the Lord Jesus Christ for the remission of sins, and the baptism of the Holy Ghost with the initial sign of speaking with other tongues as the Spirit gives utterance. We shall endeavor to keep the unity of the Spirit until we all come into the unity of the faith, at the same time admonishing all brethren that they shall not contend for their different views to the disunity of the body." Articles of Faith, "Fundamental Doctrine," *Manual of the United Pentecostal Church International* (Hazelwood, Mo.: United Pentecostal Church International, 1990), 22.

8. The word *steps* is used by Oneness Pentecostals to identify three elements of the salvational experience: repentance, water baptism, and the infilling of the Spirit. However, since the sequence does not always follow this order (note the reverse of water baptism and the baptism of the Holy Ghost in Acts 10), the word *steps* is functional but not ideal. The use of *steps* corresponds to what Laurence Christenson calls "three links: repentance and faith, water baptism, and the baptism with the Holy Spirit." He states that this list is "the normal sequence with no significant time lapse. For all practical purposes it is one unified experience with three distinct aspects." Christenson identifies the pattern of this "unified experience" as: "The Word of salvation in Christ is proclaimed; the hearer receives the word, believes, and is baptized with water; the believer is baptized with the Holy Spirit." L. Christenson, *Speaking in Tongues and Its Significance for the Church* (Minneapolis: Bethany Fellowship, 1968), 37–38.

9. Early Pentecostals used the word *full* to stress the distinctive experience of the Holy Ghost. It appeared in such phrases as "full gospel" and the "fullness of the Spirit." [Cf. D. W. Dayton, *Theological Roots of Pentecostalism* (reprint, Peabody, Mass.: Hendrickson, 1991); Ed.] Oneness Pentecostals

often use *full* to indicate the completed process of salvation, including repentance, water baptism, and Spirit baptism. The word is not intended to indicate that a person is half or partly saved, but it simply recognizes the genuineness of a person's experience in faith, repentance, and water baptism, all of which lead toward the infilling of the Spirit.

10. D. K. Bernard, *The New Birth* (Hazelwood, Mo.: Word Aflame Press, 1984), 85–101. Bernard presents the view of most Oneness Pentecostals on the new birth.

11. L. Ford, "The 'Finger of God' in Evangelism," in J. I. Packer and P. Fromer, eds., *The Best in Theology* (Carol Stream, Ill.: Christianity Today, 1987), vol. 1, 292–93. Ford states, "A true and complete conversion must involve both the sweeping clean that takes place in forgiveness and the occupying of the cleansed spirit when the Holy Spirit takes up residence. Certainly for the first Christians it was clear that a complete conversion included accepting the Word of God, being baptized in the name of Jesus, and receiving the Holy Spirit."

12. Christenson makes this same point: "This [the event in Samaria] is our clearest indication in Scripture that the baptism with the Holy Spirit is an aspect of our relationship to Christ which is distinct from repentance and baptism. It is closely linked to both, but is possible to have one without the other, as the text clearly indicates. However, *it is not considered normal to have one without the other*" (Christenson, *Speaking in Tongues*, 49–50 [emphasis is Christenson's]).

13. The scriptural analogy of being buried with Christ in baptism before being raised together with him to walk in the newness of life (Rom. 6:3–5) indicates that water baptism normally precedes Spirit baptism. While this order prevailed in two events (Acts 8:16; 19:5–6) and perhaps in others (Acts 2:38–41; 9:17–18 and 22:16), the reverse order in Acts 10:44–48 reveals that people can and do receive the Holy Ghost before water baptism. In other words, receiving the Holy Ghost is not contingent upon water baptism. At the same time, Acts 10:44–48 stresses the necessity of water baptism, for those who received the Holy Ghost were commanded to be baptized in the name of Jesus Christ.

14. Bernard, *New Birth*, 129–36. Oneness Pentecostals do not teach baptismal regeneration but that water baptism is "for the remission of sins" (Acts 2:38). Regeneration is the work of the Holy Ghost.

15. G. D. Fee, "Baptism in the Holy Spirit: The Issue of Separability and Subsequence," *Pneuma* 7 (1985): 89–90. Fee notes that exegetical problems make tenuous the interpretation of John 20:22 as a regenerational experience of the Spirit.

16. P. Hocken, "The Meaning and Purpose of 'Baptism in the Spirit,' " *Pneuma* 7 (1985): 131, 133. Hocken suggests that the implied tritheism in separating Jesus and the Holy Ghost could have caused the doctrinal division that produced the Oneness Pentecostal movement. He contends that the argument of receiving the Spirit of Christ at conversion and the Holy Ghost at Spirit baptism is not satisfactory.

17. A. A. Hoekema, *Tongues and Spirit-Baptism* (Grand Rapids: Baker, 1981), 57–58; R. M. Riggs, *The Spirit Himself* (Springfield, Mo.: Gospel Publishing House, 1949), 43–61, 101; D. and R. Bennett, *The Holy Spirit and*

You (Plainfield, N.J.: Logos International, 1971), 56, 64–65; H. M. Ervin, *This Which You See and Hear* (Minneapolis: Bethany Fellowship, 1968), 42; Christenson, *Speaking in Tongues*, 37, 48.

18. Fee, "Issue of Separability and Sequence," 91–96. Although not arriving at the same conclusions concerning the Oneness of God, Fee writes, "Note, finally, that nowhere does the New Testament say, 'Get saved, and then be filled with the Spirit.' To them, getting saved, which included repentance and forgiveness obviously, meant especially to be filled with the Spirit. That all believers in Christ are Spirit-filled is the *presupposition* of the New Testament writers. . . . They simply did not think of Christian initiation as a two-stage process. For them, to be a Christian meant to have the Spirit, to be a 'Spirit person' " (emphasis is Fee's).

19. Riggs, *Spirit Himself,* 58–59. In an attempt to distinguish the word *baptize* in 1 Corinthians 12:13 from its use in reference to the Spirit in the Gospels and Acts, Riggs interprets the clause, "For by one Spirit are we all baptized into one body," to mean regeneration and not Spirit baptism. Oddly, he interprets the last clause of this verse, "and [we] have all been made to drink into one Spirit," as the baptism of the Spirit. He states: "The two clauses of this verse, then, speak of two experiences: salvation and Baptism in the Spirit." That the verse uses two analogies to describe the same experience appears to be more logical.

20. R. Lovelace, "Baptism in the Holy Spirit and the Evangelical Tradition," *Pneuma* 7 (1985): 119; Menzies, *Anointed to Serve*, 37, 39; S. E. Parham, *The Life of Charles F. Parham* (Joplin, Mo.: Hunter Printing Company, 1930), 52, 58–58.

21. Parham, *Life*, 52–53, 59, 66. Although some confusion exists about the date Ozman received the Holy Ghost (she apparently spoke a few words in tongues during prayer several days earlier than January 1, 1901), it was her experience of speaking in tongues when Parham laid hands on her that sparked the Pentecostal outpouring in Topeka.

22. Ibid., 53, 61.

23. E. E. Goss, *The Winds of God*, rev. ed. (Hazelwood, Mo.: Word Aflame Press, 1977), 104. Goss relates that at a conference in Waco, Texas, in February 1907, a group of Pentecostals agreed on a test to determine if speaking in tongues was the evidence of Spirit baptism. Goss said the test "satisfied even the most skeptical among us" that speaking in tongues is the evidence. Agnes Ozman made the same experiential test: "It was some months later I was persuaded in my own heart about the evidence of the baptism of the Holy Spirit and I proved the Lord nine times concerning it" (Parham, *Life*, 67). One prominent early Pentecostal leader, F. F. Bosworth, created a crisis in the Assemblies of God when he disagreed with the initial evidence doctrine. After a debate on this subject at the General Council in 1918, the Assemblies of God adopted a firmer statement supporting speaking in tongues as the initial evidence of Spirit baptism. Bosworth withdrew from the organization (Menzies, *Anointed to Serve*, 126–30).

24. Since the Greek word *glōssa*, meaning tongue or language, appears in Acts 2, 10 and 19, it seems conclusive that the disciples in Jerusalem, the Gentiles in Caesarea, and the disciples in Ephesus spoke in languages. In Jerusalem, the people understood the languages, but there is no indication

that anyone understood the languages spoken in Caesarea and Ephesus. Moreover, since the same word occurs in 1 Corinthians 12 and 14, it appears that the gift of "divers kinds of tongues" and the "unknown tongue" also refer to languages, unknown perhaps by those present and not necessarily identifiable among the thousands of languages and dialects spoken on earth today.

25. Hoekema, *Tongues*, 70. A critic of Pentecostalism, Hoekema nevertheless concedes that speaking in tongues was the sign of the Spirit's reception among the Samaritans.

26. F. L. Arrington, "The Indwelling, Baptism, and Infilling with the Holy Spirit: A Differentiation of Terms," *Pneuma* 3 (1981): 2–3.

11

NORMAL, BUT NOT A NORM: "INITIAL EVIDENCE" AND THE NEW TESTAMENT

Larry W. Hurtado

This is a departure from the sort of essay* that I usually write. On the one hand, those contributing to this "exegetical" section of this volume have been asked to discuss the New Testament material concerning tongues speaking—basically a scholarly assignment in exegesis. On the other hand, we have been asked to consider this material with reference to the modern Pentecostal doctrine that speaking in tongues constitutes the "initial physical evidence" of the "baptism in the Holy Spirit." This changes the task from a simple description of New Testament texts to an exercise in biblical theology (tinged with potential for polemical tensions). Moreover, we have been invited to contribute to this collection in part because we represent different personal histories and stances toward tongues speaking, which invests these essays with considerably more of an explicitly autobiographical element than a simple exercise in exegesis or biblical theology.

In the spirit of such candor, therefore, I offer a summary of my own relationship to the Pentecostal movement. I received my initial spiritual

---

* I dedicate this essay to William Jesse Burton (my maternal grandfather), who first taught me the importance of careful study of Scripture in doctrinal matters.—LWH

formation in Pentecostal circles and was involved in Assemblies of God churches between 1957 and 1975. In the subsequent years, my church fellowship has been in a Baptist church and now (for about a decade) in an Anglican church.

I am by choice, therefore, not a member of a Pentecostal group, though I once was. I suppose that I could be called an "ex-Pentecostal," if my formal associations are the criterion. But this term could suggest that one wishes to be completely disassociated with anything "Pentecostal"; but, in my case, that suggestion would be incorrect. I was asked to write this essay because I represent a different stance toward Pentecostalism and associated phenomena such as tongues speaking. I suppose, in the parlance suggested by one recent analyst of the worldwide Pentecostal-influenced renewal movements, I could be called a "Post-pentecostal," though any label is of limited value in understanding people and important issues.[1] Succinctly put, my own posture with regard to Pentecostalism and tongues speaking involves the following combination: (1) a gratitude and appreciation for features of Pentecostalism that shaped my spiritual life in my earlier years; (2) an affirmation of the legitimacy of such phenomena as tongues speaking as a feature of Christian spirituality and church life; and (3) a doctrinal understanding of the Holy Spirit's work and of the significance of tongues speaking in particular that prevents me from accepting the traditional formulations of the Pentecostal churches with which I am directly familiar.

In place of a traditional Pentecostal view that tongues speaking constitutes the requisite "initial physical evidence" of a special endowment with the Spirit, I take the position that tongues speaking can be affirmed as an acceptable, even salutary, feature of Christian devotional life, but in itself does not constitute "evidence" of any special spiritual status or of a separate experience of the Spirit beyond regeneration. I do not regard tongues speaking as abnormal, unhealthy, or to be avoided. It is, to use the language of the behavioral sciences, "normal," within the range of Christian devotional behavior that is compatible with legitimate spirituality and healthy personality. As I shall attempt to show briefly, the New Testament suggests that tongues speaking can be "edifying." Controlled studies on modern Christians whose religious life incorporates tongues speaking indicate no reason to see any connection between the phenomenon and unhealthy personality.[2] But I do not see how tongues speaking can be made a "norm," as is done when the phenomenon is required as "the initial evidence" of being "Spirit-filled" or of a special experience called "the baptism in the Holy Spirit."

In place of the traditional Pentecostal formulations about tongues speaking, and instead of the usual rejection or benign disdain of the phenomenon among Christians outside of Pentecostal and charismatic circles, there is this third alternative. In what follows, I propose to explain why I have found it to be the most cogent and appealing as a reflection of the New Testament data. In order to do this, unfortunately, I shall have to show why I find the traditional Pentecostal view of tongues unpersuasive. One of the most impressive emphases of my Pentecostal background was that Scripture is the most important criterion of the validity of doctrines. In the following discussion, therefore, I shall focus on the scriptural data concerning tongues speaking to determine what sort of doctrine about this phenomenon is warranted.

THE "INITIAL EVIDENCE" QUESTION

Perhaps the first exegetical observation to offer is a negative one. The question of what constitutes "the initial evidence" of a person having received the "baptism in the Spirit" simply is not raised anywhere in the New Testament. Of course, those who hold traditional Pentecostal views will not find this a surprising or controversial statement. The case for the view that tongues speaking is the initial evidence of a special experience of the Spirit was never presented as based upon explicit teachings in the New Testament. Instead, the traditional Pentecostal doctrine amounted to inferences urged as appropriately drawn from certain passages, particularly in the book of Acts.

Now it would be the most severe form of biblicism to refuse to deal with any theological question not treated explicitly in the Scriptures or to declare a doctrine invalid simply because it is not explicitly taught there. To mention an obvious example, the doctrine of the Trinity is not taught explicitly in the New Testament either; but nearly all would agree that this by itself neither renders the doctrine invalid nor makes the questions associated with the doctrine inappropriate to address.

But, to pursue the example cited a bit further, the major reason why the New Testament can be investigated with regard to the doctrine of the Trinity is that it is clear that the faith and teachings about God and Christ reflected in the New Testament represent early stages of a religious and theological process that resulted in the developed doctrine of the Trinity and the accompanying two-natures Christology of the first five centuries A.D. That is, though a period of time elapsed before the classical doctrine of the Trinity was fully formulated, earlier stages of the issues and forces that led to this formulation can be traced back into the New Testament itself and are directly reflected in the many passages in which God and Christ are explicitly the focus. It appears that the Christian movement, from its earliest observable stages, was engaged in attempting to understand God in the light of Christ, and accorded Christ the veneration normally reserved for God alone in the biblical tradition within which Christianity arose.[3] And from the earliest observable stages of the Christian movement onward in an unbroken line, it is clear that doctrinal questions about God and Christ's relationship to God were central issues.

In the case of the "initial evidence" question, however, we are dealing with an issue that arose in connection with developments in certain North American renewal movements of the late nineteenth and early twentieth centuries, particularly holiness movements and the Keswick-influenced movements represented by figures like R. A. Torrey.[4] In the face of widespread perceptions of a lack of spiritual vitality in major Christian denominations of that period, questions of whether there is a separate and superior level of Holy Spirit empowerment subsequent to regeneration, how this subsequent experience is understood, and what phenomena are the "evidence" of this experience all became pressing matters in various circles committed to renewal.

It is not my purpose to dwell on the historical background of the modern Pentecostal movement and its theological formulations. My point is simply that the question of "the initial evidence" of the "baptism in the Spirit" is foreign to the New Testament and reflects relatively modern church struggles and group formation. Unlike such matters as the Christian doctrine of God, the question of whether there is a separate level of Spirit empowerment subsequent to regeneration, with a required "evidence" of it, seems not to be reflected at all in the New Testament. We do not find early stages of a discussion leading to such a question in the New Testament; and the claim that the New Testament teaches such an experience and that tongues speaking is to be taken as the initial evidence of this experience amount to eisegesis, the inappropriate reading of one's views into the biblical text.

Few if any Christians set out to misrepresent the New Testament, however, and the standard Pentecostal views on "initial evidence" are to be seen as resulting from zealous but misguided handling of the biblical data. In the next section, therefore, we examine the key biblical material in order to sketch its proper interpretation.

ACTS AND TONGUES SPEAKING

As indicated already, the usual argument for the Pentecostal view of tongues speaking as the required "initial evidence" of baptism in the Spirit amounts to inferential treatment of certain passages, particularly in the Acts of the Apostles.[5] Essentially, the argument proceeds as follows.

First, among five passages in Acts where people are "filled" with the Holy Spirit or are given the Spirit, tongues speaking is mentioned in three cases as an immediate result (2:1–4; 10:44–47; 19:1–7). In the two other passages usually considered (8:14–19; 9:17–19), no specific phenomena are highlighted. Thus, where specific phenomena are linked with the gift of the Spirit in Acts, tongues speaking is mentioned. In the other cases, tongues speaking is not mentioned but may be inferred (so the argument goes) as having happened on the basis of its explicit mention in the three clear cases.

Second, it is assumed and urged that the Acts passages describing the gift of the Spirit are to be taken as sufficient basis for formulating a doctrine of the reception of the Spirit good for all time, including a doctrine of the "initial evidence" of the reception of the Spirit. That is, the descriptions of Spirit-reception and infilling in Acts are taken as having didactic, prescriptive force, pointing to a doctrine of the reception of the Spirit in the life of believers. This too is basically an inference, as the author of Acts nowhere explicitly indicates such an intention. This inference is really the more crucial, it seems to me, for only by assuming that Acts is intended to provide the basis for formulating a doctrine of the reception of the Spirit in the life of the believer can one marshall the particular passages mentioned above so as to develop a doctrine of the way the Spirit is received and to be manifested at reception. As mentioned earlier, there is no disputing the observation that the doctrine of "initial evidence" is not explicitly taught anywhere in the New Testament. The whole argument depends, then, on whether it is proper to make the inferences about the Acts passages summarized here.

Within the limits of this essay, it is neither possible nor necessary to try to treat in depth the Holy Spirit in Acts.[6] I shall restrict myself to a discussion of specific matters directly relevant to the focus of this volume.

The major question begged by the Pentecostal use of Acts passages summarized above is basically as follows: What is the apparent purpose of the Acts accounts of Spirit-receptions? To put the question this way is to recognize as a hermeneutical principle that our use of Scripture in theological argument should be consonant with the historical intention of the author/editor of the scriptural writing we are studying. Gordon D.

Fee has, I think, already argued this point quite cogently with particular
reference to Pentecostal use of Scripture.[7]

The scholarly investigation of the purposes of Luke–Acts amounts to a
considerable body of material and yet has not produced unanimity.[8] But
it is generally recognized that the portrayal of the progress of the gospel
from the Jerusalem church, across various cultural, geographical and
ethnic lines, to Rome, the capital city of the Roman Empire, forms at
least an important part of the intention in Luke–Acts. Throughout Acts,
the progress of the gospel is accompanied and prompted by the Holy
Spirit, and the passages focused on in the Pentecostal tradition are simply
examples of this larger pattern.

In Acts the reception and manifestations of the Spirit in Jerusalem at
Pentecost (2:1–4), in Samaria (8:14–19), and in the conversion of the
Gentile Cornelius (10:44–48) are all dramatic scenes showing the gospel's
progress to new ethnic and cultural groups. The Spirit's bestowal on Paul
in Damascus (9:10–19) is part of the author's larger focus on Paul as the
great agent of the progress of the gospel, whose career consumes the
second half of Acts (chs. 13–28), where the Spirit directs and aids Paul at
every turn. And the account concerning the disciples of the Baptist in
Ephesus fits the pattern too. Together with the preceding account concerning Apollos (18:24–28), Acts 19:1–7 shows how the gospel fulfills
and eclipses the ministry of John the Baptist.[9]

It is this emphasis on the Spirit's role in the gospel's progress at these
crucial, dramatic points that is the author's main concern in the passages
singled out in Pentecostal teaching. The author's purpose was not to
provide a basis for formulating *how* the Spirit is received, but rather it
seems to have been to show *that* the Spirit prompted and accompanied
the progress of the gospel at every significant juncture and was the power
enabling the work of Christian leaders.

This explains why the author sometimes does and sometimes does not
(8:14–19; 9:17–19) bother to describe specifically *how* the Spirit was
manifested when people are described as "filled" or otherwise gifted with
the Spirit. When the author does emphasize specific phenomena, he does
not seem to do so in order to teach a doctrine of the Spirit's reception. At
least, there is no hint that this was his purpose. His intent instead seems
to be to show the validity of the gospel developments described. For
example, in 10:44–48, the tongues speaking and extolling of God among
the Gentiles of Cornelius' household are taken as signs that the Spirit has
really prompted the proclamation to Gentiles and that welcoming them
into Christian fellowship is proper. The issue is the legitimacy of the
proclamation of the gospel to Gentiles and is not a doctrine of "initial

evidence" of a Spirit empowerment distinguishable from regeneration. This is evident from the immediately following passage (11:1–18), where Peter's statement that the Gentiles had been given "the same gift" of the Holy Spirit as was given to the Jerusalem church is part of Peter's argument for the propriety of his fellowship with the Gentile Christians. This can only indicate that Cornelius' household has been made partakers of the same eschatological salvation as the Jerusalem church. In 19:1–7, the mention of tongues speaking and prophesying in connection with the gift of the Spirit to the disciples of the Baptist seems to be intended to illustrate the superiority of the gospel of Christ to the message of John, whose disciples, says the author, had "never even heard that there is a Holy Spirit" (19:2).

In Acts 4:31, a sixth passage narrating a bestowal of the Spirit, usually overlooked in traditional Pentecostal discussions, the apostles Peter and John and additional Jerusalem Christians are described as "filled" with the Spirit and are thereby enabled to speak boldly "the word of God." Thus, the phenomena mentioned as accompanying the Spirit (tongues, prophecy, boldness, etc.) vary in the six Acts passages, showing that the author was not concerned with any one phenomenon, such as tongues, and suggesting that he did not see the Spirit's bestowal in terms of consistent "evidence" of any one phenomenon.

The most that one could legitimately infer from the descriptions of the bestowal of the Spirit in Acts about the author's view of such phenomena as tongues speaking, prophecy, and courageous declaration of the gospel is that these phenomena were all familiar features of early Christian spiritual life and were manifestations of the Holy Spirit. If one were seeking to use the Acts passages for didactic purposes, one might suggest also that such phenomena are therefore to be regarded as among the legitimate, "biblical" manifestations of the Spirit in the continuing progress of the gospel and life of the churches. But the claim that these passages reflect a fixed doctrine of how the Spirit is to be received in the lives of believers, including a doctrine of "initial evidence" of the Spirit's reception, has no basis in the apparent intention of the author of Acts. To the degree that the traditional Pentecostal view of "initial evidence" rests on these Acts passages (and these passages are the biblical basis offered), the view must be regarded, I suggest, as an unfounded assertion. In short, the Pentecostal doctrine of "initial evidence" rests on an unexamined and simplistic notion of the purpose of the Acts narratives and involves the dubious procedure of extrapolating selectively from the three references to tongues in Acts to a doctrine purporting to capture the required manner of being "filled" with the Spirit.

TONGUES SPEAKING IN 1 CORINTHIANS

The other significant New Testament body of material directly concerned with tongues speaking is 1 Corinthians 12–14, and to these passages we now turn.[10] In traditional Pentecostal thinking, the tongues speaking described in 1 Corinthians 12–14 is different from the tongues speaking in Acts. Pentecostals have traditionally found the tongues speaking of Acts to be the phenomenon they call "initial evidence" of Spirit baptism; but the tongues speaking mentioned in 1 Corinthians 12–14 is a special ministry gift of utterance intended to edify the congregation. I suggest, however, that this schematization imposes an artificial dichotomy on the New Testament references to tongues, and that the real picture is at once more complicated and more simple. I have already indicated above that I find the traditional Pentecostal view of tongues in Acts to be unpersuasive; in what follows I attempt to show the relevance of 1 Corinthians 12–14 for understanding the New Testament phenomenon of tongues.

First, Paul's references to tongues indicate that the phenomenon is familiar to his original readers. He never defines the phenomenon, but proceeds with putting it in its proper context over against the apparent misuse and misguided estimation of tongues among at least some of the Corinthian Christians. Indeed, as is commonly recognized among scholars, the Corinthian fascination with tongues speaking was probably the reason Paul devoted such attention to the phenomenon in this epistle. Now, though it may be something of an argument from silence, one would think that in his rather detailed instructions about tongues speaking Paul would have included a reference to its supposed significance as "initial evidence" of Spirit baptism, if such an understanding of tongues were current at that time. It should at least give pause to those who hold the traditional Pentecostal view that Paul gives not the slightest hint of such a teaching.

Second, although it is correct that Paul includes tongues speaking among various "gifts" or "manifestations" of the Spirit to be used "for the common good" (12:4–11), he goes on to qualify the operation of tongues speaking in such ways that seem to distinguish it from the other Spirit gifts he mentions. One gets the impression that Paul includes tongues speaking among the phenomena that might be manifested in the congregational gathering, mainly because the Corinthians were bent on the exercise of tongues in this setting. Paul's tactic is to admit the legitimacy of tongues as a congregational "gift," but only when its manifestation conforms to his rules, which seem intended to avoid the abuses promoted among the Corinthians. Because Paul views tongues speaking as a genuine manifestation of the Spirit, he cannot forbid the phenomenon (14:39–40). But, because of the Corinthian abuse of tongues speaking, and because of its inherent limitations as a "ministry gift," he discourages its use in the congregation in preference to other gifts such as prophecy, as we shall now see.

Note how Paul limits the exercise of tongues as a congregational "gift." In 12:27–30, Paul limits the significance of any of the "gifts" listed (including tongues) by emphasizing that they are all divinely given (vv. 27–28) and that none of them (including tongues speaking) is intended to be exercised by all Christians (vv. 29–30).

Later, however, Paul proceeds to single out tongues speaking, imposing particular limits on its operation in the congregation. In 14:1–12, Paul underscores the incomprehensibility of tongues speaking as the major limitation of its usefulness in the church. In short, in Paul's view, if the listener cannot understand rationally the meaning of what is said, the listener cannot be "edified." The tongues-speech is no "gift" to the listener unless it can be made comprehensible by an interpretation (esp. 14:5). Christians who seek to exercise manifestations of the Spirit should aim to edify others (14:12), and this means that any tongues speaking in the Christian gathering must be interpreted so that the others can share in the gift (14:13). Indeed, in view of the importance of speaking intelligibly to others in the congregation, Paul advises avoidance of tongues speaking in favor of speech in the vernacular (14:18–19). If "outsiders" (*idiōtai*) or "unbelievers" (*apistoi*) are present, Paul warns, tongues speaking is likely to be counter-productive, leading them to write off the congregation as mad (14:23).

Thus, in fact, Paul discourages tongues speaking as a congregational "gift," permitting the phenomenon in the congregation only with reservations and firm restrictions (especially, tongues must *always* be interpreted when manifested in church). We catch his hesitation and reluctance about the public manifestation of tongues in 14:26–33. Paul includes tongues speaking in the sampling of phenomena that might be contributed "when you come together" (v. 26). But note the subtle way Paul downplays the importance of tongues speaking in comparison with prophecy in this passage. Paul uses imperative verb forms to urge mutual edification (14:26, *ginesthō*), to promote prophecies and the "weighing" of what is said by others (14:29, *laleitōsan, diakrinetosan*), and to order speakers to give way to one another (14:30, *sigatō*). In 14:27–28, Paul uses imperatives to insist on interpretation of tongues-speech (*diermēneuetō*) and to direct the tongues-speaker to be silent (*sigatō*) and to speak (*laleitō*) "to himself and to God" if there is no one present to interpret.

In contrast to all these imperatives, the almost diffident way Paul mentions tongues speaking in 14:27 seems deliberate and striking. "If any speak in a tongue" (*eite glōssē tis lalei*), suggests at most a somewhat reluctant permission for congregational exercise of tongues, and then only under a series of restrictions: two or three utterances at most, one at a time, and interpretation always required.[11] And 14:29–33, with its several references to prophecy and its benign neglect of tongues, suggests what is clearly stated earlier (14:1–5), that prophecy (inspired utterance in the vernacular) is Paul's preferred mode of charismatic utterance for congregational ministry.

All this means that, contrary to the traditional Pentecostal view, in 1 Corinthians 12–14 we do not have advocacy of a special "gift" of tongues speaking intended to be used in the congregation. Instead, we have Paul discouraging tongues in the church, permitting the phenomenon reluctantly and only if the tongues-speech is interpreted so that the church might derive some benefit. And we get the impression that the exercise of tongues in the church was never suggested by Paul but has been promoted by the Corinthians.

Paul freely grants the spiritual validity of tongues and its personal benefits to the speaker (14:2, 4) and confirms his own exercise of tongues speaking (14:18). He clearly includes the phenomenon as one of the manifestations of the Spirit that characterized the Christian spirituality he knew and approved. If, then, for Paul tongues speaking does not seem to be the "initial evidence" of Spirit baptism, and if for him the phenomenon is likewise not really a preferred ministry gift for the congregation, what role does he seem to assign tongues speaking?

The answer, which comes out at several points in 1 Corinthians 14, is that tongues speaking is essentially a distinctive form of prayer and praise, mainly of value, therefore, in private devotion.[12] In 14:13–19, Paul's illustrations of the use of tongues speaking are restricted to praying in tongues (v. 14–15), giving thanks (to God) in tongues (vv. 16–17), and singing (praise) to God in tongues (v. 15). Praying and singing in tongues, which Paul can also refer to as praying and singing "with my spirit," are mentioned as variations to praying and singing "with my mind."[13] In the context, "with my mind" must mean prayer and song in the language(s) understood rationally by the speaker. Accordingly, Paul's references to prayer/praise "with my spirit" suggests that he thought of what we would call human personality as having more than one layer or level, the human "spirit" being a kind of inner level or realm not fully accessible to the "mind" of rational knowledge.[14]

This understanding of tongues as prayer and praise makes sense of 14:2–4, where Paul says that the tongues-speaker communicates "not to men but to God," that in tongues one utters (but does not understand) "mysteries [*mystēria*] in the Spirit,"[15] and that one who speaks in tongues "edifies himself." That is, because tongues speaking is prayer and praise, it can be described as directed to God, unlike prophecy, which is a divinely inspired address to people. Paul offers no explanation of how tongues speaking edifies the speaker here, and his conviction that the practice is edifying may very likely be experientially based, given his own statement of his personal familiarity with tongues speaking (14:18).

The Spirit-inspired quality of tongues speaking means that it must be productive, edifying, even if one does not understand "with the mind" how it can be. But the fact that the rational mind cannot make sense of tongues speaking means that it cannot be of value to anyone else other than the speaker. This in turn means that tongues must be seen as essentially a distinctive form of prayer/devotion for use privately, "one to one with God" we might say, and not in the gathered Christian community. This is the preferred role for tongues speaking as far as we can tell from Paul; and this was probably the major use of tongues speaking in the early church, where Corinthian misuse of tongues was avoided. Paul makes it plain that violations of his restrictions on tongues speaking are not acceptable (14:37–38!).

CONCLUSION

In sum, the material in Acts does not justify a doctrine of "initial evidence" in which tongues speaking is the requisite for all Christians as the seal of some sort of post-regeneration spiritual status or experience. There is a Lucan use of tongues in certain episodes of Acts as part of the author's intention to show the genuineness of the spread of the gospel to new people and groups. And 1 Corinthians 12–14 cannot be understood as referring to another type of tongues speaking, a supposed ministry gift for congregational use. In 1 Corinthians 12–14, Paul tries to redirect the Corinthians away from their fascination for tongues speaking as a congregational phenomenon by promoting the understanding of tongues speaking as prayer and praise fit mainly for private devotions and by insisting that any manifestation of tongues in the congregation can be permitted only under strict conditions (two or three at most, one at a time, *always* interpreted).

The Lucan use of tongues as a sign of the gospel's advance, and Paul's own familiarity with tongues (in Corinth, in his own life, and probably elsewhere in his churches) combine to lead us to the conclusion that tongues speaking was a familiar and accepted feature of early Christian spirituality. And in light of this and modern studies of tongues speaking mentioned earlier, I suggest that we can regard the phenomenon as "normal," within the range of Christian spirituality that can still be approved or even encouraged. But there is no basis for making tongues speaking the earmark of any special gift or spiritual state, however much Paul and subsequent Christians have testified to its edifying effect for the individual who prays and praises "with the spirit."

Moreover, I suggest that it trivializes what can be a precious experience of personal, almost mystical, devotion to make tongues speaking into some requisite phenomenon that admits one into full status, "Pentecostal" or otherwise. Surely the great contributions of the Pentecostal movement to modern Christianity will be seen to be its emphasis on the reality of the power of the Holy Spirit, the intensity of its devotional and worship life, and its commitment to world evangelism. Within these contributions, the recovery of tongues speaking as a legitimate expression of Christian spirituality surely fits; but the doctrine of "initial evidence," whatever its historic significance for institutionalized Pentecostalism, should be set aside as a sincere but misguided understanding of Scripture.

NOTES

1. D. B. Barrett, "Statistics, Global," *DPCM*, 810–30, esp. 824.
2. K. McDonnell, *Charismatic Renewal and the Churches* (New York: Seabury Press, 1976), is still the most complete survey of social-scientific studies of glossolalia.
3. See, e.g., L. W. Hurtado, *One God, One Lord: Early Christian Devotion and Ancient Jewish Monotheism* (Philadelphia: Fortress, 1988).
4. See, e.g., the summary and bibliography in K. Kendrick, "Initial Evidence, A Historical Perspective," *DPCM*, 459–60; see also ch. 6 in this volume.
5. The most extensive defense of a classical Pentecostal viewpoint known to me is C. Brumback, *"What Meaneth This?" A Pentecostal Answer to a Pentecostal Question* (Springfield. Mo.: Gospel Publishing House, 1947), esp. 191–287. For more sophisticated (and more guarded) treatments of the Acts passages from a "classical" Pentecostal perspective, see, e.g., W. G. MacDonald, *Glossolalia in the New Testament* (Springfield. Mo.: Gospel Publishing House, ca. 1964); idem, "Pentecostal Theology: A Classical Viewpoint," *Perspectives on*

the New Pentecostalism, ed. R. P. Spittler (Grand Rapids: Baker, 1976), 58–74; and B. C. Aker, "Initial Evidence, A Biblical Perspective," *DPCM,* 455–59.

6. See esp. J. H. E. Hull, *The Holy Spirit in the Acts of the Apostles* (London: Lutterworth Press, 1967); J. D. G. Dunn, *Baptism in the Holy Spirit* (London: SCM, 1970); idem, *Jesus and the Spirit* (Philadelphia: Westminster, 1975); R. Stronstad, *The Charismatic Theology of St. Luke* (Peabody, Mass.: Hendrickson, 1984).

7. G. D. Fee, "Hermeneutics and Historical Precedent—A Major Problem in Pentecostal Hermeneutics," in Spittler, *Perspectives,* 118–32.

8. For an analysis of work, now slightly dated, see I. H. Marshall, *Luke: Historian and Theologian* (Grand Rapids: Zondervan, 1970). For a more recent investigation of the question, see R. L. Maddox, *The Purpose of Luke–Acts* (Edinburgh: T. & T. Clark, 1985).

9. Note that the disciples of the Baptist here are specified as twelve in number, corresponding to the number of the Jerusalem apostles. This suggests that the author intends this passage to be seen in comparison with the Pentecost episode in Acts 2, where the Jerusalem apostles receive the Spirit.

10. For the most recent and helpful commentary discussion of this material, see G. D. Fee, *The First Epistle to the Corinthians,* NICNT (Grand Rapids: Eerdmans, 1987), 569–713. For another treatment of the material reflecting sympathy with Pentecostal spirituality, see, e.g., A. Bittlinger, *Gifts and Graces, A Commentary on 1 Corinthians 12–14* (Grand Rapids: Eerdmans, 1967).

11. See Fee's discussion of the restrictions placed on tongues in 14:27–28 (*First Corinthians,* 691–92).

12. Once again, I refer readers to the incisive treatment by Fee, *First Corinthians,* 670–76.

13. On the translation and meaning of the terms *pneuma* (spirit) and *nous* (mind) in 1 Cor. 12–14, see esp. ibid., 578 (n. 43), 669–71.

14. On the term "spirit" as an anthropological category, see, e.g., J. D. G. Dunn, "Spirit," *NIDNTT* 3:693–95.

15. As Fee notes, the term "mysteries" of 1 Cor. 14:2 may be seen in light of the same term in 13:2 (*First Corinthians,* 656). But we should note that in 13:2 Paul refers to the possibility of understanding divine mysteries, whereas in 14:2 the mysteries spoken of in tongues cannot be understood, even by the speaker in tongues.

12

EVIDENCES OF THE SPIRIT, OR THE SPIRIT AS EVIDENCE? SOME NON-PENTECOSTAL REFLECTIONS

J. Ramsey Michaels

Terms such as "new birth," "election," "sanctification," "imputed righteousness," and the "victorious life" were common enough in the theological vocabulary on which my faith was nurtured, but "initial evidence" never was. I cannot recall even hearing the phrase until I began teaching Pentecostal students in an interdenominational seminary. I soon realized that the expression was important to them in assessing their own religious experience and their relationship to the tradition out of which they had come. Teaching now in a state university, I have little occasion to discuss "initial evidence" in the classroom, yet no one who teaches the Bible or religion in Springfield, Missouri, can be unaware of the term's importance to certain friends and colleagues. "Initial evidence" is part of Pentecostal self-definition, and Springfield is home to the largest of Pentecostal denominations, the Assemblies of God.

How does one examine critically the religious terminology of others, especially when the "others" are good friends and disciples of the same Lord? "Very carefully." It is well to proceed in exactly the same way one would proceed to examine one's own traditions and cherished formulations of belief or experience—with honesty, fairness, and respect. This requires beginning where the Pentecostal tradition itself begins, with the book of Acts and the Pentecost experience. It also requires not ending there.

"INITIAL EVIDENCE" IN THE BOOK OF ACTS

The Pentecostal argument for tongues as the "initial physical evidence" of baptism in the Holy Spirit rests above all on the experience of Cornelius and his companions in Caesarea in Acts 10. Peter's sermon (10:34–43) was interrupted when "the Holy Spirit fell on all who heard the word" (10:44).[1] Luke does not explain precisely *how* "the Holy Spirit fell," but he does tell us that the reaction to it was clear and immediate: "And the believers from among the circumcised who came with Peter were amazed because the gift of the Holy Spirit had been poured out even on the Gentiles. For they heard them speaking in tongues and extolling God" (10:45–46).

The Pentecostal argument, as I understand it, is that the phenomenon of "speaking in tongues" was the audible (i.e., physical) evidence that "the gift of the Holy Spirit had been poured out." Peter seems to confirm this with the rhetorical question, "Can anyone forbid water for baptizing these people who have received the Holy Spirit just as we have?" (v. 47), and with the command that they be "baptized in the name of Jesus Christ" (v. 48). The words, "just as we have," in verse 47 link the incident to the earlier coming of the Spirit among Jewish believers at Pentecost in Acts 2:1–4, where those who were "filled with the Holy Spirit" similarly "began to speak in other tongues" (2:4). The phenomenon of tongues speaking on the day of Pentecost in Acts 2 provides the reference point for validating the experience of Cornelius and his companions in Acts 10. To Pentecostals, the story of Cornelius provides the classic biblical *example* of "initial evidence," and on it the Pentecostal *doctrine* of initial evidence is largely based.

There is nothing wrong in principle with deriving normative beliefs and practices from narratives.[2] The primary documents of Christian faith are, after all, the four Gospel narratives of the life and teaching of Jesus. Their testimonies to God's work of salvation through Jesus Christ do not have to be confirmed by the discursive logic of the apostle Paul in order to be valid. Paul's letters are just as "occasional," just as much rooted in specific historical situations as the Gospels are—more so, in fact. There is no reason why things Paul wrote to his churches in the heat of controversy should necessarily take precedence over stories used by the Gospel

writers to nurture the faith of their communities. The problem with the
Pentecostals' use of the book of Acts is not that they have built a doctrine
of "initial evidence" from an isolated incident (the coming of the Spirit
on Cornelius in the book of Acts is hardly that!). The problem lies rather
in the way in which the move from narrative to doctrine is made.

The first question to ask is, "What is meant by *evidence?*" A typical
dictionary definition is "That which serves to prove or disprove something," or "That which serves as a ground for knowing something with
certainty," or "An outward indication of the existence or fact of something."[3] Such definitions assume "something" as unknown or invisible,
with "evidence" as the tangible or visible pointer to its existence, reality,
or truth. In the Acts narrative, then, what is the "evidence" and what is
the "something" toward which the evidence points? According to most
Pentecostal interpretations, tongues speaking is the outward evidence and
the baptism of the Holy Spirit is the inward reality to which the tongues
phenomenon points. But is this the case in the narratives themselves? In
the account of Peter in the house of Cornelius, the point is *not* that
tongues were the "outward" and "physical" evidence of the "inward" and
"invisible" work of the Holy Spirit. Quite the contrary. The Spirit itself[4]
is nothing in this passage if not "outward" and "physical." It is no "still,
small voice" within the hearts of individuals. Rather, it is visible enough
and noisy enough to bring Peter's sermon to an abrupt end! In retelling
the story a chapter later, Peter indicates that he was only beginning to
preach when the Spirit suddenly stopped him (Acts 11:15).

It is true that Luke pauses momentarily to explain what all the commo-
tion was about: "For they heard them speaking in tongues and extolling
God" (10:46). This parenthetical comment, more than anything else in
the passage, is what suggests to Pentecostals that tongues are the "initial
evidence," while the Spirit is the reality to which the evidence points.
There is no doubt that "speaking in tongues" and "extolling God"[5] are
accompaniments of the Spirit's coming (at least in this instance), but
accompaniments are not quite the same thing as evidence. Peter states for
Luke the conclusion to be drawn from the evidence in Acts 10:47 ("Can
anyone forbid water for baptizing these people *who have received the Holy
Spirit just as we have?*) and again in 11:17 ("If then God gave *the same gift*
to them as he gave to us when we believed in the Lord Jesus Christ, who
was I that I could withstand God?"). The "same gift" mentioned in Acts
11:17 is the decisive evidence to which Peter appeals, but the gift is clearly
not the gift of tongues. It is rather the "gift of the Holy Spirit" mentioned
in Acts 10:45, as well as earlier in 2:38.[6] Tongues speaking (like other
phenomena such as prophecy, visions, or miracles) may *accompany* the

gift under certain circumstances, but in itself tongues is not the gift, and therefore not "evidence" of anything.

This is true also in Acts 19, the only other reference to tongues speaking in the book of Acts. When Paul came to Ephesus, he asked a group of disciples, "Did you receive the Holy Spirit when you believed?" He assumed that if they had received the Spirit they would know it, and indeed they know that they have not: "No, we have never even heard that there is a Holy Spirit" (Acts 19:2). There is not a trace in the book of Acts of the soul-searching of modern Christians who keep asking themselves, "Do I have the Spirit? Do I feel it? Have I been baptized in the Spirit? Am I filled with the Spirit?"—and are never quite certain of the answer. After Paul explained to them the testimony of John the Baptist to Jesus Christ, these disciples "were baptized in the name of the Lord Jesus" (19:5). Then, when Paul laid hands on them, "the Holy Spirit came on them" (19:6). Again the text adds that "they spoke with tongues and prophesied." Once again, tongues and prophecy (not just tongues)[7] are the accompaniments of the reception of the Spirit, yet there is no hint that they were regarded as "evidence." Rather, *the Spirit itself* is the evidence of a decisive change in the experience and commitment of these disciples.

If the Holy Spirit itself is the evidence in Acts 2, Acts 10–11, and Acts 19, the question remains, "Evidence of what?" In the house of Cornelius, the Spirit's coming is evidence that "to the Gentiles also God has granted repentance unto life" (11:18; cf. 10:47). For Peter, the Spirit simply confirms and carries one step further what he had already learned from a vision: i.e., "that I should not call any man common or unclean" (10:28), and "that God shows no partiality, but in every nation any one who fears him and does what is right is acceptable to him" (10:35). In Acts 2, the Spirit is evidence of something quite different, though here too it is Peter who provides the explanation: that "*this* is what was spoken by the prophet Joel" (2:16), and finally that Jesus of Nazareth, "exalted at the right hand of the Father, and having received from the Father the promise of the Holy Spirit, he has poured out *this* which you see and hear" (2:33). In Acts 19, the Spirit is evidence that God has established in Asia Minor a new community of believers, twelve in number like the Twelve in Jerusalem. In each instance *the Spirit itself,* not some particular gift or manifestation of the Spirit, is the evidence ("initial evidence," if you will) of what God is now doing in the world.

From a distance, it has always seemed to me that the strength of the Pentecostal movement lay in its insistence on the empirical, almost tangible, reality of the Holy Spirit. The Spirit of God is a Person, to be sure, but first of all the Spirit is Power, power that can be felt, heard, and even sometimes seen. If you have the Holy Spirit in you, you will know it, and others will know it as well. This is, I believe, an insight profoundly true to the book of Acts, difficult though it may be to square with present-day Christian experience. If it is a fair statement of Pentecostal belief, then the doctrine of "initial evidence" is actually a subtle compromise of that belief. Why? Because the doctrine of "initial evidence" presupposes that the Spirit is just the opposite of what the narratives in Acts imply—i.e., that the Spirit in itself is an inward, invisible "something" that must be *inferred* from a certain outward, audible phenomenon—an individual's ability to speak at least once in foreign or unintelligible languages.

To this extent, American Pentecostalism has bought into an evangelical or pietistic understanding of the Spirit that is inconsistent with its own distinctive character. The evangelical tradition views the Holy Spirit as an inward, invisible reality known by its "fruits," usually defined by an appeal to Galatians 5:22–23: "love, joy, peace, patience, kindness, good-ness, faithfulness, gentleness, self-control." American Pentecostalism, to the degree that it is preoccupied with "initial evidence," views the Holy Spirit in much the same way except that the inward, invisible Spirit is known by its "gifts," or rather by one gift in particular, the gift of tongues. Although tongues are given pride of place as "initial evidence" of the Spirit's baptism, other gifts, as well as the "fruits of the Spirit," are also recognized as valid signs of the Spirit's work in the lives of individuals. These observations suggest that some strands in American Pentecostalism have in common with the evangelical tradition a tendency quite foreign to the New Testament to internalize and (strange as it may sound) "spir-itualize" the Holy Spirit. In the book of Acts, the Spirit needs no "evi-dence" (initial or otherwise) to lead us to it. The Spirit is itself the evidence of the reality of God and of the resurrection and lordship of Jesus Christ.

If there is a problem with the use of the word "evidence" in Pentecostal interpretations of Acts, there is no less a problem with the word "initial." The phrase "*initial* evidence" leads us to expect a preoccupation with the *first* work of the Spirit in the lives of individuals or groups. This is in fact the case in the narratives of Acts, but not in most versions of Pentecostal theology. Tongues are normally regarded by Pentecostals as the physical sign not of the first, but of the *second* stage of the Spirit's ministry in the life of the believer. The first stage, both in Pentecostal and evangelical theology, is regeneration, or the new birth, and most Pentecostal groups that I know do *not* require tongues as initial evidence that a person has been "born again." All that is required is the willing confession of Jesus as Lord, in the tradition of Romans 10:9–10. Tongues belong more often to the second stage (as Pentecostals understand it), the "baptism of [or in] the Holy Spirit." Only when (as sometimes happens) the two stages are telescoped into one do tongues occur in connection with Christian initiation.

In the book of Acts, however, tongues do occur in connection with a group's *first* reception of the Spirit. The Pentecost experience in Acts 2 is the fulfillment of Jesus' promise that "you shall receive power *when the Holy Spirit has come upon you* (Acts 1:5), a statement implying that they did not yet have the Spirit when Jesus spoke those words. Pentecostal exegesis tends to argue that the disciples already had the Holy Spirit in them from the day of Jesus' resurrection, but did not have the Spirit's fullness or power until fifty days later. This is possible only through a rather forced harmonization of Acts with John 20:22, where Jesus breathed on his disciples and said "Receive the Holy Spirit." The long-disputed issue of the relationship between Acts 2 and John 20 is not going to be resolved here. Still, there is a subtlety to the Pentecostal solution of this difficulty which seems to this outsider both contrived and contrary to the genius of the Pentecostal tradition itself. Christian initiation in the New Testament is linked to "baptism," a once-for-all ritual bath in water. The application of the same term to the reception of the Holy Spirit by an individual or group suggests that this "baptism" too occurs at the moment of conversion or initiation into the Christian community, not at some indefinite later time. Although modern Pentecostalism claims to base itself squarely on the accounts in Acts, its doctrine of "initial evidence" differs from that of the Acts narratives in two respects: first, in its emphasis on "evidence of the Spirit" rather than on "the Spirit as evidence"; second, in divorcing "initial evidence" from Christian initiation, so that it is not truly "initial."

"INITIAL EVIDENCE" IN PAUL

The Validation of Ministry

The idea of "initial evidence" can be found even earlier than the book of Acts in the letters of Paul. Near the beginning of 1 Thessalonians, Paul's first letter and the earliest Christian writing that we possess, the apostle states that "our gospel came to you *not only in word, but also in power and in the Holy Spirit* and with full conviction" (1 Thess. 1:5). In a similar context in 1 Corinthians, he claims that "I was with you in weakness and in much fear and trembling; and my speech and my message were *not in plausible words of wisdom, but in demonstration of the Spirit and power,* that your faith might not rest in the wisdom of humans but in the power of God" (1 Cor. 2:3–5).

The apparent equation between the Holy Spirit and power in both these texts[8] recalls Luke–Acts (e.g., Luke 24:49; Acts 1:8), yet Paul makes no explicit mention of tongues speaking in connection with the beginnings of his ministries in Thessalonica or Corinth.[9] The "demonstration," or "evidence" (Greek: *apodeixis*) of the Spirit to which he refers is probably to be understood rather as the performance of miracles or healings, and it is possible that miracles are implied already by the word "power" itself (Greek: *dynamis*). Miracles are even more clearly in view in 2 Corinthians 12:12, where Paul looks back on his Corinthian ministry and states: "The signs of a true apostle were performed among you; in all patience, with signs and wonders and mighty works."

With regard to the "demonstration" or "evidence" mentioned in 1 Corinthians 2:4, Gordon Fee considers it "possible, but not probable, given the context of 'weakness,' that it reflects the 'signs and wonders' of 2 Corinthians 12:12."[10] Yet there is nothing incompatible in Paul between "weakness" and the performance of miracles. The "weakness" (Greek: *astheneia*) mentioned in 1 Corinthians 2:3–4 is, if anything, even more conspicuous in the context of 2 Corinthians 12:12: "On behalf of this man I will boast, but on my own behalf I will not boast, except of my *weaknesses*" (2 Cor. 12:5); "Three times I besought the Lord . . . but he said to me, 'My grace is sufficient for you, for my power is made perfect in *weakness.*' I will all the more gladly boast of my *weaknesses,* that the power of Christ may rest upon me. For the sake of Christ, then, I am content with *weaknesses,* insults, hardships, persecutions, and calamities; for when I am *weak,* then I am strong" (12:9–10; cf. verse 11b, " . . . even though I am nothing"). The contexts of the two passages are not so different after all.

The term "evidence" is appropriate in connection with Paul's references to his Corinthian ministry both in 1 Corinthians 2:4 (where the word *apodeixis* might be so translated), and in 2 Corinthians 12:12 (where the word *sēmeia,* normally translated "signs," carries a similar connotation). Although no comparable term is used in 1 Thessalonians 1:5, the contrast between Paul's gospel and a gospel "only in word" suggests an implicit appeal to "evidence" there as well. Moreover, the evidence to which Paul appeals in these passages is "initial evidence," in that he has in mind phenomena that took place when he first came to Thessalonica and

Corinth respectively. Where it differs from the doctrine of "initial evidence" as taught in modern Pentecostalism is that it has to do with the validation of a movement or a ministry, not with the religious experience of individuals. Paul's ministry in these cities was valid because his message was "not only in word, but also in power and in the Holy Spirit" (1 Thess. 1:5). Consequently, those who accepted his message "accepted it not as the word of human beings but as what it really is, the word of God" (1 Thess. 2:13; cf., 1 Cor. 2:4–5). In the same way, he claimed that whoever disregarded his commands "disregards not a man, but God, who gives his Holy Spirit to you" (1 Thess. 4:8).

Here Paul seems to have applied to himself the promise Jesus had given to his immediate followers that "He who hears you hears me, and he who rejects you rejects me" (Luke 10:16; cf., Matt. 10:40; John 13:20). The "power" of Paul's gospel, expressed in "full conviction," in "joy inspired by the Holy Spirit" (1 Thess. 1:5–6), and probably also in the performance of miracles (2 Cor. 12:12), was to Paul evidence of his own authority as "apostle of Jesus Christ," an authority signalled at the very start of nine of the letters attributed to him in the New Testament. Aside from 2 Corinthians 12:12, Paul is very reserved about basing his claim to apostolic authority on the performance of miracles. He is more inclined to base it on "revelation" given him by Jesus Christ (Gal. 1:12, 16; 2:1), but even in this regard he is unwilling to speak explicitly about actual visions or revelations that he has seen (cf., 2 Cor. 12:1–6). When he mentions the "signs of an apostle" in 2 Corinthians 12:12, he seems to be making a minimal, and reluctant, concession to what Christians at the time—certainly in Corinth—were expecting.

The standard early Christian expectation of what should characterize a truly apostolic ministry is probably reflected in Hebrews 2:3–4, with its reference to a salvation "declared at first by the Lord" and "attested to us by those who heard him, while God also bore witness by signs and wonders and various miracles and by gifts of the Holy Spirit distributed according to his will." A later list of the same kinds of expectations is echoed in the ending that finally became attached to the Gospel of Mark, where Jesus is represented as promising that "these signs will accompany those who believe: in my name they will cast out demons; they will speak in new tongues; they will pick up serpents, and if they drink any deadly thing, it will not hurt them; they will lay their hands on the sick; and they will recover" (Mark 16:17–18). In this passage, two differences are noticeable: first, the list of "signs" is more specific (and longer); second, the "signs" seem to be performed not by the apostles, but by "those who believe" (in the eight preceding verses it is clear that the apostles do *not* believe!). Whoever is responsible for the longer ending of Mark seems to have applied the promises to certain post-apostolic prophetic or charismatic movements, not to the apostles or to those who followed the apostles. In Paul's day, however, and in the letter to the Hebrews, the "signs" are still the "signs of an apostle," given to validate the ministries of those who have seen Jesus. Paul claims these signs for himself with considerable reserve, and in the context of his "weakness," probably in fear of an undue fascination with "power," and the evidences of power, among the congregations at Thessalonica and Corinth.

It is important to recognize that in the view of the New Testament writers, including Paul, the "initial evidence" validating the ministries of apostles and prophets could be counterfeited. False prophets and false messiahs are said to perform "signs and wonders" (Mark 13:22a), and even the antichrist comes with "pretended signs and wonders" according to Paul (2 Thess. 2:9–10), or with "great signs" according to the book of Revelation (13:13–15). Miracles, even extravagant ones, prove nothing. They may "lead astray, *if possible*, the elect" (Mark 13:22b), but the assumption is that this is *not* possible. The "elect" are defined as elect precisely by their resistance to such "evidence" (cf., Mark 13:23). The antichrist's miracles will not deceive true believers, but only "the dwellers on the earth" (Rev. 13:14), "those who are to perish, because they refused to love the truth and be saved" (2 Thess. 2:10). The validity of evidence always depends in part on the predisposition of those for whom it is intended. Because Paul knows this, he gives primary attention in his Thessalonian and Corinthian letters to the disposition of his readers toward him and his message, rather than to the "objective" evidence of miracles or revelations that accompanied his ministry when he first arrived among them.

The Validation of Christian Experience

If Paul on occasion mentions "demonstration of the Spirit and of power" in connection with the validation of his ministry (1 Cor. 2:4), does he mention evidence of any kind in connection with the personal religious experience of believers, whether himself or others? Probably the closest he comes to this is in Romans 8:14–16:

> For all who are led by the Spirit of God are sons of God. For you did not receive the spirit of slavery to fall back into fear, but you have received the spirit of sonship. When we cry, "Abba! Father!" it is the Spirit himself bearing witness with our spirit that we are children of God."

Here as in the book of Acts the primary emphasis is not on "evidences" pointing to the Spirit, but on the Spirit as evidence of something else—in this case, evidence that individuals or communities belong to God in a special way as God's "children." Although the Spirit testifies with the words, "Abba! Father!" the Abba-prayer is viewed not as evidence of the Spirit or Spirit baptism, but as evidence of a relationship to God as Father (cf., Gal. 4:6, "And because you are sons, God has sent the Spirit of his Son into our hearts, crying 'Abba! Father!' ").

That his readers have received the Holy Spirit, Paul has no doubt, and his assumption is that they have no doubt of it either. He assumes it as a given: "Any one who does not have the Spirit of Christ does not belong to him" (Rom. 8:9). If they have a doubt, it has to do with their hope for the future. Therefore he writes to assure them that "If [i.e., assuming] the Spirit of him who raised Jesus from the dead dwells in you, he who raised Christ Jesus from the dead will give life to your mortal bodies also through the Spirit which dwells in you" (Rom. 8:11). The indwelling Spirit is a firm basis on which he can assure them not only that they are children of God, but "heirs, heirs of God and fellow heirs with Christ," provided only that "we suffer with him in order that we may also be glorified with him" (Rom. 8:17). This thought is thoroughly developed in Romans 8:18–39. Nowhere in the entire discussion does Paul express the slightest doubt that his readers "have" the Spirit of God in every sense possible; neither is there the slightest doubt that they know it (see, e.g., v. 23, "we ourselves, who have the first fruits of the Spirit"; v. 26, "the Spirit helps us in our weakness . . . the Spirit himself intercedes for us with sighs too deep for words"; v. 27, "the Spirit intercedes for the saints according to the will of God"). No "evidences" are needed to prove any of this to Paul, to God, or to the readers themselves. Paul uses his readers' presumed confidence in the presence and ministry of the Spirit to assure them of a secure eternal destiny with God through Jesus Christ (Rom. 8:28–30, 35–39).

In a quite different context, Paul appeals to the Galatians' certainty of having received the Holy Spirit in order to convince them to rely on faith and not the law in living the Christian life: "Let me ask you only this: Did you receive the Spirit by works of the law, or by hearing with faith? Are you so foolish? Having begun with the Spirit, are you now ending with the flesh? Did you experience so many things in vain?—if it really is in vain. Does he who supplies the Spirit to you and works miracles among you do so by works of the law, or by hearing with faith?" (Gal. 2:2–5). Here as in Romans, the readers' reception of the Spirit is a *datum*, the presupposition of an entire series of rhetorical questions. No "evidence" for it is needed, and Paul gives none.[11] Once again he assumes that his readers have received the Spirit, that they know it, and that consequently they know exactly what he means.

"INITIAL—AND CONTINUING—EVIDENCE" IN JOHN.

No group of New Testament writings is more interested in evidence than the Gospel and three "epistles" traditionally ascribed to John the apostle. The Gospel of John builds the story of Jesus around a series of "signs" (Greek: *sēmeia*) by which he gave evidence of his identity and mission. Sometimes the "signs" brought people to genuine faith in Jesus, sometimes not. Near the end of the first half of the Gospel, the author concludes, "Though he had done so many signs before them, yet *they did not believe in him*" (John 12:37). Near the end of the book, however, after the resurrection appearances in Jerusalem, he adds for the benefit of his readers, "Now Jesus did many other signs in the presence of his disciples, which are not written in this book; but these are written *that you may believe that Jesus is the Christ, the Son of God*, and that believing you may have life in his name" (John 20:30–31). Signs in the Gospel of John can lead either to genuine faith (2:11; 4:54; 6:26), or to questionable faith (2:23; 3:2; 6:2, 14; 7:31; 9:16; 10:41; 11:47), or to no faith at all (4:48). In two instances (2:18, 6:30), requests for tangible evidence in the form of a "sign" are assumed to be motivated by unbelief. Yet for the readers of the Gospel, the "signs" performed by Jesus are decisive evidence that he is indeed "the Christ, the Son of God."

It is perhaps for the sake of the "signs" that the author has chosen to present his testimony to Jesus Christ in the form of a Gospel narrative. In the "Johannine" writings that are not Gospels (i.e., 1, 2, and 3 John), signs are not mentioned, yet the author is still preoccupied with "evidence"—evidence not of the identity of Jesus, but of the reality of Christian salvation. Although the author of 1 John has no specific word for "evidence," he presents in this work a series of characteristics or "tests" by which the life of God in recognized in individuals or communities. Robert Law writes that

> Life, according to the Johannine conception, is the essence or animating principle that underlies the whole phenomena of conscious Christian experience, *and cannot itself be the object of direct consciousness. Its possession is a matter of inference, its presence certified only by its appropriate effects* [italics mine]. It may be tested simply as life, by the evidence of those functions—

growth, assimilation, and reproduction—which are characteristic of every kind of vital energy.[12]

The three "tests of life" that Robert Law proposes are righteousness, love, and belief.[13] Believers can be sure they have the life of God if they obey Jesus' commands (e.g., 1 John 2:3–4), if they love one another—which amounts to the same thing—(e.g., 1 John 2:7–11), and if they believe in Jesus Christ "come in the flesh" (e.g., 1 John 4:2). In some instances, the author of 1 John introduces the phrase, "by this we know," or some equivalent, in order to make the notion of "evidence" explicit. The number of such examples varies depending on what one considers an explicit appeal to "evidence." The following list is fairly complete, and in general supports Law's proposal:

(1) *And by this we may be sure* that we know him, if we keep his commandments (1 John 2:3).

(2) Children, it is the last hour; and as you have heard that antichrist is coming, so now many antichrists have come; *therefore we know* that it is the last hour (1 John 2:18).

(3) *By this it may be seen* who are the children of God, and who are the children of the devil: whoever does not do right is not of God, nor he who does not love his brother (1 John 3:10).

(4) *By this we know love,* that he laid down his life for us; and we ought to lay down our lives for the brethren (1 John 3:16).

(5) *By this we shall know* that we are of the truth, and reassure our hearts before him whenever our hearts condemn us (1 John 3:19).

(6) *And by this we know* that he abides in us, by the Spirit which he has given us (1 John 3:24).

(7) *By this you know* the Spirit of God: every spirit which confesses that Jesus Christ has come in the flesh is of God, and every spirit which does not confess Jesus Christ is not of God (1 John 4:2–3a). *By this we know* the spirit of truth and the spirit of error (4:6b).

(8) *In this the love of God was made manifest among us,* that God sent his only Son into the world. . . . In this is love, not that we loved God but that he loved us, and sent his Son to be the expiation for our sins (1 John 4:9–10).

(9) *By this we know* that we abide in him and he in us, because he has given us of his own Spirit (1 John 4:13).

(10) And we have seen and testify that the Father has sent his Son as Savior of the world. . . . *So we know and believe* the love God has for us (1 John 4:14, 16).

(11) *By this we know* that we love the children of God, when we love God and obey his commandments. For this is the love of God, that we keep his commandments (1 John 5:2–3a).

(12) I write this to you who believe in the name of the Son of God, *that you may know* that you have eternal life (1 John 5:13).

Law's "test of righteousness" can be clearly seen in (1), (3), and (11); his "test of love" in (3), (4), and (11); his "test of belief" in (7), (8),[14] (10), and (12). This leaves (2), (5), (6), and (9). The first of these, (2), stands somewhat apart from all the rest, in that the "evidence" in question (i.e., the presence of "many antichrists") is not introduced as evidence of "life" or of "knowing God," but simply of a prophetic assertion: "it is the last hour" (1 John 2:18). In the case of (5), it is not altogether clear what the evidence is. Probably the words, "By this we shall know," in 1 John 3:19 are intended to refer back to verse 18, "Little children, let us not love in word or speech but in deed and truth."[15] If so, then (5) is an example of "the test of love."

This leaves (6) and (9), in which the evidence of God dwelling in Christian believers and believers dwelling in God is said to be the Spirit that God has given (1 John 3:24; 4:13). Here Law's categories are difficult to apply. Is this to be considered a test of righteousness, of love, or of belief? What is clear in any event is that 1 John stands squarely in the tradition of the book of Acts and the letters of Paul, where the Spirit itself is evidence of something. Once again the author's assumption is that his readers have the Spirit and know that they have it. Because the mutual indwelling of God (or Christ) and the Christian believer is a conspicuous Johannine theme (cf., e.g., John 6:56; 14:20, 23; 15:4–7; 17:21; 1 John 2:24; 5:20), it is not surprising that indwelling is the invisible reality of which the Spirit is the outward evidence. In 1 John, as everywhere else in the New Testament, it is not a matter of "evidences of the Spirit" but of "the Spirit as evidence."

Yet in 1 John there is a further question to be pursued. As soon as he has written (6), "And by this we know that he abides in us, by the Spirit which he has given us" (1 John 3:24), the author continues, "Beloved, do not believe every spirit, but test the spirits to see whether they are of God; for many false prophets have gone out into the world" (4:1). This introduces (7) from the preceding list: "By this you know the Spirit of God: every spirit which confesses that Jesus Christ has come in the flesh is of God, and every spirit which does not confess Jesus is not of God. This is the spirit of antichrist, of which you heard that it was coming, and now it is in the world already" (4:2–3). Here it seems the author *does* after all introduce "evidence," or a "test," of the Spirit. If the Spirit is evidence of something (i.e., the reality of mutual indwelling), then the Spirit in turn is itself put to the test of Christian belief (i.e., the confession that "Jesus Christ has come in the flesh").

Is it fair to say on the basis of this passage that the "initial evidence" of the Spirit's work in the believer is the Christian creed or confession? Not exactly. The author of 1 John is proposing a test of Christian prophecy, not of Christian experience. The problem is not the validity of any individual's reception of the Spirit, but the validity of certain utterances given as utterances of the Spirit. A specific doctrinal test is necessary because "many false prophets have gone out into the world" (4:1). There is a "spirit of error" as well as a "spirit of truth" in the Christian communities (4:6), and the author of 1 John wants the readers to be able to tell the difference.[16] As far as the readers themselves are concerned, however, the author's assumption is that their experience of the Spirit is self-authenticating.

The thought of 1 John 3:24 is repeated in 4:13: "By this we know that we abide in him and he in us, because he has given us of his own Spirit" (9). Once again, the Spirit is not something to be tested, but is itself one of the tests. The question posed in connection with 3:24, however, has not yet been answered: in Robert Law's categories, is the test of the Spirit a test of righteousness, of love, or of belief? The terminology of 1 John 4:13 is slightly different from that of 3:24, and the difference is instructive:

> *1 John 3:24*—And by this we know . . . by the Spirit which he has given us.

> *1 John 4:13*—By this we know . . . because he has given us of his own Spirit.

In the first instance the test is the Spirit; in the second it is the *giving* of the Spirit. The author immediately goes on to remind his readers that "the Father has sent his Son as the Savior of the world" (4:14), and that "Whoever confesses that Jesus is the Son of God, God abides in him and he in God" (4:15). Probably the giving of the Spirit, no less than the sending of the Son, belongs to what Law describes as the test of belief.[17]

Despite the helpfulness of his discussion, however, Law's conclusion limits too much the Spirit's role in 1 John. He claims that "the Spirit, throughout these passages, is regarded simply as the inspirer of the true confession of Jesus. If we make this confession, it is evidence that the spirit in us is the Spirit of God."[18] The difficulty is that the thought of the passage runs parallel to that of Paul in Galatians 4:4–6, where the affirmation that "God sent forth his Son" (4:4) is shortly followed by the reminder that "God has sent the Spirit of his Son into our hearts, crying 'Abba! Father!' " (4:6). The point is not that creedal orthodoxy is "evidence" of the reality of the Spirit, but just the opposite: the believer's possession of the Spirit is evidence that God has given the Spirit and consequently that God sent the Son into the world. The sending of the Son and the giving of the Spirit are two stages of the same redemptive event. The reality of the Spirit in the believer's life is assumed rather than proven in 1 John (cf., also 2:20, 27) and serves as the author's safeguard against any kind of dead orthodoxy.

CONCLUSIONS: TRACKING THE WIND

This investigation has uncovered considerable uniformity among New Testament writers on the Christian experience of the Holy Spirit. In the book of Acts, in the letters of Paul, and in the writings attributed to John, the Spirit is presented as empirical evidence of the reality of God and of the work of God in individuals and communities. As a non-Pentecostal, I have long appreciated the witness of Pentecostals and the Pentecostal tradition to that empirical reality. Jesus said to Nicodemus in John's Gospel, "The wind blows where it wills, and you hear the sound of it, but you do not know where it comes from or whither it goes; so it is with every one who is born of the Spirit" (John 3:8).

Quite properly, most Christians have heeded the note of caution in Jesus' statement. We are all too aware that the Spirit is a mystery and that we "do not know where it comes from or whither it goes." We are less certain that we can "hear the sound of it." The Pentecostal tradition is here to remind us of the Spirit's sight and sound, the faint echoes in our world of "the rush of a mighty wind" on the day of Pentecost (Acts 2:2). The fact that the rest of us have "spiritualized" the Spirit to the point that we cannot hear or see it, or cannot even be quite sure of its presence among us, is no reason for Pentecostalism to do the same thing. The rest of the church needs the testimony of Pentecostals to the "evidence" that *is* the Spirit, not to this or that phenomenon pointing to something inward, invisible, or abstract. Just as there is a danger in other traditions of reducing the Spirit to liturgy, ethics, mystical experiences, or doctrine, so there is a danger in the Pentecostal notion of "initial evidence" of reducing the Spirit to tongues speaking. But in the New Testament, the Spirit is not reducible to anything. It is what it is. Like the wind, the Spirit blows wherever it will.

A final observation: I know it is irritating for a non-Pentecostal to try to tell Pentecostals how to be more true to their own traditions. It is like Protestants advising Roman Catholics how to be better Catholics. The viewpoint of an outsider may be right or it may be wrong. In the last analysis, that is for the insiders to determine. What I have tried to present here is not only the testimony of the New Testament, but also the distinctive testimony (as I perceive it) of Pentecostalism to the rest of the church. I deeply appreciate that testimony, and—"initial evidence" aside—I find a remarkable correspondence between the Pentecostal perspective on the Spirit and that of the New Testament.

NOTES

1. Quotations are from the RSV, with slight revisions in a few places for the sake of inclusive language.

2. Cf. J. R. Michaels, "Luke–Acts," *DPCM*, 545.

3. *Funk & Wagnalls Standard College Dictionary* (New York: Funk & Wagnalls, 1977), 460.

4. In using "it," or "itself," for the Holy Spirit in this essay, I do not at all intend to deny the personality of the Spirit. The neuter pronouns simply indicate that in these particular passages the personality of the Spirit is not being emphasized. The introduction of masculine or feminine pronouns would not only give the impression that these early recipients of the Spirit were consciously aware of the Spirit's personality (which is unlikely), but would also raise unnecessarily the question of the Spirit's gender.

5. There is room for honest disagreement over whether the phrases "speaking in tongues" and "extolling God" refer to the same phenomenon or to two distinct or overlapping phenomena. Grammatically they appear to be distinct, but the parallel with Acts 2:11 suggests that they may be the same (i.e., extolling God in other languages). The text does not address the more specific question of whether or not the same diverse languages represented at Pentecost were also represented at the house of Cornelius, and whether or not each of the Jewish believers again "heard them speaking in his own language" (2:6).

6. Cf., the expression "the gift of God," used of the Holy Spirit in Acts 8:20 and John 4:10.

7. In Acts 2 as well, the phenomenon of tongues speaking is identified in Peter's use of the quotation from Joel as prophecy ("and your sons and your daughters shall prophesy," 2:17; "and they shall prophesy," 2:18).

8. See, e.g., G. D. Fee, *The First Epistle to the Corinthians*, NICNT (Grand Rapids: Eerdmans, 1987), 95; C. K. Barrett, *The First Epistle to the Corinthians* (New York: Harper & Row, 1968), 65–66; F. F. Bruce, *1 and 2 Thessalonians*, Word Biblical Commentary 45 (Waco, Tex.: Word Books, 1982), 14.

9. Fee, *First Corinthians*, 95, argues that tongues are implied here in connection with the conversion of the Corinthians, but Paul's discussion of tongues at Corinth (1 Cor. 12–14) is as a spiritual gift for worship, not as the

accompaniment of conversion or as evidence for Spirit baptism. The debate over tongues in Corinth takes place in the context not of Christian initiation but of communal worship and mutual ministry. All have been "baptized into one body" (1 Cor. 12:13) but not all speak in tongues.

10. Fee, *First Corinthians*, 95.

11. "Miracles" are mentioned in v. 5 not as evidence of the Spirit's work but simply as its accompaniments, just as in 2 Cor. 12:12, and (implicitly) in 1 Cor. 2:4 and 1 Thess. 1:5. In appealing to the religious experience of the Galatians, Paul cannot help but appeal indirectly to the validity of his own ministry among them.

12. Robert Law, *The Tests of Life: A Study of the First Epistle of St. John*, 3d ed. (Edinburgh: T. & T. Clark, 1914), 208.

13. Law, *Tests*, 208–77. For my own summary and further development of Law's thesis, see G. W. Barker, W. L. Lane, and J. R. Michaels, *The New Testament Speaks* (New York: Harper & Row, 1969), 413–25 (reprinted as "Reflections on the Three Epistles of John," in *A Companion to John*, ed. M. J. Taylor [New York: Alba House, 1977], 257–71).

14. The point of (8) is not that the life of Christian believers is tested by their love for each other, but that the love of God for believers is proved by his act of sending the Son into the world—an object of Christian belief.

15. See the discussion in R. E. Brown, *The Epistles of John*, Anchor Bible 30 (Garden City, N.Y.: Doubleday, 1982), 454.

16. Paul had proposed a similar test for prophetic utterances in 1 Cor. 12:3: "Therefore I want you to understand that no one speaking by the Spirit of God ever says, 'Jesus be cursed!' and no one can say 'Jesus is Lord' except by the Holy Spirit" (cf., the preceding discussion of false prophets and prophecy in 2 Thess. 2, Mark 13, and Rev. 13).

17. Law, *Tests*, 258–79. Law himself states that "the possession of the Spirit of God—the Spirit that confesses Jesus as the Christ (4:2)—is the objective and infallible sign that God is abiding in us" (263, n. 1).

18. Ibid., 263, n. 1.

INDEX OF NAMES

INDEX OF ANCIENT SOURCES